Russell Herman Conwell

History of the Great Fire in Saint John in 1877

Vol. 1

Russell Herman Conwell

History of the Great Fire in Saint John in 1877
Vol. 1

ISBN/EAN: 9783337340681

Printed in Europe, USA, Canada, Australia, Japan

Cover: Foto ©ninafisch / pixelio.de

More available books at **www.hansebooks.com**

HISTORY

OF THE

GREAT FIRE IN SAINT JOHN,

JUNE 20 AND 21, 1877.

BY

RUSSELL H. CONWELL,

AUTHOR OF "HISTORY OF THE GREAT FIRE IN BOSTON," "LIFE OF
PRESIDENT HAYES," "WOMAN AND THE LAW," "WHY
AND HOW THE CHINESE EMIGRATE," ETC.

"Fire, commissioned by the winds,
Begins on sheds, but, rolling in a round,
On palaces returns."

BOSTON:
PUBLISHED BY B. B. RUSSELL, 55 CORNHILL.
SAINT JOHN, N.B.: JONES & MORRISON.
TORONTO: MIGHT & TAYLOR.

1877.

TO THE

HON. SAMUEL LEONARD TILLEY, C.B.,

*LIEUTENANT-GOVERNOR OF THE PROVINCE
OF NEW BRUNSWICK,*

THE FRIEND OF HUMANITY EVERYWHERE, AND AN ACTIVE PRO-
MOTER OF ALL LEGITIMATE MEASURES FOR
THE RELIEF OF SAINT JOHN,

This Volume

IS MOST RESPECTFULLY DEDICATED

BY THE AUTHOR.

PREFACE.

It is a hideous story at the best, full of the very saddest events and the most exciting scenes. The contemplation of that disastrous evening, that lurid night, that pile of spectral ruins, makes us hesitate to dip the pen; yet it should be written. The history of the terrible scourge, with all its frightful details, should be preserved in historical form, to hand its lessons down to other generations, to show that the active sympathy of the civilized world was not misplaced, and to immortalize the good and brave deeds of that noble people to whose homes this awful visitation came. R. H. C.

ACKNOWLEDGMENTS.

THE most sincere thanks of the author are due to the gentlemen named below, who so kindly, at such personal sacrifice, furnished us with facts concerning the great fire, and contributed so much to make our stay in the afflicted city comfortable, profitable, and pleasant. It is a pleasure as well as a duty to write about such a people; and we tremble lest we shall fail to make a suitable return herein for the universal hospitality of every man we met in St. John. To him whose fortunes we mainly follow in the opening chapters of this book, we may owe an apology for making so free with his narrative; and while we have tried to disguise it by adding incidents, which, while each one related actually happened, he perhaps did not see, yet doubtless many in St. John will recognize the actor.

Our thanks are tendered to Mr. John Boyd, E.

Lester Peters, James W. Lawrence, John E. Turnbull, James Hannay, Thomas S. Simms, Messrs. Jones and Morrison, Frank C. Smith, Thomas Marter, Matthew Lindsay, and the Rev. W. Mitchell.

ILLUSTRATIONS.

STEEL PLATE (Portraits of Lieut.-Gov. Tilley, Mayor S. Z. Earle, and John Boyd) . . . . *Frontispiece.*
VIEW OF ST. JOHN BEFORE THE FIRE 25
ST. JOHN IN FLAMES 58
PLAN OF ST. JOHN 81
ACADEMY OF MUSIC. — VICTORIA HOTEL 153
VIEW OF RUINS (Prince William Street and Victoria Hotel) . 176
NORTH WHARF AND MARKET SQUARE (in ruins). — MARKET SQUARE (before the fire) 212
REED'S POINT. — POST OFFICE 230
SKATING RINK. — BEACON LIGHT 270

CONTENTS.

CHAPTER I.

A HOME IN SAINT JOHN.

PAGE

House on Queen's Square. — The Inside of a Merchant's Residence. — Furniture and Keepsakes. — Prophecy of the Old Indian. — Forebodings of coming Disaster 17

CHAPTER II.

THE BEGINNING OF THE FIRE.

York Point Slip. — The Fire Department. — The Progress of the Flames. — Scenes of Excitement. — Burning of Dwellings and Warehouses. — Destruction of Vessels. — Strange Behavior of Panic-stricken Ones 27

CHAPTER III.

BURNING HOMES.

Caught by the Flames. — Running the Gauntlet of Fire. — Burning of the Dead. — The Ruins of a Home. — Searching for Loved Ones. — Surrounded by Fire. — Queen's Square . . 36

CONTENTS.

CHAPTER IV.

INCIDENTS OF THE FIRE.

The Culmination of the Destruction. — Death by Fire. — A Life, or a Dwelling? — Saving a Handful of Wood. — Losing Gold Sovereigns. — Birth of Children amid the Flames and on the Bay. — Escape by Raft. — The Scene from Ballast Wharf . 50

CHAPTER V.

IN THE VICINITY OF KING'S SQUARE.

The Stationary Vehicle. — The Merchandise in King's Square. — Appearance of the Refugees. — The Old Burying-Ground. — The Shelterless Ones. — Removal to New Homes . . 60

CHAPTER VI.

THE PEOPLE BEFORE THE FIRE.

The Metropolis of New Brunswick. — Character of its Founders. — Culture of the People. — Public and Private Enterprise. — Public Buildings, Commerce, Manufacturing, &c. . . . 71

CHAPTER VII.

THE CITY BEFORE THE FIRE.

The Situation of the City. — The Dwellings. — The Public Buildings. — The Churches. — The Environs. — The Scenery. — The Harbor. — The Business Enterprises 76

CHAPTER VIII.

HISTORICAL SKETCH OF SAINT JOHN.

From 1604 to 1775. — Discovery by the French. — Fort La Tour. — Contest between La Tour and Charnisay. — Grant of

CONTENTS. 13

PAGE

Lands. — Indian Wars. — Pirates. — Expeditions from Boston. — War between the English and French. — Naval Engagements. — Capture of Fort La Tour. — Erection of a Blockhouse 80

CHAPTER IX.

HISTORICAL SKETCH OF SAINT JOHN.

From 1774 to 1874. — Establishment of Government. — War between the Colonies and Great Britain. — Indian Warfare. — The Opening of Trade. — Landing of the Loyalists. — Great Fires in Saint John. — First Church. — First Newspaper. — Visits from Distinguished Persons. — War with France. — War of 1812. — Facts and Incidents of Recent History . . 105

CHAPTER X.

THE GREAT FIRE.

The Origin unknown. — The Sudden Appearance of the Flames. — The Spread of the Calamity. — The Fire Department. — The Streets and Wharves destroyed. — The Public Buildings. — The Shipping. — The Churches. — Explosions, Deaths, Accidents, &c. 146

CHAPTER XI.

SCENES ATTENDING THE CONFLAGRATION.

Similarity to the Fire in London. — The Description of that Calamity applied to this. — Scenes of Confusion. — Acts of Heroism. — Effect of the Fire upon Men's Natural Dispositions. — Thieves. — Deaths by Fire. — Sheltering a Homeless People. — All Things common 160

CHAPTER XII.

AFTER THE FIRE.

The Ruins?—Obliteration of Streets.—Appearance of the Squares.—Exodus of the People.—Establishment of Business Quarters.—Absence of Food.—Danger of Starvation . 175

CHAPTER XIII.

EXTENT OF THE CALAMITY.

Estimated Loss.—Great Extent of the Destruction in Proportion to the Size of the City.—Names of the Owners of Buildings.—Names of Occupants.—Business Firms burned out.—Roster of Losers by Streets.—The Effect on the Working Classes.—Summary of the Property destroyed . 179

CHAPTER XIV.

THE DEAD AND WOUNDED.

The Number of Deaths unknown.—Eighteen suddenly killed.—Deaths in the Hospital.—Mention of Individual Cases.—Accidental Burning.—The List of the Injured.—The Dependent Families 217

CHAPTER XV.

PUBLIC BUILDINGS AND SHIPPING.

Description of the Public Buildings.—Trinity Church.—Germain-street Baptist Church.—Other Church Edifices destroyed.—City Hall.—The Custom House.—The Post Office.—Public Halls.—Academy of Music.—Temperance Halls.—Masonic Hall.—Hotels.—Gas Works.—Shipping destroyed 223

CONTENTS.

CHAPTER XVI.

FRIENDS IN NEED.

First Assurances of Help. — The Liberality of the People. — Telegrams from Cities in America and Europe. — Returning Past Kindnesses. — The Behavior of the Recipients. — List of Contributors. — The Amounts given and received. — How Chicago, Boston, and London responded. — Other Cities and Towns 242

CHAPTER XVII.

ADMINISTRATION OF RELIEF.

The First Distribution. — The Random Applications. — The Danger from Impostors. — The First Organization. — Ineffectiveness of Original Plan. — The Great Number of Applicants. — How they were supplied. — The Introduction of the Chicago System. — The New Committee — The Tents and Barracks. — Independent Shanties. — How Assistance could be obtained 268

CHAPTER XVIII.

REBUILDING THE CITY.

Character of the People. — Peaceableness of the Inhabitants. — Beginning to clear away the *Débris*. — Temporary Dwellings. — Temporary Storehouses. — General Clearing of the Burned District. — Measures for securing Money. — Speech of Mr. John Boyd 278

CONTENTS.

CHAPTER XIX.

CHURCHES AND SERMONS.

The Sad Worshippers. — The Meetings for Consultation. — Sad as Funerals. — The Sermon of the Rev. D. M. Maclise, D.D.: "Shall there be evil in a city, and the Lord hath not done it?" — Sermon of the Rev. John Wills: "Shall a trumpet be blown in the city, and the people not be afraid?" — Sermon of the Rev. G. M. Armstrong: "I know, O Lord, that thy judgments are right" 287

CHAPTER XX.

MISCELLANEOUS MATTERS OF INTEREST.

The Newspapers of Saint John. — Historical Notice. — Biographical Sketch of the Life of Lieut-Gov. Tilley, C. B. — The Life of John Boyd, a Private Citizen. — Examples of Saint John's Sterling Men. — The City Government. — The Fire Department. — The Insurance Companies. — Little Wanderers' Home. — Incidents of the Fire. —Conclusion . . 338

GREAT FIRE IN SAINT JOHN.

CHAPTER I.

A HOME IN SAINT JOHN.

House on Queen's Square. — The Inside of a Merchant's Residence. — Furniture and Keepsakes. — Prophecy of the Old Indian. — Forebodings of coming Disaster.

DAVID TOURNAY stood before one of the large parlor-windows of his spacious and somewhat imposing residence on Queen's Square, Saint John, looking out upon the park. He was a man of dignified bearing, having a body short and stout, a face round and large, with chin and forehead of the recognized English pattern, and wearing his gray side-whiskers and thick hair neatly trimmed. The accurate cut of his gray coat and lighter-colored pants, the gloss of his cuffs and collar, the whiteness of his teeth, the bright restless movement of his blue eyes, together with his general appearance of scrupulous neatness, denoted a cultivated and wealthy gentleman. He held in one hand a new Manilla hat, and in the other a rattan cane with an ivory handle secured by a band of gold.

It was the twentieth day of June, 1877. The trees and grass wore their liveliest color and their thickest foliage. The fresh sea-breeze which rippled the broad river and bay, and shook the leaves on the shore, also swung the lace curtains in the open windows of Saint John's most elegant homes. The hot sun which had gleamed for several days with unpleasant directness upon the valleys and hillsides of the undulating city seemed intent upon crumbling the rocks into dust, and parching the trees into easy playthings for the increasing wind. Impartially did the sun inflame and the breezes fan the poor and the rich; the ignorant and the educated alike hid from the sun, and welcomed the western wind. In the favors and neglects of air and light, no man can boast exclusiveness. But the breezes were none the less welcome to David Tournay for having skimmed the lowly roofs of many an honest laborer, and ruffled the hair of numerous human beings lower in the social scale than himself, before they slammed the shutters and flapped the curtains of his mansion. He was not the man to wish others poorer than himself, and had none of that exclusiveness in his manner or his home to indicate that he was particularly proud of his possessions or of his ancestry. Yet he might have been vain in the consciousness of having been honored in both; for he was one of that large class of wealthy merchants who have made Saint John their home, and who for nearly a hundred years have been known as careful, earnest, honest men, having a taste for culture, and making generous, hearty good-fellowship a fundamental article in their social and religious creed.

That he was in possession of enough to make him boastful, could have been clearly established by glancing about him as he stood waiting for his carriage that day. The parlor where he waited was furnished in the most elegant and costly manner. Neither Nottingham nor Alençon produced a prettier design in lace than the curtains at his windows exhibited. No velvet carpet made to order in Benares or Brussels would have exhibited more exquisite taste, or harmonized more perfectly with the rich plush of the sofas and the artistic decorations on the walls, than did the carpet his good taste had chosen. The chandeliers, the mirrors, the rugs, the carved tables, the works of art in painting, sculpture, and books, the piano and its embroidered cover — all were of the richest type. Throughout the house, from the spacious cellar to the conveniently furnished upper chambers, in drawing-room, library, dining-room, hall, sleeping-apartments, bath-rooms, and closets, there was no lack of the comforts, conveniences, and elegances of the most advanced civilized life.

For twenty-four years David Tournay and his wife had been steadily and carefully selecting articles with which to furnish that home. There were the heirlooms that told the history of two hundred years. There was a sword in the library, which an ancestor of Mrs. Tournay captured at Bannockburn. There was a musket or blunderbuss hanging near it, which an ancestor of David Tournay carried in the romantic days of De la Tour, when St. John was but a fort, and that fort could contain less than a hundred followers of that adventurous knight. In bed-chamber and hall, in dining-room and kitchen, were vases in Parian, cups of ancient china, baskets of curious finish, specimens of heathen workmanship in iron, gold, ivory, and sandalwood, ancient clocks, brackets, quilts, laces, toys, and coins, each the gift of some friend or relative more or less dear or celebrated. The Bible from mother, an old portrait of himself from grandfather, an autograph of Henry VIII., a commission signed by Oliver Cromwell, and a violin used once by Paganini, were among the interesting reminders of near and dear donors long since sleeping in the tomb.

On the marble table in the parlor lay volumes in beautiful bindings, the gifts of authors or distinguished men; and there were the autograph and photograph albums, with the names and faces of all the loved friends of boyhood, girlhood, school days, years of travel, and years of hard labor. On the shelves of his library were two thousand volumes, and each had been selected with care. Curious books, strange and antique, purchased by the owner on his commercial trips to England, France, and the United States; old manuscripts of his own writing, letters from friends and public officials, poems, histories, essays, novels, works upon science, art, and commerce, — told the beholder how the culture of the mind and the accumulation of wealth had moved on hand in hand, neither crushing the other, or leaving its companion behind. Yet this home, with all its comforts and valuables, was but one of many that stood in the city of Saint John on that day, and which would disappear in a cloud of fire and smoke before another dawn.

David Tournay tells the writer (and we call him by that name because he shuns the notoriety such a book as this would give him) that as he stood looking out upon the lawn, and carelessly watching the boys and girls as they romped through the park, a feeling of gloom seized upon him so unexpectedly and so forcibly that he thought he had been taken suddenly ill. He put his hand to his heart, then to his head; tried his eyesight by looking toward the hills away beyond the bay; and then, turning quickly to his wife, who sat near him, exclaimed, —

"Mary, I feel strangely to-day: I believe my luncheon was too hearty. I have no reason that I can recall for feeling despondent, yet I do feel as if every friend I have was under the sod."

Mrs. Tournay looked up with a startled expression, her pale face flushing for a moment, and her dull eyes brightening unnaturally, and quickly responded, —

"I feel so too, David. But I felt it just as strongly before I ate to-day. It may be that watching with Ethel, poor girl! has made me low-spirited. David," — and Mrs. Tournay's lips trembled, and the tears came as she spoke, — "do you think it possible that Ethel will — will — not live?"

"Oh, nonsense, Mary, nonsense! The doctor says that she is better, and he ought to know; and, what is more, she appears better. She wanted her book and her needlework to-day. She asked after the cat and her birdie when I was up there just now. Don't think of her dying, Mary: you or I, or both of us, may go first, you know."

"Yes, it is possible we may, I know; but I do feel as if something awful were going to happen. I suppose I am foolish; but that story Harry told the kitchen-maid caused my heart to beat quick, although I know it is impossible. Every thing makes me gloomy, now that Ethel is so sick."

"What story did Harry tell? I did not hear of it. Did he say any thing about Ethel? What does he know about her?"

"No, no!" said Mrs. Tournay. "I thought you were listening too when he talked with Katie in the yard. He said that an old Indian chief told him and a number of other boys last Saturday that Saint John was going to be destroyed on Tuesday of this week (meaning yesterday, of course), and told them to advise their parents to move out. He said he told his school-teacher about it, and she scolded him for believing such nonsense, and lectured the whole school upon superstition. She did right in that, of course; and, as the day has already gone by, there was nothing in it any way. But for some reason it has troubled me so that I think about it, and dream about it when I get time to dream about any thing. I do wish that I could get over it."

David walked across the room, through the folding-door, into the drawing-room, and looked out the window instinctively, as if he thought the boy might be still there talking to the maid. Then meditatively returning, he put his hand tenderly on his wife's head, and affectionately stroked her silvered hair.

"Mary," said he, "we have no right to be down-hearted and solemn to-day. Just think back through the years, and see how we have been blessed. You cannot forget those two rooms we began to live in; you cannot forget those long years of ceaseless work, trying to earn an honest living. Now we have all we want. I was thinking this morning, as I went into the warehouse, that, were Ethel restored to health, there is nothing more that I desire. Of course we are not rich, as the people of New York and London estimate riches; but we do have all we can use; and I think it is time that I close out my business, and retire, to enjoy with you and Ethel the accumulations of all these hard years. Gloomy! I scout the idea when I stop to think. Oh, no, Mary! what cause have we to be sad? Come, cheer up! cheer up! I wonder what keeps Jim so long. He ought to have been here some time ago. Lord! it is now almost three o'clock. I'm afraid I shall have to walk down."

David had left the parlor, and had placed his hand upon the knob of the front-door, and his wife was just about to ascend the stairs, when he heard a

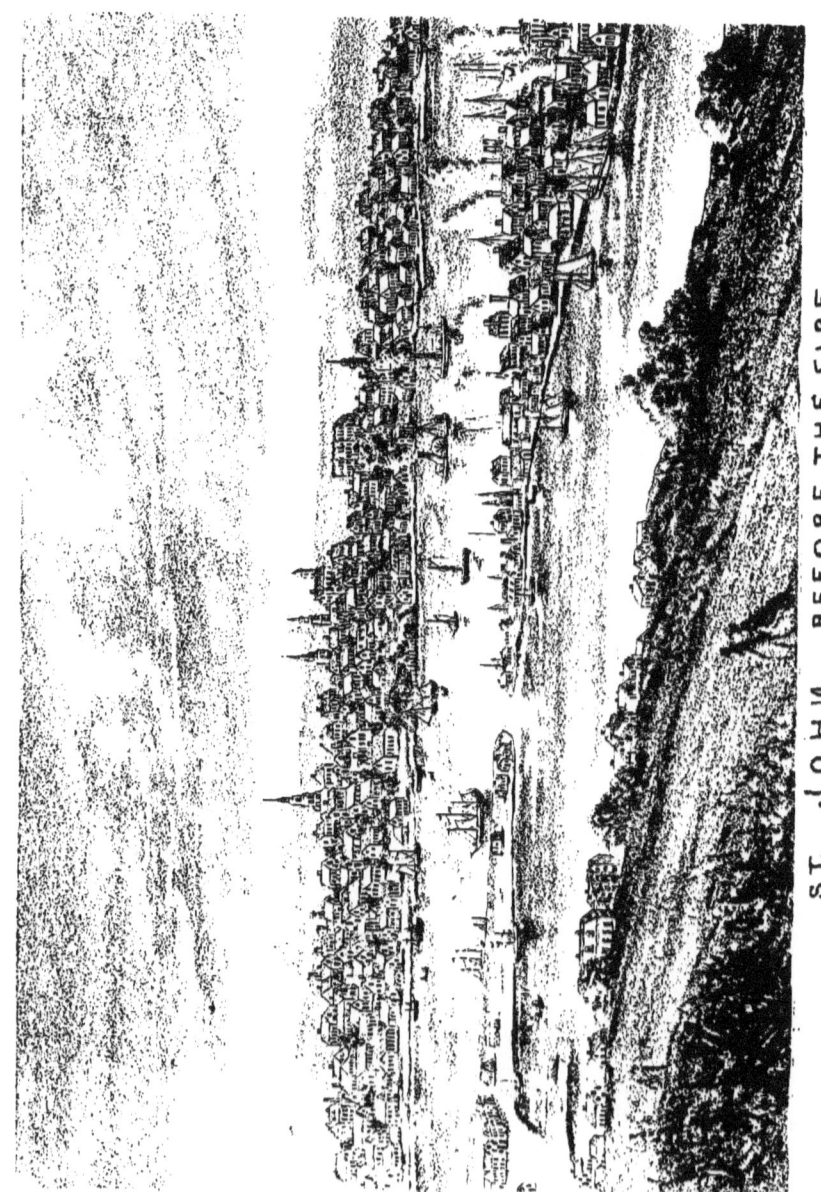
ST. JOHN BEFORE THE FIRE.

stroke of the bell on the Germain-street Baptist Church near by, which was instantly echoed from the Centenary Church, and from the old Bell-Tower half a mile away.

"The deuce!" shouted David, "there's a fire!". and then, feeling that he was unusually nervous, and could not find any thing peculiarly excitable in an alarm of fire, as the Fire Department usually put out the conflagrations in four or five minutes, he suddenly assumed a calmer demeanor, and counted the strokes. "Two, three, four, five. Oh, that is over on Union Street, somewhere down by the wharf, I think. It is not within three or four blocks of the warehouse, so we are all right. Wish I had my property insured in something besides a mutual company. But I must go: Jim has come with the carriage. Good-by, Mary; take good care of Ethel. I will be back by five o'clock; she will be better then, I know. Good-by."

So saying, he hurried out to the carriage, and, hastily seating himself, was driven briskly in the direction of Charlotte Street. Had he looked back, as he usually did, and as his wife expected he would do then, he would have seen her pale face at the window, wearing a startlingly ghastly look of foreboding and dismay. Ah, could he have had even the foresight of the wild man of the forest, he would have known that the repeated alarm-bells, still ringing out till twenty-five strokes were tolled in chimes of five strokes each, was the knell of a city; while, over his own home, disasters frightful as war menaced every thing that he loved.

CHAPTER II.

THE BEGINNING OF THE FIRE.

York Point Slip. — The Fire Department. — The Progress of the Flames. — Scenes of Excitement. — Burning of Dwellings and Warehouses. — Destruction of Vessels. — Strange Behavior of Panic-stricken Ones.

HAD David Tournay returned to his residence an hour after he left it, he would have found his wife lying asleep on the bed in little Ethel's chamber, with the sick girl beside her; while the dark-eyed pallid invalid, without moving her head, gazed cautiously at whatever of furniture or decoration came within range of her eyesight. The fever which had raged in her body for so many days had left her but a few hours before; and the consciousness of the fact that she was better, permitted the mother to sleep, and gave the daughter patience to lie quiet and disturb not her dreams. It would have been fortunate for David if he could have seen them, as his quick and experienced ear would have detected the clamor of distant crowds, the cries of

"*Fire, fire!*" and the shrill whistle of steam fire-engines. His nostrils would have detected the odor of smoke and steam; and his eyes would have seen the enormous black cloud which rolled upward and eastward, hiding the heavens, and casting an ominous shadow on house and park, street and bay. He would not have waited long after he had detected the deep mutterings of that volcano, before he would have aroused his companion, carefully wrapped his darling girl in her cloak of ermine, and hastened away from the doomed city. Alas! he was not there; and the wife unconsciously awaited the coming flames, in a deep refreshing sleep, while the daughter attributed the unusual tumult she seemed to hear, and the darkening of the sky which she seemed to notice, to her own feeble and nervous condition.

David, however, with thoughts of bundles and packages of merchandise, of accounts unsettled and capital uninvested, was driven to his warehouse, where, after bidding his partners and clerks a cheerful "good-morning," he soon lost himself in the usual pile of correspondence. He had been engaged thus for a few moments only, when the rush of an excited crowd of boys along the street, and the repeated cry of "Fire, fire!" drew him with others to the warehouse door.

"That fire seems to be gaining headway, sir," said a gentleman, pointing at the columns of vapor which rolled upward in great scrolls and banks, like the first upheavals of an approaching thunder-cloud.

"I think I will go and look at it," said Mr. Tournay, hastily entering his counting-room, crowding his letters under a paper-weight, and seizing his hat and cane. "Some poor fellow is meeting with a sad loss, I fear."

"How thankful we ought to be that it is not our property!" said he to himself, as he joined the current of human beings which flowed down King Street, and westward along Dock Street, toward York Point. "Whoever it is," continued he to himself, "I shall propose that we make up a purse for him. We will show him how good and how pleasant it is for brethren to dwell together in unity."

With such reflections as these Mr. Tournay worked himself into quite a cheerful mood, and was half hoping for an opportunity to display the good-will of his firm, when he came to the corner of Dock and Union Streets. Here a gust of wind carrying a stifling load of ashes burst upon him, driving him suddenly back behind the corner house to regain his breath.

"Great God!" exclaimed he as he glanced again around the corner in a momentary lull of the whirlwind. "The whole wharf is on fire. Smyth Street and Nelson Street will go, as sure as fate! Sir," said he to a policeman who came up just then, "how did such a fire as this begin?"

"No one seems to be able to tell," said the officer. "It was first seen at one side of McLaughlin's boiler-works, down there on the slip, and probably began in a little building alongside. Hare's Wharf is going fast. The engines work well, and I see they have ordered out old engine No. 3. But water does not seem to have any effect. There! They are shifting new No. 3 now. This is a fatal locality for fires. Sir, this block back of us has been burned six times in seventy years; and it is about here somewhere that the great fires of 1837, 1840, and 1845, began. I think you had better look sharp to your warehouse, for the air is full of burning brands and cinders. Just see that storm of them going away over to Market Wharf! My God! Mr. Tournay, this is going to be a terrible fire."

Mr. Tournay waited to hear no more; for the wind was increasing to a gale, the blinding smoke hissed around the corner, the air was dense with sparks and dust, and little puffs and jets of smoke appearing on the shingles, in crevices of clapboards, and joints of window-casings, showed him that in a few moments the wooden stores and dwellings all about him would be in a flame. Yet he could not believe that his warehouse was in any danger. He was confident the steam fire-engines would stop the conflagration. They were the pride of the city. In two minutes only after the clerk struck this alarm, the engines began to throw water upon McLaughlin's factory; and he did not see how a fire could get away from them. He could scarce credit what he himself saw, but under-estimated the danger, in whatever form it presented itself. He even so far forgot his own property, and had such a feeling of confidence in the fire-department, that he delayed some time to help a man lift a piano down a flight of doorsteps on Union Street, and, with habitual business caution, tied up the end-board of the wagon as the instrument was being carted away. When he reached Prince William Street, and turned toward Market Square, the highway before him presented a strange scene. The people had begun to be excited over the prospect of an extensive conflagration. Every one seemed to be moving his or her effects, each in a different direction, and none appearing to know whither. As he himself began to give way to the panic which was now spreading among the people, he quickened his pace to a trot, and then to a downright running chase; thinking then, for the first time, that it was among the possibilities that neither the fire-department nor the intervening blocks of brick and stone would prevent the destruction of his warehouse. He ran against old ladies with cradles and babies, tongs and dolls; against men with beds, boxes, clothing, chairs, and crockery-ware; overturned boys enveloped in piles of table-linen, dragging toy carts and tin hose-carriages. He stumbled over heaps of merchandise, broken furniture, stacks of books and picture-frames, which the owners, with shouts and screams, were endeavoring to convey to a place of safety. Some few cool-headed ones were quickly and systematically stowing their goods in wagons, or carrying them across the street; but many others were excited and unreasonable, doing the strangest and most unreasonable things, which at any other time would have strained his sides with laughter.

When he reached Market Square, it seemed as if the whole city had instantly started to move. Every available vehicle from a dray to a buggy was called into requisition, and came crowding into the square. The sidewalks were being piled with goods from the wholesale houses. Some packages were being hastily deposited on the vessels at the wharf; others were carried up King Street to King's Square; while the teams hurried hither and thither, taking goods to other stores, or to private houses, or into open lots, some to be finally saved, and others to be burned even in their place of refuge. Men were upon the roofs, and on almost every projection of the buildings, pouring on water, or extinguishing with rags the lodging sparks which showered down upon the buildings far and near. The wind was blowing in a hurricane, and fanned the furnace behind them until with volcanic throes it belched forth burning brands of pine which a strong man would have found it difficult to carry, and, shooting them high in the heavens, let them fall far to the windward, crashing into roofs and windows, or threatening the lives of the crowd, about whose heads they whirred and hissed as they fell to the pavement. So hot became the gusts, and so full of sparks was the air everywhere in the path of the tempest, that bundles of goods tossed from second-story windows were on fire before they reached the hands of those who caught them in the yard below.

Here were strange scenes. One man, too faithful to his employers to think of leaving them for his wardrobe and valuables at the burning hotel, or too excited to make much account of his feelings or his life, stood on the window-casement of the store, and passed out goods, unmindful of the fact that his hat of straw was blazing and singeing into his scalp. One elderly merchant was seen tying up an old umbrella with a clothes-line, and had to be severely shaken by his son before he recovered from his temporary lunacy. One seized the hose which threw a powerful stream, and began driving away at the broken packages of dry-goods passing him in the street.

But the action of some of the sailors in the vessels at the wharves exhibited the strangest freaks of absent-mindedness. The harbor was crowded with vessels; and the wharves in the vicinity where the fire began were closely lined with ships of various tonnage. Some of these were in such close proximity to the fire, and their rigging ignited so quickly, that many were destroyed, or badly damaged, before they could be pushed out into the bay. Some were towed away from the shore, some were forced into the stream by men along the wharves, and some were drawn out of the slips by sailors in small row-boats. One old sailor, whose vessel lay at Market Wharf, became so agitated, that when the sail caught fire he could not wait for tug or tide, and taking a small tow-line in his teeth leaped overboard, and, as he stoutly claims since, actually towed the vessel to safe anchorage by swimming against the tide. The officers seem to think that the men with spike-poles on the wharf had something to do with the movement of the ship; but the sailor does not admit that such was the fact. Another at the end of a Water-street slip tried to draw water with a cord hammock to extinguish a flame in a bundle of tarred rags. Another ran up aloft, and seated himself on the yard, to get out of the flames on deck, and was only saved by being persuaded to leap into the bay. Another poor fellow, whose family reside at Halifax, rowed alongside a burning wharf, and saved a man and a woman clinging to the timbers; but in so doing was so burned, and drew into his lungs so much smoke, that he died but a few hours later.

Mr. Tournay did not stop to ponder upon the events transpiring about him; but, as he crossed Market Square, he saw at a glance the great tongues of flame rise over the distant blocks, and, with a hiss like that of a bomb, dart over and downward upon mast and sail and lumber piles. He saw the sailors leaping from rope to rope with pail and sponge. He saw the water surging along the half-submerged boards, as bucket after bucket was emptied upon the decks. He heard the shouts of captains, the yells of men along the wharves, the bustle on the piers, the confusion which characterized everybody and every thing on dock, street, sidewalk, or warehouses; but they made no fixed impression on his mind.

He hastened, puffing and sighing, from store to

store; and at last, almost paralyzed with fatigue and agitation, he rushed into his warehouse. A few minutes had changed every thing without and within. Without were eager hurrying masses of people, all excited and noisy; while within were busy hands, trained to be systematic and cautious, tying bundles, nailing cases, stowing goods near the rear windows preparatory to a precipitate removal; and with a celerity which only comes from a thorough training in arranging, packing, and economizing room, the clerks and porters secured for safe transportation the vast collection of valuable merchandise which the building contained.

Still believing that the fire might be stayed, as it was burning within the fire limits where brick, stone, and mortar formed the principal building-material, Mr. Tournay's associates hoped to save the building, and avoid the expense of removal. They, however, took the precaution to send out men to hire express-wagons for the removal of their merchandise, having but one or two teams of their own. They also sent men to the roof and windows to saturate with water all the exposed wood-work about the structure. The messengers who were sent after the teams soon returned, saying that no money could hire a drayman or expressman; that the fire was demolishing the stone buildings as if they were but mortar; and that wildest confusion reigned in every business street.

Then it was decided by all that the time had come to remove the goods as fast as possible. But they had waited a few minutes too long. When they attempted to raise the windows on the side towards the fire, the rush of smoke and cinders was so great as to make it impossible to work there, even had not the safety of the building been dependent upon keeping all such avenues closed. So they tried the windows at the rear end of the warehouse; but the change caused such delay in getting the teams within reach, that the roof was blazing high when the first packages were handed down to the wagons. The employees young and old stood by the burning building like sailors by a ship, and would not forsake their revered employers, though they felt sure their own property in other places was perishing for the need of their protection, and that the men they served might be too poor on the morrow to pay them their wages for even that day. They staid after the proprietors told them to go. They threw out hundreds of cases and bales after the approaching heat had broken the glass in the windows, and let in great billows of fire. They staid until the merchandise was ablaze; and then with scorched faces and blistered hands they leaped from the windows into the alley, and, hiding from the smoke and flame, crawled between old sheds and fences, and thus picked their way, more dead than alive, into King's Square.

CHAPTER III.

BURNING HOMES.

Caught by the Flames. — Running the Gauntlet of Fire. — Burning of the Dead. — The Ruins of a Home. — Searching for Loved Ones. — Surrounded by Fire. — Queen's Square.

DAVID TOURNAY was the last person to leave the warehouse, as he lingered behind to be sure that the safe was locked, and that all valuable papers were taken away or deposited. And when he reached the rear entrance, and opened the door, he was confronted by a solid sheet of flame. It was impossible to escape that way; and he felt his heart leap as it occurred to him that those who had left but a few moments before by that same way must have been burned to death. For it was only a short time since they had called him to follow. He forced the door back into place, and pressed down the latch, catching full in his face as it closed a furnace-blast that singed his whiskers, and punctured his cheeks with a thousand stings.

Now what was he to do? Should he try to gain

an upper window? No: the second and third floors were already on fire, and the smoke even then began to curl in curious rifts along the ceiling of the ware-room in which he stood. The front doors had been shut and bolted some time before, to keep out both thieves and fire; but through the crevices in the drawn shutters he could see the rushing clouds of dust and smoke, with an occasional glare like the gleams of lightning at night, which for a moment illuminated the store in a lurid, ghastly manner, and then left it gloomier than before. This warehouse in which he had accumulated his wealth, this building from which he was so soon to retire with a competency, to be happy all his days with his wife and Ethel, was now to be his grave, and the great city was to be his funeral pyre.

Let the writers of romance describe imaginary scenes as they may, let poets collect their most affecting numbers, and relate with all the license of their calling; but they will not approach any thing akin to accuracy in describing a scene like this. The pen is powerless to picture the dismay, the horrid apprehensions, which must torture the man or woman in Mr. Tournay's situation. There are emotions which are so horrid, and which so seldom come, that man has no language with which to express them. To be burned to death while in complete health; to die with every thing in his possession to make life a pleasure; to leave his wife and child alone; and — ah! could it be possible? Would this fire reach Queen's Square? Might not his wife and Ethel be burned for lack of a protector, — no one to move the poor ill girl?

How many men there are, who, before the Saint John fire, have been wrought up to desperate deeds, as Mr. Tournay says that he was, by the care and love they felt for others, when the thoughts of themselves only weakened their resolution, and confirmed their fear! When he thought of his loved ones in distress, he became desperately in earnest, and feared not to attempt any thing which might lead to them. He instantly decided to go by the front door, for that led into the open street, while the rear passage was crooked and uncertain.

Glancing about him for some protection, he saw a woollen blanket lying upon a box. He seized it at once, swung it over his head, wrapped it close about his shoulders; and, turning the key, he quickly opened the door, and darted desperately into the street. The spot was like a smelting-furnace. Ashes, dust, smoke, and pieces of crumbling ruins, went whistling, dashing by, forced on by a typhoon which had arisen after the fire began. It seized him, whirled him, lifted him, choked him, but bore him onward, onward, whither he hardly knew. With his head completely wrapped in the woollen blanket, seeing nothing, hearing nothing, he ran with the wind, scarce getting a breath, and uncertain whether the next step might not drop him over a precipice, or into a burning dwelling. He could feel the flame's hot breath scorching his limbs and feet, and knew it was a fearful gauntlet he was running. He could smell the burning blanket, and knew that his race must be a short one, or he would be lost.

Soon he stumbled against a stone which lay beside the street, and, falling headlong, went sprawling in the muddy gutter. Here he threw off the blanket to see where he had fallen; and he found himself several blocks from the warehouse, but with the fire burning in the buildings about him on all sides. The houses, however, were smaller, and the danger from falling walls was passed. He found too, — strange he had not thought of it before, — found that as he lay on the ground he was clear of the smoke, except when the strongest gusts went by. He also found that which was nearly an equal blessing, — the gutter filled with running water coming from hose or hydrant left open by the retreating people.

He had the presence of mind to dip his blanket in the filthy water, and, blessing the Yorkshire operators who wove that covering, concealed his head again, and ran on as before. It was an easy matter now. He could drop to the ground and get fresh air at any time, while the wet cloth protected him from the smoke as well as from the flame.

As he turned into Duke Street he ascertained that he was leaving the fire behind; and, after crossing Germain Street, he found himself again in the midst of human beings: yet the smoke and flying cinders were still almost intolerable.

At that time the whole water-front upon the river side of the city was on fire. The conflagration had spread in a most unusual and astonishing manner. For while the original flames were coursing down Dock and Nelson Streets, and demolishing the structures on Market Wharf, live coals were carried long distances, and dropped into tarred roofs, or bales of hay, or slyly inserted by the wind under casings, shingles, or shavings, to spring up into hundreds of bonfires wholly unexpected, and consequently wholly at liberty to grow into wildfires without obstruction. In this way the large establishment of Daniel and Boyd on Market Square was ignited. In this way the wooden buildings half a mile distant and near the Custom House were set on fire. So that it was the work of but a short space of time, not exceeding forty-five minutes after the fire was in Dock Street, before the whole of the city lying between Prince William Street and the water was burning nearly as far down as Reed's Point. The steam fire-engines had done most excellent service in preventing the spread of the flames up Union Street beyond Dock Street, as that block where they stopped the fire was the key to all that part of the city north of King Street, and all of which was saved; at a great sacrifice, however, as we shall see hereafter.

Intent upon nothing but reaching his house, Mr. Tournay hurried into Germain Street; but he saw the huge columns of smoke back of the Victoria Hotel; and he noticed also that old Trinity Church was giving way to the devouring element, which had not more respect for things sacred than it had for things profane. Even old Trinity, with almost a century of history clinging to its walls, with the same timbers the Loyalists hewed when they made Saint John their home,— even that could burn! The swift progress of the disaster thus shown warned him not to try to reach Queen's Square by Germain Street: and, quickly turning back, he hastened toward Charlotte Street, one block farther removed from the fire. The air was thick with sparks, which kindled into flame on the roofs and porches on either side of his way; but, with the aid of his blanket, he made comparatively safe progress.

He had not proceeded far, however, from Germain Street, before he was rudely seized by a stout hand; and a hoarse sailor's voice shouted, —

"Say, friend, give us a hand! We have moved the corpse three times, and it's likely to burn after all. Come, give us a lift! just a minute!"

"My house is burning: my wife and sick child are in it! I can not, will not stop!" said Mr. Tournay, impatiently shaking off the hold of the stranger upon his arm.

"Sorry for you, sir," said the same voice. "It is better to be dead than alive in such an hour as this. Then I must let the dead past bury its dead," he added, following closely upon Mr. Tournay's heels, and evidently abandoning the body of the dead to be burned to ashes.

At the next corner two young women, frenzied with terror, seized Mr. Tournay, and pleaded with tears and shrieks that he would save their father.

"I cannot stop! I must save my wife! I must save my child!" screamed he, as he pulled and dragged at the blanket they so tenaciously held.

"Oh, come with us! He was dying when the flames drove us away. We took him out of his sick-bed: we carried him two blocks; we could not carry him farther. Oh, my God! my God! he is burning, and no one will help us!"

Mr. Tournay hesitated. But the thought that this man, whoever he was, might be already dead, while his own wife and child, if saved from the fire, would be safe from such a fatal disease, increased his determination to go on. He shook them off with a desperate jerk, and started down the street. His journey was not an easy one, for his path was often blockaded by bundles, beds, tables, mirrors, wagons, wheelbarrows, books, kettles, and lumber, that the doting owners were trying to hurry, in an immense variety of conveyances and methods, to a place of safety (which, by the way, the greater part of the property never found).

Imagine, if you can, the dismay and heart-sickness of that great number of St. John's merchants, when they gazed, as Mr. Tournay gazed, upon the crumbling ruins of their homes, — the walls enclosing a furnace hot and seething, — and when they felt, as he felt, that in all probability the family he loved were flayed in its bed of coals. We follow the steps of Mr. Tournay, not because his experience was more thrilling or more disastrous than that of thousands of others, — for we believe that, were the details known to those who write or those who print, there would be found men whose adventures on that afternoon and night were of a much more interesting and exciting character, — but we follow him as a representative of the many, and because his story happened to be heard under circumstances favorable to its perpetuation in history. If the reader will multiply Mr. Tournay's sufferings by fifteen thousand, and add five thousand for those who suffered less but lost their homes, he may, in a measure, obtain an idea of this appalling disaster.

Queen's Square, when David Tournay at last reached it, was enveloped in flame upon three sides; and the westerly front was fast succumbing to the heat and whirling brands. He could not see his house when he entered the square, so thick was the intervening cloud. But with a heart aching until he half determined to rush into the embers of his home and die as *they* had probably died, he wrapped the blanket again about his head, and rushed into the middle of the square. The shade-trees and the grass were parching with the heat; and long wings of flame swooped down upon them from the roofs of the houses, as the countless whirlwinds wrestled and fought around the walls of those beautiful homes. In the centre of the park, cowering upon the grass and among piles of furniture, was a small company of women and children, crouching with fear, and unable to move.

Mr. Tournay thought at first that he detected the velvet-trimmed dress of his wife among their number, and hasted with an eagerness he never knew before, to scan the smoke-begrimed faces. But those he sought were not there. Disheartened, he started toward his house; but the shifting of the wind showed him that nothing was left of his beautiful residence, with all its priceless treasures, except the front wall; while through the ghastly apertures, once the windows of a mansion, he could see and hear the hideous, remorseless flames. In the single glance which he had of his house before the smoke returned, he saw that a part of the front door still clung to its hinges, and that *it was partially open.* He knew that it had a stout spring lock. He knew that he closed it firmly when he left it. Hence *some person must have opened the door from the inside*, or it would not then be open and swinging upon its hinges. He saw enough to give him a hope of their escape. Yes, they might have been warned in time! They might have found friends! And thus attempting to quiet his dreadful apprehensions he turned away, hoping to escape while yet there was an opportunity. But as he noticed again the women and children, and heard them so pitifully calling after him, he said to himself, " These are some other men's loved ones, and I will do by them as I so much hope some one has done by mine." Then he hurried them upon their feet, told them he could take them to a place of safety, called to another forlorn searcher like himself for assistance; and, with many a burn and heavy tug with the fainting ladies and fear-stricken children, they managed to avoid other disasters, and landed the little company safely in Carmarthen Street, and started them on their way toward the barracks.

CHAPTER IV.

INCIDENTS OF THE FIRE.

The Culmination of the Destruction. — Death by Fire. — A Life, or a Dwelling? — Saving a Handful of Wood. — Losing Gold Sovereigns. — Birth of Children amid the Flames and on the Bay. — Escape by Raft. — The Scene from Ballast Wharf.

THE shadows which slowly fell upon the ocean and on the distant hills found David Tournay, in common with thousands of his townsmen, still searching for his loved ones. With an unnatural display of endurance, he had passed swiftly from street to street, had encountered the fire again and again, as it steadily but quickly advanced from house to house. He had seen the destroying flames, with one flank resting upon the parade-ground at the end of the peninsula, and the other upon King Street, marching onward with solid front, and sweeping every thing before them from the harbor on the west to Courtney Bay on the east. He had witnessed terrible scenes of suffering. Men, women, and children had been often carried by him with burned faces or scorched limbs. The faces of the killed, so ghastly and horrible, glared from under their uncertain covering, as the uncouth, steaming bearers hurried them on to those anxious but hopeful groups which in health and joy the dead had left but a few hours before. He had anxiously stared into humble cottages, had unceremoniously burst into the doors of deserted mansions, had scanned the groups at the water's edge, and the crowds in the park, and had called upon all he met with whom he claimed any acquaintance, and upon many who knew and cared nothing for him, everywhere asking for his wife and child.

Once there came rushing toward him an old acquaintance, known to all the people as one of nature's noblemen, who though far along in years, sadly deaf, and bereft by this calamity of his house of stone, and his factory in which for years he and his sons had driven a profitable trade in window-sashes, doors, and blinds, was yet so generous, so forgetful of self, as to be unceasingly active in saving the lives and property of others.

"John," said Tournay, putting his lips close to the ear of his friend, "have you seen or heard any thing of my wife or child?"

"No, I have not seen *your* wife and child; but I have seen many wives and children of other men, looking for their husbands and fathers: sorry yours were not among them. O David! I have seen such a sight to-day!" continued he. "I tremble as I think of it. I saw a woman burned to death, — an old lady, the mother of the ex-mayor. It was hard, hard, hard! She came into my house after I had sent all my folks away except my son James; and she sat down in the back room, just as if she was making a call. James told me she was there; and, as the houses were burning all around mine, I told James to tend the hose, and keep the roof wet, while I went down to see what she was doing there. I walked right in where she was, and saw her rocking back and forth, talking to herself; but of course I could not hear what she said. I told her that everybody had left the street, and that my house was likely to burn with the others, though I intended to die by it; and I took hold of her, and tried to lift her up, but she would not move. I saw, as she looked up at me, and refused to take a step, that she was insane. The fire, with all its horrors, had actually driven her mad. I saw through the window that the rear buildings were burning; and I was then almost suffocating with the smoke that sifted into the house, although I kept a wet silk handkerchief constantly tied over my mouth. 'Come,' I said: 'you must go.' But when I tried to lift her out of the chair, she sank upon the floor. I tugged away for a while, but I soon concluded that I could not save her and the house too; and the house was a doubtful matter at the best. So I called to James, and told him we must get this woman away. So we pulled her to the door; but when she saw the buildings all on fire about us, and blazing terrifically as far as we could see up and down the street, she kicked and screamed, and urged us to let her die just there. But we dragged her into the street, and abandoned the old home to the fire. It was so hot, the wet handkerchief over my mouth steamed like a boiling kettle, and my hands prickled and smarted, and every breath seemed to singe the inside of my throat and lungs. Oh, it was so hot! James took the old lady on his back, after we got into the street; and I kept alongside, to shelter him and her from the heat; and he carried her some distance that way. But there seemed to be no end to the destruction. As far as we could see, nothing but fire, fire, fire. It was of no use. James could not hold out. I saw he was tottering, and I told him to stop, and let the woman down a moment; then I thought I would take her myself. But she resisted so much, and was so determined to be burned, that I could not possibly manage her alone. James was fast giving way to the heat and smoke: so I says, 'Run, James, run! Keep close to the ground. Get under the smoke, and take breath. Keep down Main Street to the bay, and get into the water as quick as you can. Then I did not know what to do next. I knelt down, and pleaded with her to get up. 'My God! you and I will both be burned here in a moment, if you don't get up and come along.' But she was only the more determined to remain. So I drew her alongside an overturned boat which lay near by, and threw a piece of tarpaulin over her, hoping something might happen to save her; and ran for my life. But it was not five minutes before the boat and tarpaulin were seen blazing like a tinder; and she must have burned to ashes alive right there."

But David Tournay could not wait to hear more of his old friend's details, and abruptly left the speaker in order to scrutinize a company that had waded into the water alongside the railway dikes skirting the bay; but his wife and child were not there. He hurried up the bank to a vacant lot, where stood an abandoned horse-car. Smoke and cinders which beat upon it, and the floods which volunteer firemen showered upon it, made it an uncomfortable but safe place of refuge. Within that strange tenement, a poor fainting, exhausted woman had been thrust by those who could no longer carry her; and there, amid the thunders and screechings of the conflagration, and the equally unearthly screams of women and hallooing of men, she gave birth to a child. Of all the terrors and pains of that night, it would seem as if such an event was the culmination of all woe; yet both mother and child survived.

Still searching along the shore, wading into the water, and running around falling walls, until every fibre of his clothing sent out puffs of steam, he hurried toward the International Steamship Wharf, where he was told a crowd of women had collected.

Night had come, but the lurid peninsula melting with heat illuminated the landscape for a hundred miles. Ships far out at sea showed their white sails tinged with red. The Penitentiary across the bay, the Insane Asylum on Carleton Heights, Reed's Castle on the Portland cliffs, the residences along Manawaggonish Road, the St. John River for many, many miles inland, Partridge Island in the bay, and the Carleton Wards on the western shore, were all radiant with light. The glare upon distant lawns, windows, and towers, was spectral, red as blood, and strangely mingled with flickering, uneasy shadows; but yet so bright that the clearest noonday was hardly more searching and distinct. It gave a weird, unreal aspect to the forms of men and women as they flitted on the banks, or hastened away from the melting shore in boats, scows, and rafts.

At one point the approach of the fire was so swift that the bewildered refugees sought an asylum on rafts of lumber, and floated awkwardly out into the bay. On one of the most crowded of these, where men were holding on and swimming because there was no room for more to stand, another child was born. Another lumber-float with no male adult upon it, but bearing a score of women and children, drifted helplessly out to sea, and would soon have been lost, had not the red glare of the burning city showed them to an approaching schooner. When rescued, the conflict between wind and tide had whirled them around and around, until all were too giddy to stand upon their feet. Upon all such rafts as these along the shore, David Tournay bent his anxious gaze; but his wife was not there. He leaped into boats near the shore, and shouted to others in the stream, but no tidings of her did he find; but many a wretched sufferer did he meet, and many groans and sighs and prayers did he hear, until, as he says, all such exhibitions of terror or grief lost their force, and became stale and irksome to him.

One person stopped him as he ran, to tell how he had been so crazed by the sudden approach of the calamity, that he unaccountably left all his valuables and keepsakes in the house, and ran half a mile with a handful of cord-wood. Another told him how he had piled his best furniture into his cellar, and turned on the water, hoping to fill the cellar from the aqueduct. One woman had laid up, in past years, an old coffee-pot full of gold sovereigns; and, when she left her house that afternoon, she poured the gold into the pocket of her dress, and, seizing a heavy iron fender, lugged that heavy piece of metal out of danger. She found, however, when she was so far out of the heat as to recover her self-possession, that the weight of the gold had torn away her pocket, and her sovereigns were gone. All she had saved from a house full of valuable articles of furniture and decorations was a useless iron fender which the fire might not in the least have harmed. Several other ladies he afterwards saw who had lost money and jewelry by the tearing of their pockets in the same way.

But it is to be feared that Mr. Tournay did not listen very deferentially, or wait long for the completion of such tales. His mind was pre-occupied with a great, inexpressible sorrow. Yet, when he found himself baffled in his search around the shores of the bay, and stood hesitating at the extreme end of the peninsula where the earthworks and the cannon furnished a temporary shelter from the heat of the burning barracks, he could not avoid giving expression to his wonder, as he gazed up the sloping hillsides on which the city had stood.

> "By Heaven! it is a splendid sight to see,
> For one who hath no friend, no brother, there."

The magnificence of the spectacle could not escape the dullest mind. The red clouds hanging above, the columns and shoots of flame below, the widespread glow of the still bright embers, the strange outline of the Germain-street Church in its picturesque ruins against the illumined smoke beyond; the Gothic arches of the Orphan Asylum, resplendent in living red; the infinite variety of shape and color the ruins had everywhere assumed; the shifting banks of smoke, the delicate blushes of the water on either hand; the intermingling of blue, carnation, crimson, yellow, and white, with kaleidoscopic changes in ruin, cloud, and sea, made an impression which the beholder can never efface. It was not lost upon Mr. Tournay. A whole city in embers! Such a bonfire may the world never see again! Those streets he knew so well were undistinguishable from the foundations of dwellings. All alike seemed burning. Those houses, those churches, those trees, those warehouses, those banks, which had grown so familiar to him, were reduced to dust and crumbling heaps of coals.

ST. JOHN IN FLAMES.

How was it with himself, — he that was so happy, so rich, so successful, so loved, so respected, in the morning? How is it now with him? Can it be that so soon he is wifeless, childless, penniless? A mourner and a beggar! Yet he was but one of many. Sad hours are often seen by all mankind; but where are there any sadder than those of that long night to the homeless, stricken people of Saint John?

CHAPTER V.

IN THE VICINITY OF KING'S SQUARE.

The Stationary Vehicle. — The Merchandise in King's Square. — Appearance of the Refugees. — The Old Burying-Ground. — The Shelterless Ones. — Removal to New Homes.

IT was late in the night when Mr. Tournay succeeded in fighting his way against heat, water, and human crowds, back to the foot of Orange Street on the shore of Courtney Bay; but the fire was not even there wholly overcome. Here and there houses caught and blazed most furiously, which had been up to that hour successfully defended. But the few buildings which were left at the water's edge were so accessible to the steam fire-engines, and the force of the aqueduct was so great at these low points, that water was to be had in abundance. So many people had opened the faucets in their houses, and were using their hose so generally when the fire approached the principal streets, that the supply on the highest portion of the mountainous city ran short for the fire-engines. The water would scarcely flow while the fire raged the fiercest, so great was the quantity taken and wasted by the people. But in the lower and outlying districts there was water in abundance, and buildings there could be saved; yet, when Tournay passed by Orange Street, the heat was still so intense that any house fronting the conflagration, though constantly saturated with water, would dry in one moment, and spring into a flame the next. One such house had been defended for more than an hour, when the draft of water by the fire-engines on Pitt Street lessened the supply at this point. Almost instantly the structure ignited along the whole front.

The men, seeing it useless to work longer upon the building, drove a horse close to the rear door, and backed the wagon upon the sidewalk. When Mr. Tournay came up, they had heaped the vehicle with household goods, had shouted themselves hoarse at the motionless animal, had kicked and clubbed him, pulled at his bridle, and pushed at the wheel; but the load did not, would not, move. The beast seemed to try his strength, and although the load stood on an inclined plane it would not move. Almost beside themselves with surprise and vexation, the laborers danced about and screamed at that horse; and at last, driven away by the increasing heat, they left the poor beast and his load to the destroyer. They felt sure, however, that the horse would soon start rather than stand and be burned to death; and they lay by and watched for him. Mr. Tournay was hastening to their assistance, when the falling of a roof near by them drove them farther away; and, availing himself of his charred blanket which he still carried, he ran up to the trembling animal, and took hold of the bridle. But the horse would not start, or could not do so; yet the beast seemed to appreciate his danger, and shivered like an aspen, looking at his load with a frightened and pleading expression, and making a plaintive whining noise. The load was blazing high, when Mr. Tournay groped along to the hindermost wheels, thinking to try one push, and if unsuccessful to release the animal from the shafts. There, as the smoke drifted for a moment another way, he saw the difficulty. For the driver in his haste had dropped the chain he used to secure the end-board of the wagon, over the crown of an iron post or hydrant; and a dozen horses could not break that chain, or extract the post. A sharp pull at the wheel, a quick lifting of the chain, and the wagon was released. Who knows but the horse understood the situation, and was thankful as he was led by the bridle into Crown Street, and the fire in the load extinguished?

From Crown Street, Mr. Tournay proceeded

through Union Street and Sidney Street to King's Square, stopping frequently at some doorway on these remaining streets where little companies were assembled, and asking for news of his wife and child. In the glare of the now dying fires, he recognized many old friends, some who spoke cheerfully of their prospects, some who appeared wholly disheartened, some who had lost all their property, some who had no hope of payment although insured in various small companies, some who were badly burned, some whose friends had been killed or badly maimed; but not one of them had seen Mr. Tournay's companion or daughter.

No one in the city slept that night; all came into that section of the city which had been saved from the destroyer, and in subdued whispers and half-concealed undertones talked of the calamity, and magnified its horrors by rumors of many terrible things which could not possibly happen. King's Square presented a motley scene indeed, — half human beings, half merchandise, interminably entangled, so that any man whom the police allowed to enter was in a continuous state of doubt whether the bundles and heaps about him were animate or inanimate. This had been the general depository of all the property saved from the fire; and stacks of merchandise, of enormous value, at one time covered its walks and lawns. But at the first opportunity furnished by some neighbor who opened his house, store, manufactory, or stable, to their reception, the goods were as hastily removed as they had been delivered; so that teams and porters were coming and going in endless procession, while the fear of thieves kept a strong force of volunteer watchmen about each owner's stock. Here were men searching for lost articles, the location of which they had forgotten. Here were women and children with quilts and shawls over their heads, seated on a heap of household property, so hastily thrown together, guarding their only remaining possessions. Here were a number of trunks, whose owners believed them destroyed, and on one of which two little girls sat crying for their father and mother; while all about the greensward men, women, and children were sitting, lying, or standing, not knowing where to go, or waiting the return of some messenger sent out for succor. Over the whole space were scattered pieces of almost every thing merchantable. All trades, professions, and occupations had contributed toward the motley collection; and in the hasty removal with such uncertain light (the lamps being extinguished) specimens of almost every deposit were left behind to clog the feet of those who followed.

But the saddest scenes of all were witnessed in the old burying-ground situated on the other side of Sidney Street and nearly opposite King's Square. To the numbers who crowded that dismal locality, especially so in the dead of night, thousands of homes had contributed.

No real home needs velvets, laces, or diamonds, to make it dear. The forlorn one who had parted with but a few dollars' worth of household articles was as deeply pained at the loss of that as he who counted the value of his mansion's trimmings by thousands of pounds. The husband whose beard was rough, whose hands were calloused, and whose speech was untutored and coarse, had the same value in the eyes of his wife as that which the wife of the rich and cultured man placed upon his life. The child of the fisherman or lumberman was as dear to his parents, and, under the thorough free-school system of such a city, was as sure of arriving at distinction, as the son of the wealthiest official. Here they were huddled among the graves, broken scattered families; a son, a daughter, a sister, a brother, a parent, in the list of missing. Sad field of sorrow! the very sward was wet with tears. It is certain that never before since the cemetery was consecrated had such things been witnessed there; and it is doubtful if the old Loyalists themselves, whose imposing tombs tell of so much adventure and privation, ever witnessed such keen and heart-breaking anxiety as that possessing the minds of those who that night trod thoughtlessly upon the Loyalists' graves, nearly all waiting for some dear one who might never, never come.

"Katie! Katie! Is that you?" asked Mr. Tournay, as he entered the cemetery, and thought he saw the form of his kitchen-maid passing under the trees.

"O Lord! have you come alive, — sure?" almost screamed Katie, as she recognized the voice, and rushed toward him with a bound. "Where is mistress? where is Ethel?" added she, in the same breath.

"O Katie! haven't you seen them? Where did you leave them? Did they escape?" frantically pleaded the husband and father, as he seized the shoulder of the girl with a grasp that made her cringe.

"I don't know, sir," said she. "I heard the fire a-coming, and I ran out the front way; and I didn't see them at all."

He turned from her as if he had been stung by a serpent. It was Katie, then, who opened the front-door of his dwelling, and not his wife, as he had so much hoped. Hope gave place to dismay; and the exhausted, heart-broken man dropped upon the grass, and groaned.

Strangers came, and tried to comfort him. They told him that many had escaped from Queen's Square; that his wife might be off in a boat or schooner. But he would not be comforted. At last there came by him a gentleman who had known Mr. Tournay, and had been a visitor at his house. As he heard Mr. Tournay wailing so piteously, he stopped to ascertain the cause. Kneeling by the mourner, and failing to recognize him because of his torn coat, singed whiskers, sooty face, and the uncertain light, he bade him look on the brighter side. Mr. Tournay, however, recognized the voice, and, discovering that his friend did not know him, said, "Manseur, don't you remember me since yesterday? Oh, my wife and child! oh, my poor child!"

"Heavens, David! I can hardly believe your own lips. Are you really alive? Why, we heard you were burned in the store after the others had left. And your wife, too, thinks you are dead."

"My wife!" shouted David. "Have you seen her? and Ethel? Are they living? If you say no, I certainly shall die."

"Come with me, and I will show them to you," said his friend, leading the way briskly around the tombs to the other side of the cemetery. David

Tournay followed in silence. He could not speak. The re-action was so great that he gasped for breath, and great tears rolled down his cheeks. Under a small shade-tree in one corner of the city of the dead, in the shadow of the Court House, which stood between them and the ruins, was a blanket spread upon the grass; and upon it lay the sick and almost dying girl. Kneeling beside her, and holding one of her hands, with transparent face and closed eyes, was her grief-stricken mother.

"Mrs. Tournay," said the guide in a half-whisper, "don't disturb your daughter, *but I have brought you your husband.*"

"O David, David!" was all that was said.

Soon they took up the feeble girl, and carried her tenderly to a hospitable though humble home, where they laid her on a bed soft as her own, and called the nearest physician. Long and anxiously they awaited his coming; and when he had made his visit, and left his prescription, they were as uneasy and uncertain about the invalid as before. He said it *might* be all right, but she was exhausted: she might rally, and "the best thing to do was to hope for the best."

As the hours passed, and morning came, little Ethel slept; and the father and mother watched by her bedside, telling each other in whispers their adventures in the fire. She told him how Ethel had awakened her to see the fire along the window-casings; how in terror she seized the coverlet, and, wrapping the girl in it, carried her in great fright to the front stairs, where she saw so much smoke entering by the open door that she retreated into the front chamber. She told how she screamed for help from the window; how at last she desperately dropped from the window into the yard, with Ethel held by one hand; and how near she came to losing her hold upon her precious charge. She told how she ran to the house of a friend; how they were driven from that by the flames; how she sought and found another place of refuge, from which she was again driven; and how she determined to go to no more dwellings, but seek the burial-ground, where she was told the smoke and fire could not come. But a short time before he came to her, they had told her that he was dead.

They talked it over and over again, enumerated their losses, sighed when they thought of their home, wept when they talked of their all swept thus suddenly away; but gathered hope as they planned for years of work instead of the rest they had anticipated, and realized of how little consequence, after all, property was to them who had each other — and Ethel.

Alas, poor little Ethel! The agitation, the exposure, the heat, the smoke, all combined to overcome her feeble strength, and their effects were fatal. Twelve hours later, a little company of friends gathered at her bedside, where her parents held her pale hands as she calmly, peacefully, after twelve years of life, left this world of terror, for that realm of beauty where terrors of earthquake, tempest, and fire never come.

She was none the less a victim of the fire, because her name appears not in the list of the killed. How many, many others there were who suffered and died in the same way, the world will never know.

CHAPTER VI.

THE PEOPLE BEFORE THE FIRE.

The Metropolis of New Brunswick. — Character of its Founders. — Culture of the People. — Public and Private Enterprise. — Public Buildings, Commerce, Manufacturing, &c.

IT is a most difficult task to write a history of such an event as this, with that conciseness of detail which would please the people living in the locality of the disaster, and at the same time make a volume of sufficient interest to attract and hold those readers who are unacquainted with the city, and take no interest in local names and places; but to inform by facts and please by completeness both of those classes, will be the writer's earnest endeavor. Yet, as we write mainly for readers who are strangers to St. John, expecting to find our audience more in the United States, England, and Canada, than in New Brunswick, and as a gifted writer who is a resident of St. John[1] will produce a most valuable record of the great disaster, as we sincerely hope

[1] Mr. George Stuart.

and believe, we try to look upon the people and the calamity as an impartial stranger would view them, and write more especially of those things which a foreigner might wish to see and understand.

Although the city of St. John was not the legislative capital of New Brunswick, it was socially, intellectually, and commercially, the metropolis of the Province. Its fifty thousand people were unusually cultivated and enterprising. The rocky peninsula was selected as a site for a city by those expatriated loyalists from Massachusetts, New York, and Virginia, who were known at the time of their exile in 1783 as the most polished and learned men on the continent. They sought these huge, uninviting cliffs as the Pilgrim Fathers sought the ledges of Plymouth Rock.

> "Ay, call it holy ground, —
> The soil where first they trod:
> They have left unstained what there they found, —
> Freedom to worship God."

They were men who loved old England, and had no faith in the success of the dangerous experiment being tried by the colonies; men who revered old institutions, and despised iconoclasts; men to whom Chaucer, Raleigh, Milton, Taylor, Lamb, Goldsmith, and Shakespeare were patterns of literary excellence, and to whom William Pitt was a model statesman. They clung with ardent affection to the land and the nation which had produced such characters, and cared not to exchange it for a commonwealth which had no name, no history, no literature, and no art. They were sincere enough to fight for their convictions: thence the short-sighted people of the United States sent them away, and in so doing made the great, liberal, tolerant, generous nation they founded often blush with shame.

Such men as these, including in their number distinguished lawyers, orators, statesmen, soldiers, professors, merchants, and hardy tradesmen, were they who founded the city. Such as they have been their descendants. As like produces like, as men of similar tastes seek the society of each other, so the children of the founders, and the companions they drew to them from the mother country, were men and women who respected genuine worth, encouraged education, and assisted the industrious.

Such were the people to whom this great horror came. Public schools they had, and private academies. Libraries they had, both public and private, and were eminently a reading people. Churches and an imposing cathedral they had, being no less a church-going, God-fearing people, than a studious and industrious one. Banks they had, whose paper was current in the whole circuit of the world, and in the vaults of which when the visitation came were over fifty millions of dollars. Wharves they had, to which every clime and land had been tributary, and from which their own ships departed for almost every known port. Manufactories they had, competing with the imports from Europe. Hospitals they had, for the disabled in body and the deranged in mind; asylums for the orphan, the widow, the pauper; halls for public assemblies; theatres for dramas, lectures, and balls; markets with the products of every climate; hotels that were commodious; newspapers published by enterprising, conscientious men; and all the conveniences of light, water, sewerage, and communication, which are the pride of modern civilization. Connected with all these were the plainest indications of economy; born, no doubt, from the frugal, unostentatious habits of the people, combined with the enormous expense they necessarily incurred in cutting down the cliffs and hewing their streets and sewers through solid rock. They were a happy people. They were not possessed of enormous wealth; but they had enough, and they knew it. They were active, yet contented.

Why, in the providence of God, such a desolation should come to such a people, sweeping away in its unsparing malignity Bible depositories, religious schools, and beautiful churches, on which the prosperity of the faith seemed to depend, is one of those questions which every one asks, but no one can answer.

CHAPTER VII.

THE CITY BEFORE THE FIRE.

The Situation of the City. — The Dwellings. — The Public Buildings. — The Churches. — The Environs. — The Scenery. — The Harbor. — The Business Enterprises.

THE city of St. John was not a beautiful city to the eye of the merely æsthetical observer, although there were squares, parks, and shaded streets, to relieve the monotony of the landscape. Situated upon a peninsula which projected far into the bay, and confined to that promontory by more barren and almost inaccessible cliffs upon the landward side, the people availed themselves of every attainable spot within the city limits to build their houses, stores, and shops. This gave to the streets a somewhat crowded appearance, more especially outside of the fire precinct, where the buildings were largely constructed from wood, and without that unity of design which would have resulted from a greater desire for architectural effect, and less attention to the necessities and expenses of the constructors. But within the fire-limits, where the owners of land were confined to the use of non-combustible material in the construction of their buildings, the streets had a neat and thrifty appearance. Some of the warehouses were imposing and commodious buildings, arranged and ornamented after the drawings of the most skilful architects on the continent.

The churches were usually small, but the number of them was very large in proportion to the number of inhabitants. There were several exceptions, however, to the general rule as to the diminutiveness of church structures, including St. Stephen's Church (Church of Scotland), Trinity Church (Church of England), and the Germain-street Baptist edifice; while the Catholic Cathedral of the Immaculate Conception, on Waterloo Street, still standing, is a grand edifice two hundred feet long and one hundred and ten feet wide, and cost one hundred thousand dollars. There were various public school buildings, a spacious skating-rink, a Mechanics' Institute with a hall that seats twelve hundred auditors, a fine Court House, Custom House, a gymnasium and a lyceum; but so scattered were these, that they could not be counted as adding much to the beauty or symmetry of the city.

Yet, set as it was within a circle of attractive

suburbs, with a river on one side, which rises and falls, surges and roars, between precipitous cliffs in a most romantic manner; with a bay that shimmered and sparkled between gently receding shores of forest and lawn, and cheerfully bubbled and gurgled about the rocky island which bears the light-house tower; with views of summer retreats, hedged fields, and cultivated hills, to the eastward, beyond which the eyesight was lost in mountainous forests of evergreen; and with rocks that rose in towers to the northward, upon which were suburban parks, mansions, and, beyond them, plateaus of field and grove stretching away to the wide raft and schooner dotted river, — the city was, after all, one of the most inviting and exhilarating of resorts for those who admired the beauties of nature in their most varied forms.

Looking upon the city with a view to its commercial advantages, visitors found commodious wharves, ample anchorage, and a thicket of masts, with all the activity in the streets and wholesale warehouses which accompany such enterprises. In the ship yards there were vessels on the stocks; in the tributary waters there were countless rafts of manufactured lumber, and indications everywhere of active, permanent business growth.

Manufactories of edge-tools, nails, boots and shoes,

brick, carriages, furniture, iron-work, leather, lumber, woollen and cotton cloths, brushes, watches, books, spices, pianos, cigars, rope, and many other articles, were in a flourishing condition.

Upon such a city as this did the dread destroyer come. What a commentary upon the instability and uncertainty of man's most permanent institutions! and what an admonition its history contains, enjoining us to be profoundly thankful that we who write and we who read have been spared, while a people our equal in every thing that is deserving and noble have been so greatly afflicted!

CHAPTER VIII.

HISTORICAL SKETCH OF SAINT JOHN.

From 1604 to 1775. —Discovery by the French. — Fort La Tour. — Contest between La Tour and Charnisay. — Grant of Lands. — Indian Wars. — Pirates. — Expeditions from Boston. — War between the English and French. — Naval Engagements. — Capture of Fort La Tour. — Erection of a Blockhouse.

IT will give the interested inquirer a more comprehensive idea of the extent of the destruction, to insert here a condensed sketch of the history of Saint John and its environs. Such a chronicle must, however, be greatly condensed to admit of its publication in a book of this character; and, should the student desire to follow the matter into its exciting and romantic details, he cannot find a volume so complete, or peruse a story more delightfully told, than "The History of Acadia," by James Hannay, soon to be published. To the author of that interesting work we are indebted for the facts which follow, together with much useful information on other subjects, so kindly given during our search among

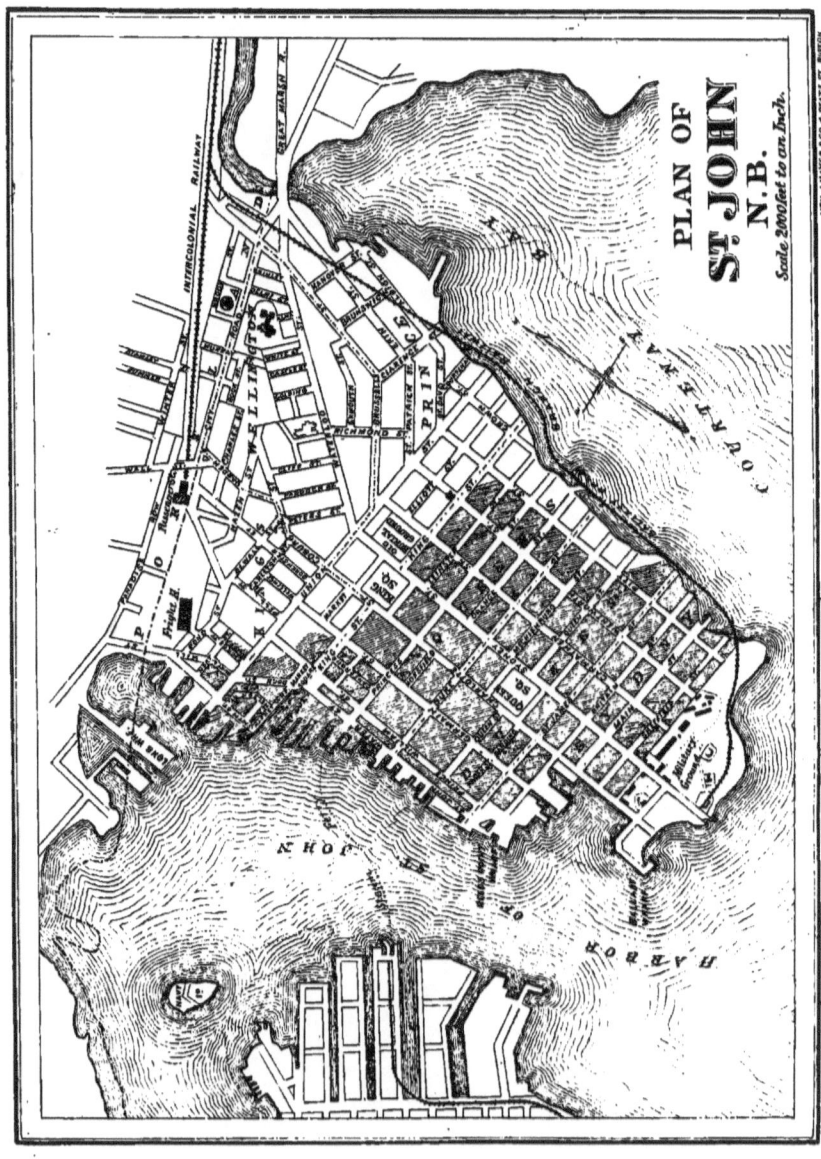

the ruins of his city and around the ashes of his home.

As early as the 24th of June, 1604, a little French ship sailed into the bay now known as the harbor of Saint John. She was a paltry craft, measured by modern standards, smaller than many of the coasting schooners of the present day; but she carried the germ of an empire, for Champlain, De Monts, and Poutrincourt, the founders of New France, were on her deck. Champlain's chart of the harbor shows how carefully he scanned his new discovery, and how little the great natural features of the place have changed in 271 years. The rugged hills about Saint John were then covered with pines and cedars; and on Navy Island, which was then separated from the mainland on the Carleton side by a much narrower channel than now, was a collection of Indian wigwams surrounded by a high palisade.

The savages who then dwelt at the mouth of the Saint John were Micmacs, called by the French Souriquois, the Malicetes or Etchemins being then confined to the upper parts of the river, which they called *Wollastook*, or Long River. By the Micmacs it was called *Wigoudy*, or the Great Highway. Champlain regarded himself as its first discoverer, and in honor of the day, that of Saint John the Baptist, gave the river the name which it has ever since retained.

But, though bent on founding a colony, he did not linger at the mouth of the Saint John, but spread his sails for a longer flight, and turned the prow of his vessel toward the fatal Island of St. Croix. Seven years after this, in 1611, Father Edmond Masse, a Jesuit father, was found living at the mouth of the Saint John, and, in the midst of all the discomforts incidental to a life amongst the savages, endeavoring to learn their language. But his residence there was short, and then the locality is without a history for nearly twenty years.

In 1630 Charles Amador de la Tour, a French nobleman, who was lieutenant-general to the king on the coast of Acadia, as that country was then called, commenced to build a fort at the mouth of the Saint John. The spot selected was the neck of land on the Carleton side, opposite to Navy Island; and Fort La Tour, as finally completed, was a palisaded fort of four bastions two hundred feet square, and mounting twenty-four guns. La Tour lived here for many years, and generally had two or three hundred servants and retainers about him. He traded largely with the Indians, as many as three thousand moose-skins being brought in from the Upper St. John and its tributaries in a single year, besides large numbers of beaver. La Tour had an enormous territory, and held a portion of his land by a double title, from the company of New France, and from Sir William Alexander, the grantee of James I. of England. In 1640 violent differences arose between La Tour and d'Aulnay Charnisay, who had a fort at Port Royal, now Annapolis, and was also a grantee of the company of New France. He succeeded in having La Tour's commission from the king revoked, and an order issued for his arrest, under the hand of Louis XIII., which La Tour treated with contempt. In 1643 Charnisay attacked La Tour's fort with five ships and five hundred men; but the latter obtained aid from Boston, and beat him off with loss. Early in 1645, in La Tour's absence, Charnisay made another attack; but La Tour's heroic wife encouraged the garrison, and his ship was compelled to retire in a sinking condition. Charnisay, however, returned with a stronger force, and attacked Fort La Tour from the land side. For three days Lady La Tour, with her weak garrison, held him at bay; but on the fourth, which was Easter Sunday, 16th April, 1645, while the garrison were at prayers, a treacherous Swiss sentinel opened the gate to the invaders. Lady La Tour, with unfaltering courage, rallied her little band of fifty men, and made head against the enemy; but finally, to save further bloodshed, made terms of capitulation. These terms Charnisay completely disregarded, and, with incredible barbarity, hanged all the garrison except the brave woman.

This accumulation of disasters so preyed on the spirits of Lady La Tour, that in a few days she died, leaving an infant child which was sent to France. Charnisay continued to retain Fort La Tour for some years, its legitimate owner having, in the mean time, retired to Quebec. Charnisay in 1650 was drowned in the Annapolis River; and in the following year La Tour had his commission restored to him by the French king, and recovered possession of his fort. In 1653 he married Charnisay's widow, and was living at St. John in a quiet domestic way, when in 1654 an English fleet which had been sent out by Oliver Cromwell appeared before Fort La Tour, which, being in a defenceless state, was obliged to capitulate; and Acadia passed into the hands of the English. La Tour went to England, and succeeded, in conjunction with Thomas Temple and William Crowne, in obtaining from Cromwell a grant of the whole of Acadia. La Tour subsequently sold out to Temple, who strengthened and improved Fort La Tour, and built a new fort at Jemseg, where he carried on a considerable trade with the Indians. La Tour died in 1666 at St. John; and in the following year the treaty of Breda was made between Louis XIV. and Charles II., by which Acadia was to be surrendered to France.

Owing to difficulties raised by Temple as to the

limits of Acadia, the surrender was not effected until 1670. It then became a French province with royal governors. The first governor under this new order of things was the Chevalier de Grandfontaine, who resided most of the time on the River St. John. He strengthened and improved Fort La Tour, bringing cannon to it from the fort at Jemseg, which for the time seems to have been abandoned. There were at that time in all Acadia less than four hundred souls, as appears by an actual census of the inhabitants taken in the year 1671. Only two forts were then maintained in Acadia, — that at Pentagoet, where the Chevalier Grandfontaine resided, and Fort La Tour, where his lieutenant M. de Marson held command.

In 1673 Grandfontaine returned to France, and was succeeded in command in Acadia by M. de Chambly. About this time, for some reason which is not given, but probably from its greater proximity and consequent advantages for communication with the Indians, De Marson appears to have transferred his headquarters to Fort Jemseg, for in 1674 he was there surprised by a Flemish pirate commanded by an English adventurer, and compelled to surrender. De Marson was carried off a prisoner, but soon appears to have been set at liberty; and he continued to hold command on the River St. John for some years. In 1676 he received a grant from the French crown of a seigniory called Nachouac; and in the same year he also received a grant of the fort or house of Jemseg.

In 1682 M. de la Vallière was in command in Acadia, under an appointment made by Count Frontenac, the governor of Canada. About this time the king of France granted to the Sieur Bergier of Rochelle, Gautier, Boucher, and De Montes, "the lands which they shall find suitable along the coast of Acadia and the River Saint John," for the establishment of the shore fishery. Bergier came to Acadia, and proceeded to organize fishing-establishments on its coasts; but he found his operations constantly impeded by the English, who had been fishing on these coasts for years, and were not to be restrained. La Vallière the commandant, who resided at Saint John, was openly accused of being in league with these enemies of his country; and it was stated in memorials written to the French Government of that day, that he had licensed the English vessels to fish on the coast of Acadia for money payment. Whether these accusations were true or not, it is certain that the differences between Bergier and La Vallière continued to increase in violence; and finally the latter, with something like piratical violence, seized several of Bergier's vessels, and confiscated their cargoes of fish and hides.

In 1684 La Vallière was removed from the governorship of Acadia, and succeeded by M. Perrot, who was in his turn succeeded in 1687 by M. de Meuneral. Prior to this, however, a new set of adventurers from Quebec had made their appearance on the Saint John River. These were four brothers named d'Amours, sons of Matthieu d'Amours, one of the councillors of state at Quebec. Their names were Louis, René, Matthieu, and Bernard; and, notwithstanding the rank and official position of their father, at an early age they took to the woods as *coureurs de bois*, or outlaws of the bush, and at one time were actually arrested by the governor of Canada for following this employment. They obtained grants of land on the River Saint John in 1684; and two of them, Matthieu and Louis, married to two sisters named Guyon, formed permanent establishments on the Saint John. Matthieu resided on the east bank of the river, opposite to the mouth of the Oromocto; and Louis had his habitation at the mouth of the Jemseg. All the brothers traded extensively with the Indians of the Saint John River; of whom it is now time to speak, as about this time they became a power in the eastern parts of America. These Indians are part of the great Algonquin family, and were variously designated Etchemins or Malicites, names the meanings of which are now lost; they also called themselves, in common with some of the Indians of Maine, by the general name of Wabanaki, or men of the east. The Indian wars in which the Malicites took part commenced in 1689; and for the next thirty or forty years there was a state of hostility between the border settlers of Maine and New Hampshire, and the New Brunswick Indians. Year after year the work of slaughter went on; and some of the most thrilling tales of suffering and of Indian adventure belong to this period, and relate to conflicts with the Malicites of Acadia.

An event happened shortly after the commencement of this Indian war, which gave greater strength and consistency to their efforts. For some years prior to 1690, Port Royal, now Annapolis, had been the seat of government of Acadia; but in that year it was captured by Sir William Phips, and its governor and garrison taken as prisoners to Boston. When Villebon, who came to take Meuneral's place as governor, arrived at Port Royal, he found it in a ruinous condition; and he at once decided to remove the seat of government to the River Saint John, to the fort at Jemseg, which had been formerly occupied by Grandfontaine.

At this period pirates were abundant on the coast of Acadia; and one of these corsairs landed at Port Royal, and committed many depredations. They then crossed to Saint John, and captured the vessel in which Villebon had come from France, which was lying in this harbor, Villebon being then up the River Saint John. It was probably its liability to insult and attack by piratical vessels, that caused Villebon to occupy the fort at Jemseg, rather than Fort Latour at this period. Jemseg, however, proved in every way unsuitable for a garrison, having originally been intended merely for a trading-post; and Villebon shortly left it, and proceeded to build a palisaded fort at the mouth of the Nashwaak, a tributary of the Saint John, which enters it opposite to the city of Fredericton. The rise of this new fortification was deemed by the English colonists an insult and a menace; for in 1692 Sir William Phips sent a ship of forty-eight guns and two brigantines, with eighty soldiers on board, to capture it. Villebon, however, was on the alert, and, without waiting to be attacked, sent a detachment to the mouth of the river to watch the enemy; who were so much disconcerted at the appearance of the French on the alert, that they returned without attempting to make any attack.

At this period several French war-vessels were kept cruising on the coast of Acadia, partly to keep the pirates who infested its shores at a respectable distance, and partly to attack and destroy the fishing and trading vessels of the English colonists. The harbor of Saint John became a sort of dépôt for these captured vessels and their cargoes. A privateer named Baptiste was particularly active in depredations upon English commerce at this period. At the same time Fort Nashwaak on the Saint John was the focus of these intrigues against the peace and prosperity of the settlements of New England, which kept its border towns in a state of warfare, and often of ruin, for so many years. It was from Fort Nashwaak, that expedition after expedition went forth, composed of bloodthirsty and treacherous savages, and headed generally by Frenchmen, to murder and destroy in the settlements of New Hampshire and Maine. Hundreds of English colonists were slain in these bloody encounters, and many captured; and the fort at Saint John finally came to be looked upon as the cause of all these disasters, so that a very natural desire rose in the hearts of the people of New England to destroy it. This desire was hardened into a firm resolve by an event which happened in August, 1696, — the capture of Fort William Henry at Pemaquid, by a force of French and Indians from Saint John. This fort was almost new, built of stone, and had cost the Province of Massachusetts more than twenty thousand pounds. Its capture was too gross an insult to be borne. It was determined by the people of Boston, that the French should be driven from the River Saint John. That no incentive might be wanting to stimulate the pride and zeal of the men of Massachusetts, two ships of the French expedition, the " Profond " and " Envieu," had been attacked off the harbor of St. John by three English vessels, the " Sorling," " Newport," and " Province " galley. One of the latter, the " Newport," was captured, and the others put to flight. The " Newport " was carried into Saint John.

The English expedition to capture Fort Nashwaak was placed under the command of Benjamin Church, who had won distinction in King Philip's wars. Between four hundred and five hundred men were put under his command, and he sailed from Piscataqua late in August; his force, which included some Indians, being disposed in several small vessels and boats. Church, instead of steering straight for Fort Nashwaak, which he might have surprised, went up the bay to Chignecto, which he proceeded to plunder and destroy. He remained there nine days, which he employed in killing the cattle, burning down the houses, and destroying the crops, of the unfortunate Acadians. Even the chapel was not spared by this licentious soldier, who seems to have had no stomach for war, so long as booty was to be obtained. The accounts given of his scandalous treatment of these poor people would be incredible, had he not taken the pains to write and publish them himself in a book.

Church and his force returned to Saint John, where his chief exploit was frightening some workmen who were rebuilding the fort at the mouth of the river, and capturing twelve cannon that the French had buried in the beach. He then sailed for Passamaquoddy, where he was met by Col. Hathorne, who had brought a re-enforcement of three vessels; and, taking command of the expedition, bade Church return to aid him in an attack on Fort Nashwaak. Villebon, who had a guard at the mouth of the Saint John, was early informed of Hathorne's approach, and strengthened his garrison by calling in the Frenchmen who lived lower down the river. Father Simon, the Recollet missionary, who dwelt at Aucpaque, also came into the fort at the head of thirty-six Indian warriors; and when the English made their appearance before the fort, on the morning of the 18th of October, the French commander was fully prepared to receive them. After a cannonade which lasted two days, the siege was abandoned in a precipitate manner; and the English force withdrew down the river, having lost a considerable number of men. The cause of this action is said to have been the want of tents to shelter the troops, who suffered greatly from the cold.

Fort Nashwaak was strengthened during the winter, in anticipation of another attack in the spring; but Villebon had resolved to remove his headquarters to Fort Latour at the mouth of the river. In 1697 he organized an Indian expedition against the English settlements of Maine, and kept his men busy rebuilding the fort at the mouth of the Saint John. The work of rebuilding went on all that year; and in 1698 Nashwaak was abandoned, and Villebon removed with his garrison to the fort at the mouth of the Saint John. For the next two years matters in Acadia were of an uneventful character. There was little to cause excitement among its inhabitants, except the occasional appearance of a pirate on its shores.

In July, 1700, Villebon died, and was buried at Saint John; and Villieu took the command of Acadia until June, 1701, when Brouillan, who had been sent out as governor, arrived. This commander resolved to abandon the fort and establishment at Saint John, on which so much money and labor had been expended; an act of folly to which the subsequent loss of Acadia by the French may be largely attributed. He caused the fortifications to be razed, demolished the houses, and carried away the guns and every thing else of a portable character, to Port Royal. Saint John was left as deserted and desolate as it had been nearly a century before, previous to the arrival of Champlain. A deep silence fell upon the place, which was unbroken for thirty years. The Indian might wander among the ruins of a fort which had been abandoned to his care, or left to be converted into a hiding-place for the wild beasts of the forest, and wonder at the folly of the white men who had forsaken the finest river in all Acadia for the hunter, the woodsman, the fisherman, or the farmer.

The persistent attempts which were made by the French to build a great town at Port Royal, and the steady neglect of the advantages of Saint John, where nature had obviously intended that a great city should be erected, are things which may well excite our surprise; for, during the whole French occupation of Acadia, Saint John never progressed a single step towards its present condition. They built fortifications here indeed, and filled them with soldiers; but there were no private settlers at the mouth of the river, and no attempt to establish any trade at Saint John was ever seriously made in their time; the only article exported during the French period, besides the skins of wild animals, if we except pines for masts for the French navy, being limestone, which at an early date was taken from Saint John in considerable quantities to Port Royal. All the energies of the French people, for more than a century, were directed to the building-up of settlements at Port Royal, Minas, and Chignecto. The very vastness and solitary grandeur of the Saint John seem to have frightened private settlers away; and the Government of France seems to have given such persons no encouragement to settle here.

In 1710 a material change was caused in the aspect of Acadian affairs by the fall of Port Royal, which was captured by an English expedition under Gen. Nicholson. Its name was changed to Annapolis, in honor of the reigning queen; and it continued for a long time to be the seat of government of the English colony of Nova Scotia. Although the French made several attempts to recapture their beloved Port Royal, they always failed.

Although by the treaty of Utrecht Acadia was ceded to the English crown, the French contended that the name only covered the peninsula of Nova Scotia, and therefore that the Saint John still belonged to them. This claim was made officially in a letter written in 1718 by the Marquis de Vaudreuil, the governor of Canada, to John Doucett, lieutenant-governor of Annapolis Royal. The French governor also encouraged the inhabitants of Acadia to settle on the Saint John River; but none appear to have done so at this time. In 1732, however, a small

French colony from Chignecto settled on the River Saint John, and speedily made themselves obnoxious to the commander of Port Royal, by their refusal to recognize his authority. These people in 1736 numbered seventy-eight souls, besides the missionary priest, Jean Pierre Danilo. These simple Acadians were not the sort of people to make any great figure in history; and accordingly they have left little record of their existence, except a few entries in regard to them in the minutes of council and letter books of the Province of Nova Scotia. The number of French Acadians on the St. John River gradually continued to increase; and their settlements gradually grew to be a refuge for the disaffected from other parts of the Province. The Malicite Indians of the Saint John were always on good terms with the French, and, while the latter remained in the country, were always openly or secretly hostile to the English.

In 1749, after the close of the war between France and England, which arose out of the violation of the Pragmatic Sanction by Frederick the Great, Col. John Gorham was sent to the River Saint John with a force, to exact submission from the French inhabitants there. His troops on landing were fired on by the Indians, or by the French; it is not very clear which. Two Indians who do not appear to have been concerned in the attack on the English, but who rather seem to have strayed into their camp, were seized by Gorham, and detained as hostages. This act provoked a correspondence between the Count Galissionliere, the governor of Canada, and the British authorities, in which the old question with regard to the ownership of the Saint John River, which had been in abeyance for many years, was revived. The result of these conflicting claims was a determination on the part of the French governor to occupy the territory in dispute with an armed force.

Accordingly in the summer of 1749 a French officer named Boisherbert was sent down from Quebec with thirty men to occupy the old fort at the mouth of the Saint John River. Once more its ruined bastions, which had been deserted for well-nigh a half-century, were trodden by armed men; and the colors of France again waved over them. The English at Halifax, which was founded in that year, at once took the alarm; and Gov. Cornwallis ordered Capt. Rous to go to Saint John, and order the French to desist from erecting fortifications there. In July, 1749, he proceeded in the ship of war "Albany" to Saint John, and for some days saw nothing of the French. Finally a French schooner laden with provisions arrived, and was seized; but Capt. Rous offered to release her, provided the master would go up the river in a canoe, and bring down the French officer. Boisherbert, it appears, was at the time engaged in constructing a small fort at the mouth of the Nerepis, on the west side of the Saint John. The master of the schooner went up the river to find him; and on the following day the French officer made his appearance at the head of thirty troops and one hundred and fifty Indians, and they planted their colors on the shore opposite to where the "Albany" was lying at anchor. Capt. Rous ordered them to strike their colors; and this, after some demurring, was done. Boisherbert, in excuse for his presence there, produced letters from the governor of Canada, ordering him to prevent the English from settling at Saint John, on the ground that the territory belonged to France. A letter from Cornwallis, ordering him to desist from erecting forts at Saint John, was delivered to Boisherbert; and Rous retired, taking with him some of the chiefs of the Saint John River Indians for the purpose of arranging a treaty. Boisherbert afterwards wrote to Gov. Cornwallis, disavowing any intention of fortifying or building at Saint John, but stating that his orders were not to allow any one else to build at Saint John until the right of possession had been settled between the two crowns. Notwithstanding this disavowal, the fort at Nerepis, of the existence of which the

English were then unaware, was finished; and, as if to show the determination of the French to retain the continental part of Acadia, an officer named Le Corne was sent from Quebec with seventy men to take possession of the Isthmus of Chignecto. There in the following year arose the bastions of the strongest fort yet erected in Acadia, the grim and formidable Beausejour.

For the next five years there was no material change in the aspect of affairs in Nova Scotia. The French continued to fortify themselves at Chignecto and Saint John; and it was finally resolved by the British authorities in Massachusetts and Nova Scotia to dispossess them. An expedition was organized in New England by Gov. Shirley, consisting of about two thousand men, and placed under the command of Col. Monckton. They sailed from Boston in May, 1755, in thirty-six vessels, large and small, including three frigates, and on the 2d June appeared off Fort Beausejour, which they attacked; and on the 16th June it surrendered. As soon as this French stronghold was captured, Capt. Rous was sent with three twenty-gun ships, and a sloop, to look into the Saint John River, where it was reported that there were two French ships of thirty-six guns each. He anchored off the mouth of the river, and sent in his boats to reconnoitre; but there was no vessel in the harbor. As soon, however, as the French on shore saw them, they burst their cannon, blew up their magazine, burned every thing they could belonging to the fort, and marched off.

The forcible removal of the French inhabitants from Nova Scotia took place in the same year, not long after the fall of Beausejour. It was a cruel and extreme act, but was rendered necessary by their turbulent character and their determination not to live peaceably under the British flag. In some parts the deportation of the inhabitants was effected without much difficulty. At Grand Pré 1,923 French men, women, and children were collected and peaceably removed. But at Chignecto, Shepody, and other places, resistance was offered; and large numbers of the inhabitants from these parts fled to the River Saint John. It was calculated that Boisherbert, the French officer in command of the river, was at one time at the head of as many as one thousand five hundred of these French fugitives. Their presence caused no small amount of uneasiness to the authorities at Halifax. For the French, thus re-enforced, were again able to hold the mouth of the River Saint John, and they had a fortified post at Saint Ann's, ninety miles up the river, on the site of the present city of Fredericton. The destruction of both posts and the entire removal of the French from the river were objects to which the attention of the English was now directed. At all events, it was clear that the fort at the mouth of the river must be re-occupied.

Accordingly in the summer of 1758 three ships of war and two transports, with two regiments, one of Highlanders and the other of Provincial troops, on board, were despatched from Boston to recapture Fort La Tour. They landed at Negro Town Point, and cut a road through the woods to the place where the Carleton City Hall now stands, which was then used as a vegetable-garden by the French. From there they advanced against the fort in order of battle, and, after one repulse, succeeded in carrying it by assault. They captured two hundred or three hundred prisoners; and the rest of the garrison escaped across the river in boats, and finally made their way up river. Many, however, were killed in the boats by the shots of the attacking party. The loss of both French and English was heavy, especially of the former, — more than forty being killed. This ended their occupation of the mouth of the Saint John; and soon after the French were driven entirely from the river, except a few families who continued to reside near Saint Ann's. Fort La Tour was occupied and garrisoned by the English, and renamed

Fort Frederick. A blockhouse was also erected at Fort Howe.

The autumn of 1759 was distinguished by one of the most violent gales of wind that ever was known in these latitudes. The damage done was immense. Whole forests were blown down; the tide rose six feet above its ordinary level, and all the dikes were destroyed. A considerable part of Fort Frederick at Saint John was washed away. The descriptions given of this storm naturally recall the effects of the great gale and tidal wave which did so much damage throughout the maritime provinces a few years ago..

At this period Col. Arbuthnot was in command of Fort Frederick; and its garrison consisted of about a hundred and fifty or two hundred men. The commandant was very busy in keeping the Indians in order, and watching the French, and seems altogether to have had rather an uneasy time of it. He succeeded in removing some hundreds of the French inhabitants of the river to other places. His soldiers appear to have grown tired of the monotony of life at Saint John; for in the spring of 1760, in spite of all persuasion, seventy of them openly left in one schooner, and eighty in another, to return to their homes in New England. This desertion must have left Arbuthnot's garrison very weak; and he seems about this time to have given up the command of

Fort Frederick, for Lieut. Tong was in command of it in July, 1760. He represented his fort at that time as being greatly in need of repairs and alterations to make it defensible.

In 1761 the settlement of the marsh-lands about Sackville was commenced by colonists from the older English colonies, and in the following year a number of English settlers removed to the Saint John River, but in 1764 an immigration on a more extended scale took place. Mr. James Simonds, the ancestor of the present family of that name, with Mr. James White and Capt. Francis Peabody, arrived on the site of the present city of Saint John on the 16th April of that year, determined to make it their home. Simonds and White erected small dwellings at the foot of the hill, now known as Fort Howe. Capt. Peabody commenced the formation of a settlement at Maugerville in the county of Sunbury. This settlement, which was named after Joshua Mauger, an English merchant who was agent for the Province of Nova Scotia, was composed mainly of colonists from Massachusetts.

Although the date of this settlement is generally put down 1766, it is quite certain that it was completely established in 1764, as is proved by a memorandum made in that year by Mr. Grant of Halifax, who gives the number of English inhabitants then living on the Saint John at four hundred. In 1765 the settlement was erected into a county by the name of Sunbury, and accorded two representatives in the House of Assembly at Halifax. Large grants of land had been in the mean time made on the Saint John to actual settlers and to influential persons who wished to be great land-owners in Nova Scotia. But there was land enough for all, and these enormous reserves did not hinder the progress of settlement. In 1766 Ensign Jeremiah Meara was in command of Fort Frederick, which was still maintained as a post; and we find him writing to Halifax to complain of two of the settlers, Israel Perley and Col. Glazier, for injury and violence to the Indians. The latter had a large grant at the mouth of Nerepis, which is named on the plans of that day, " Glazier's Manor."

In 1768 the troops were withdrawn from Fort Frederick, except a corporal and four men; and Messrs. Simonds and White left to pursue their peaceful avocations, fishing and farming, without military protection. This measure seems to have emboldened the Indians to give trouble in a sneaking way; and in 1771 they burnt a storehouse and dwelling.

CHAPTER IX.

HISTORICAL SKETCH OF ST. JOHN.

From 1774 to 1874. — Establishment of Government. — War between the Colonies and Great Britain. — Indian Warfare. — The Opening of Trade. — Landing of the Loyalists. — Great Fires in St. John. — First Church. — First Newspaper. — Visits from Distinguished Persons. — War with France. — War of 1812. — Facts and Incidents of Recent History.

THE first representative for the county of Sunbury in the Nova Scotia Assembly was Charles Morris, son of the surveyor-general of Nova Scotia; and in 1774 James Simonds was also elected a member, the county being at that time entitled to two representatives. A court of common pleas had been held in Sunbury from the year 1766, so that the people on the River Saint John had all the paraphernalia of government; and, although they sometimes complained of the Indians, seem to have increased and multiplied, and gone about their daily routine of duty with a reasonable degree of assurance that their scalps were safe. But troublous times were at hand.

The disputes between Great Britain and her colonies on this continent, which arose out of the attempt of the mother country to impose taxes on the latter, culminated in the year 1775, and produced bloodshed. The revolted colonists, not content with recovering the independence of their own country, were ambitious enough to attempt to reduce both Canada and Nova Scotia; and at first there seemed to be every reason to believe that they would succeed. The people of Sunbury, or rather the great majority of them, were in sympathy with their kindred in New England, and, before the war was over, showed their disloyalty by stronger means than mere words. In the mean time the act of a raiding-party from Machias, Me., exhibited the extent of the danger to which Saint John and the whole Province was exposed. In August, 1775, Stephen Smith, a Machias man, and a delegate to the Massachusetts Congress, came to Saint John in an armed sloop, and of course met with no resistance. He burned Fort Frederick and the barracks, took the few men who had charge of the fort prisoners, and captured a brig of a hundred and twenty tons, laden with oxen, sheep, and swine, which were intended for the British troops at Boston. This sudden raid had the effect of putting the British authorities on the alert; and vessels of war were sent to cruise off Saint John, to protect the ports in the Bay of Fundy from these incursions. The governor of Nova Scotia also sent expresses to engage the Indians on the side of the crown.

In 1776 a bold attempt was made to capture Fort Cumberland, in which some of the inhabitants of Sunbury took part. The leader in this attempt was Jonathan Eddy, a native of Massachusetts, who had lived some twelve years on the marsh-lands about Chignecto, and represented Cumberland County in the assembly at Halifax. He conceived the idea of winning reputation by the capture of Fort Cumberland in the autumn of 1776; went to Boston, where he conferred with the council of war there; and, receiving some encouragement, he chartered a small vessel at Newburyport, and, with a few followers and some arms and ammunition, he proceeded to Machias, where about twenty men joined him. At Passamaquoddy he obtained a few more; and, going up the Saint John River as far as Maugerville, he was joined by a company of twenty-five men, a captain, lieutenant, and sixteen Indians, which brought the number of his force up to seventy-two. Eddy embarked his men in whale-boats and canoes, and in a few days reached Shepody, where he surprised a picket-guard from Fort Cumberland, capturing Capt. Walker and thirteen men. At Sackville they captured a sloop laden with provisions; and lying close, several persons who came down from the fort to the sloop, amongst others the engineer, were taken. Eddy's successes induced about a hundred of the inhabitants of the marsh district to join him in attempting the capture of Fort Cumberland, which was commanded by Col. Gorham.

The fort was summoned; but the demand to give it up was promptly refused, and an attack which Eddy subsequently made was repulsed with loss. This attack was made on the 12th November; and the investment of the fort was continued until the 28th, when Eddy and his troops were attacked by the garrison, and by a detachment from Windsor under Major Bott, and compelled to retire. Late in December they reached Maugerville, dispirited, worn out with fatigue, and half-starved.

This taste of warfare does not seem to have satisfied the disloyal people of Sunbury. Several public meetings were held at Maugerville, at which resolutions of sympathy with the people of New England were passed; and Asa Perley and Asa Kimball were appointed a committee to go to Boston, and solicit assistance and munitions of war from the people of Massachusetts, to enable them to rebel against Britain successfully. The result of this mission was that Col. John Allan, who had been obliged to fly from Cumberland for his disloyal plots, was sent by the government of Massachusetts, to act as colonel and superintendent of the Eastern Indians, and to raise the necessary force to take possession of the country on the Saint John River, and hold it for the United States. In April, 1777, Allan left Boston with some supplies, and in May took his departure from Machias with a party of forty-three men in whale-boats and canoes. They arrived at Saint John in safety, and effected a landing. Allan appears to have gone at once to Aukpaque, an Indian settlement above Fredericton, where he engaged in conferences with the inhabitants and the Indians, leaving a detachment at the mouth of the river, who made their headquarters at Simonds's house at the foot of Fort Howe. On Monday, the 23d June, the British war-sloop " Vulture " entered the harbor; and Allan's men were at once attacked. The latter, being protected, succeeded in inflicting some loss on the British as they landed from their boats, six of the latter being killed and wounded out of a force of forty men.

A few days later the British war-ship " Mermaid " arrived; and on the approach of this additional force the rebels fled to the woods, where, from their knowledge of the country, they expected to be able to maintain themselves. This, however, Capt. Hawker, who commanded the British, resolved to prevent; and he was about making dispositions of his forces to dislodge them, when a detachment of a hundred and twenty men from Fort Cumberland landed, and took them in flank. The main body of Allan's party retreated to Grand Bay, where their boats were; and Capt. Dyer, who was left with a rear-guard of twelve men to observe the motions of the British, was so closely pursued that he had three men killed and two wounded. Allan's force then retreated up the river, the British pursuing them. Allan, who had succeeded in gaining the good-will of the Indians, and promises of aid from them, was on his way to the mouth of the river, when he met his retreating force in five boats. He at once turned and fled with them, and on the 1st of July arrived at Maugerville. On the following day he reached the Indian settlement of Aukpaque, where he had been received with so much ceremony and consideration by the savages a short time before. There all was terror and confusion; for the British were still in pursuit. The Indians abandoned their settlement for the time, and fled; and the sequel was that Allan, abandoned by his Indian allies, and with his own men on the verge of mutiny, had to make a hasty retreat to Maine, by way of Eel River and the Scoudac Lakes, arriving at Machias Aug. 2, 1777. Thus ended this bold attempt to gain possession of the River Saint John.

On the 24th September, 1777, Mr. Franklin, the Indian commissioner, made a treaty with the Malicites and Micmacs at Fort Howe, Saint John; and from that time the Nova Scotia government experienced no difficulty with these tribes. The post at Fort Howe was held by a small force under the command of Capt. Studholm. He commenced the export of masts from Saint John for the use of the navy; and the first cargo of these arrived at Halifax, Nov. 22, 1780. During the following winter a second cargo was prepared at Saint John, consisting of upwards of two hundred sticks for masts, spars, and bowsprits; and they were shipped on board a transport in May, 1781. These operations, inconsiderable as they were, naturally drew workmen to Saint John, and mark the beginning of the trade of this now busy city. New England privateers were, however, very active on our coast at that time, and threatened to strangle the infant commerce of the port. In May, 1781, they captured a schooner belonging to Capt. Sheffield, laden with goods for Saint John; but she was retaken by a volunteer force from Cornwallis. In 1782 the cutting of spars on the River Saint John went on without interruption, and the settlements continued to grow in population. In this year Saint John had become a port of entry, James White being the first collector of customs.

The tonnage which entered Saint John during that year amounted to a hundred and forty-four tons; and the vessels which cleared amounted to a hundred and sixty-five tons. As a matter of curiosity, we append a list of the vessels which entered and cleared at Saint John in that year.

Entered.	*Tons.*	*Cleared.*	*Tons.*
Rosanna	17	Rosanna	17
Betsy	10	Peggy	8
Escape	10	Betsy	10
Polly	10	Escape	10
Sally	10	Polly	10
Lark	18	Sally	10
Ranger	12	Lark	18
Prosperity	10	Ranger	12
Unity	10	Prosperity	10
Speedy	7	Unity	10
Little Tom	30	Little Tom	30
		Monaguash	30
Total tonnage	144		
		Total tonnage	165

Such was the shipping of Saint John less than a century ago. A tolerably correct idea of the state of the settlements on the Saint John River at the close of this year may be gathered from a letter written by Amos Botsford, an agent for the Loyalists, who had been examining the country with a view to settlement. He says the inhabitants of the Saint John River are " computed to be near a thousand men able to bear arms." He says also, "The settlers are chiefly poor people who come here and get their living easily. They cut down the trees, burn the tops, put in a crop of wheat or Indian corn, which yields a plentiful increase. These intervals would make the finest meadows. The uplands produce both wheat of the summer and winter kinds, as well as Indian corn. Here are some wealthy farmers, having flocks of cattle. The greater part of the people, excepting the township of Maugerville, are tenants, or seated on the bank without leave or license, merely to get their living."

The year 1783 was the most memorable of any in the history of St. John, for it was the year of the landing of the Loyalists. But for them St. John might have struggled on for years through a protracted and sickly infancy; but the coming of the Loyalists brought it, in a few short months, from the dimensions of a hamlet to those of a respectable town. The war between Great Britain and her colonists was over, and the latter had gained their independence. Had they been wise, they would have tempered their triumph with moderation; they would have encouraged those who had espoused the royal cause to remain and assist in building up the new nation which they had founded. Instead of this, they committed one of the most stupendous acts of short-sighted folly ever perpetrated by a people. They passed edicts of banishment against the persons, and acts of confiscation against the estates, of the Loyalists. They drove them out, poor in purse indeed, but rich in experience, determination, energy, education, intellect, and the other qualities which build up states, and with their hearts fired and their energies stimulated with hatred of republicanism; they drove them out seventy thousand strong, to build up a rival nation at their very doors, to found new communities in British America, destined to grow before a century had elapsed into a great dominion, which would never have had an existence but for the rash folly of those who persecuted the Loyalists.

Early in the spring of 1783 the emigration of the Loyalists from the United States commenced, and the first ship-load arrived at St. John on the 10th May. Twenty vessels arrived between the 10th and 18th May. The names of these vessels were, "The Camel," Capt. Tinker; "The Union," Capt. Wilson; "The Aurora," Capt. Jackson; "The Hope," Capt. Peacock; "The Otter," Capt. Burns; "The Spencer;" "The Emmett," Capt. Reed; "The Thames;" "The Spring," Capt. Cadish; "The Bridgewater;" "The Favorite," Capt. Ellis; "The Ann," Capt. Clark; "The Commerce," Capt. Strong; "The

William;" "The Lord Townshend," Capt. Hogg; "The Sovereign," Capt. Stuart; "The Sally," Capt. Bell; "The Cyrus," "The Britain," and "The King George," twenty ships in all. These ships were all from New York. The spring was wet and cold; and, no houses or accommodations being provided for them, the Loyalists did not land until the 18th May. These men were expatriated exiles, men whose property had been confiscated, men without a country. Yet among them, as we have said, were some of the keenest intellects of the revolted colonies, the great lights of the law and of the Church, and the men who had filled high offices under the old order of things in New England and New York. Some had fought through the war in regular or partisan corps; others had not; but all were involved in one common ruin.

When the Loyalists reached St. John, civilization had made such small advances against the rugged might of nature, that, with the exception of a small clearing about Fort Howe, the whole site of the present city of Portland northward of Saint John was a dense forest. It was rocky and rough, too, beyond the ordinary rudeness of a wilderness; and those who have seen with what Titanic labor streets have been hewed through the rocks in Saint John can form some idea of the forbidding appearance it must have presented to those exiled and dispirited people who first undertook to found a city here. The Loyalists landed on the 18th May, the landing in most cases being effected at Lower Cove, near what was the old Sydney Market-House before the fire.

A few log huts were the only buildings at that time on the site of St. John; and the first care of the Loyalists was to provide shelter for themselves. Temporary sheds were at first erected, and afterwards residences of a more substantial character. The first fleet of ships brought upwards of three thousand Loyalists to St. John, so that the task of providing sufficient accommodation for so many was no light one. Large numbers also arrived in subsequent vessels in the course of the summer and autumn. They seem to have entered on their task with great industry and alacrity; and, long before the arrival of winter, comfortable provision had been made for the sheltering of all who arrived. Most of the dwellings erected were built of logs, and the first framed house finished by the Loyalists was a place of worship. It was erected on a lot (No. 121) on the east side of Germain Street, about midway between Queen and Duke Streets. It was used by the Episcopalians until Christmas Day, 1791, when Trinity Church was first opened, and subsequently as a place of worship by the Methodists and Baptists. The courts and the meetings of the Common Council were also held in this building until 1798.

The governor of Nova Scotia at the time of the arrival of the Loyalists was John Parr, Esq.; and St. John was at first named Parrtown, after this gentleman. The town was laid out in lots, and granted to the Loyalist families residing here; there being 1,184 grantees in one grant at St. John, and 93 in another.

Great jealousy soon arose among the Loyalists with regard to this matter of granting lands in the new colony. In August, 1783, the dissatisfaction was so great at St. John, that four hundred persons had signed an agreement to remove to Passamaquoddy. The exact reasons for the dissatisfaction which existed are at this day a little obscure; but there is no doubt that the undue partiality shown to some Loyalists of wealth and position, to the detriment of others who had suffered equally from the result of the war, lay at the foundation of the troubles. Abijah Willard, who settled in the parish of Lancaster, and fifty-four others, addressed a petition to Sir Guy Carleton, asking for extensive grants in Nova Scotia. They represented that their position in life had been very respectable, and that previous to the Revolution they had possessed much influence. They therefore asked for grants of land in Nova Scotia of the same extent as had been given to field-officers. This petition was made public at St. John, and caused much excitement. Many people declared their pulses beat too high for them to become the tenants or vassals of the worthy fifty-five. It is pretty evident that our fathers were no more free from political troubles than their descendants are at the present day.

The population of the Province of New Brunswick, towards the close of the year 1783, was estimated at 11,457. Upwards of twelve hundred more Loyalists had arrived from New York in November of that year. City lots in Parrtown were worth from two dollars up to twenty dollars, according to locality; but real estate, owing to the great influx of people, had at that time attained a fictitious value, which it afterwards lost. A lot on which the "Daily Telegraph" newspaper office stood before the fire was sold in 1786 to Dr. Adino Paddock for five shillings. It would now be cheap at ten thousand dollars. The date of the original plan of survey of Parrtown is Aug. 6, 1784. It is signed by Gov. Parr; Paul Bedell, deputy surveyor, and Gilfred Studholm, superintendent.

The first winter spent by the new settlers was a severe one, and many died. There is no record of the first Loyalist death in St. John; but the first man married was Andrew Stockton, and the fact is duly recorded on his tombstone. The year 1784 was rather an eventful one. The agitations, with regard to the granting of land, continued at St. John, and a new one sprung up demanding a separation from Nova Scotia. Even in Nova Scotia proper, at this time and long afterwards, there were brisk contests between the Loyalists, or new-comers, and the old settlers. In August of this year, information was received from England that that portion of Nova Scotia north of the Misseguash was to be erected into a new Province by the name of New Brunswick.

On Friday, the 18th June, 1784, the first of these calamities by fire, which have been so destructive in St. John, took place. Eleven houses were burned, the sufferers being chiefly discharged soldiers of the Forty-second Regiment. On the same day seven houses were consumed at the falls, and a woman and child burnt to death.

In August of this year Nehemiah Beckwith, afterwards a resident of Fredericton, built a scow or tow-boat to ply between Parrtown and Saint Ann's, the first attempt to establish regular communication between the two places. From such an humble beginning did the great traffic now moving on the Saint John River take its rise.

In October Mr. Thomas Carleton, the governor of the new Province of New Brunswick, arrived at

Halifax with his family from London, in the "Saint Lawrence," Capt. Wyatt, after a passage of eight weeks. On Sunday, the 21st November, at three o'clock in the afternoon, he arrived at Saint John with his lady and family, having crossed the bay from Digby in six hours in the sloop "Ranger," Cornelius Hatfield master. He received an enthusiastic welcome from the Loyalists. A salute of seventeen guns was fired from Lower Cove Battery as "The Ranger" entered the harbor; and, as he landed, a similar salute was thundered from Fort Howe. A great concourse of the inhabitants received him with shouts of welcome, and escorted him to the house of Mr. George Leonard, corner Union and Dock Streets, which had been fitted up for his reception. On his entering the house, the crowd gave him three cheers, and cries of " Long live our king and governor!" On the following day his commission was read, after which he was sworn in as captain-general and commander-in-chief. On the same day Duncan Ludlow, James Putnam, Abijah Willard, Gabriel G. Ludlow, Isaac Allan, William Hazen, and Jonathan Odell were sworn in members of his Majesty's council, and its first meeting was held. The new governor was addressed by the inhabitants, who called themselves "a number of oppressed and insulted Loyalists," and congratulated him on his arrival " to check the arrogance of tyranny, crush the growth of injustice, and establish such wholesome laws as are and ever have been the basis of our glorious constitution." They added that they were formerly freemen, and again hoped to be under his auspices. The friends of a Maritime Union will note with what resentful feelings the provinces of New Brunswick and Nova Scotia were separated. Five days after this first meeting of the council, Gilfred Studholm was sworn in, and took his seat; and, on the 4th December, Edward Winslow. In July, 1786, the number was further increased by the appointment of Joshua Upham and Daniel Bliss. The first chief justice of New Brunswick was George D. Ludlow; and the assistant judges were James Putnam, Isaac Allan, and Joshua Upham. All were sworn in on the same day, — the 25th November, 1784. The supreme court was opened for the first time in New Brunswick on Tuesday, Feb. 1, 1785. It met in the building on Germain Street, already referred to, which the Loyalists built for public worship. The Hon. George D. Ludlow and Hon. James Putnam were on the bench. After the formal opening of the court, the commission appointing the judges was read; and also the appointment of Ward Chipman as attorney-general, and of Colin Campbell as clerk of the courts. The first grand jury were as follows: —

Richard Lightfoot, John Kirk, Francis Deveber, John Camp, William Harding, John Colville, Henry Thomas, John Hazen, John Smith, Munson Jarvis, John Boggs, Oliver Arnold, Caleb Howe, David Melville, Isaac Bell, Richard Bonsall, James Ketchum, Luke D. Thornton, Anthony Narraway.

In February, 1785, Gov. Carleton selected St. Ann's Point as the future seat of government of the Province, and Douglas Campbell was directed to survey the town-plat there; the place to be called Fredericton, after the bishop of Osnaburg. On the 18th May, 1785, Parrtown and Carleton were, by royal charter, erected into a city, to be called the city of St. John. The new city was bounded "by a line to commence and beginning near Fort Howe, at Portland Point, at low-water-mark, and thence running a direct line to a small point or ledge of land at the causey by the old saw-mill; thence east-north-east until a direct line shall strike the creek running through Hazen's marsh on the east side of the eastern district aforesaid; thence along the course of the said creek to its mouth; thence by a line running south, nineteen degrees west, into the bay, until it meets a line running east from the south point of Partridge Island, and along the said line to the said point; thence by a direct line to a point on the shore, which is at the south-east extremity of a line running south forty-two degrees east from the River St. John to the Bay of Fundy, and terminating the town-lots of the western district aforesaid; thence along the said line north forty-two degrees west to the River St. John aforesaid, and continuing the said course across the said river until it meets the opposite shore, and from thence along the north shore of the said river at low-water-mark to Portland Point aforesaid."

On the 11th October, 1785, the first number of "The Royal Gazette and New-Brunswick Advertiser" was published at St. John by Christopher Sower, king's printer. This was the first weekly paper published in New Brunswick. In this year, too, William Cobbett, a man afterwards widely famed as a newspaper-writer, came to St. John from England, as a recruit, to join the Fifty-fourth Regiment, then stationed at Fort Howe; and it was here he met with the sergeant's pretty daughter, who became his wife. The block-house on Fort Howe was at that time, for want of a more suitable building, used as a jail. The elections for members to sit in the first New-Brunswick General Assembly were held in November, 1785, and in St. John were signalized by great riots. The members elect for St. John City were Stanton Hazard and John

McGeorge; for the county of St. John, William Pagan, Ward Chipman, Jonathan Bliss, and Christopher Billop. The democratic element evidently had it all its own way in the city; but it was otherwise in the county.

The first parliament of New Brunswick met in Saint John on the 3d January, 1786, in the "Mallard House," which was on the north side of King Street, on the second lot below Germain. Amos Botsford was chosen speaker of the house; and G. D. Ludlow, the chief justice, the president of the council. The first clerk of the house was William Paine. The number of acts passed at this first session was sixty-one; and they will compare favorably with those of any session held since then.

In this year Saint John made considerable advances in the appliances of civilization, although it had, as was to be expected, lost many of its original inhabitants, who merely made it a temporary abiding-place until they could select lands in the country in which to settle. Gen. Benedict Arnold, the traitor, was then a resident there, and had a lumber-yard near the old fort, on the west side of the harbor on the Carleton side. His residence was on the south side of King Street, below Canterbury Street. The lot on which his store stood has never been occupied since the destruction of the building many years ago, and was vacant at the time of the last fire. He was the first ship-owner of any pretensions in Saint John; and on the 1st June, 1786, we read that "an entire new and most noble ship called 'Lord Sheffield,'" and built for Benedict Arnold, came through the falls. In the same "Royal Gazette," June 3, it is announced that the corporation having purchased two fire-engines for the use of the city, and having directed one to be kept at the Market-Place, Upper Cove, the other at the Market-Place, Lower Cove, those who incline to join the two engine-companies will leave their names with Mr. Munson Jarvis and Mr. John Colville, merchants. On the 11th July, the schooner "Four Sisters" is advertised to sail from Saint John to Fredericton every Tuesday, wind and weather permitting. So here we have a wonderful advance on Mr. N. Beckwith's scow of two years before. Shipping did not trouble the harbor of Saint John much in its infant days; and the Loyalists could only solace each other with the utterance of the prophetic hope that "ships will come here from England yet."

In February, 1787, a post-sleigh commenced to run between Saint John and Fredericton. There being no roads, the ice on the river was made available as a highway. The enterprising proprietor of this conveyance was L. Merecreau, evidently a Frenchman. On the 13th of the same month, the second meeting of the legislature, and the last held in Saint John, took place. The acts of this session were twelve in number, the principal one being an act to establish the provincial militia. In August of this year, the lord-bishop of Nova Scotia, after administering confirmation to a great number of persons, laid the corner-stone of Trinity Church in Saint John, being the same building destroyed in the last fire, although it had been several times remodelled. It was opened for public worship on Christmas Day, 1791, and stood as a monument of the religious zeal of the Loyalists, adorned with the same royal coat-of-arms which they brought with them from Trinity Church, New York, when the British army evacuated that city in 1783. The first rector of Saint John was the Rev. Mr. Bissett.

On the 15th July, 1788, the provincial legislature was transferred from St. John to Fredericton, where its sessions have since been held. Saint John lost nothing by ceasing to be the capital, and Fredericton made a gain. For some years after this the annals of Saint John are scanty enough. The progress of a town in population and wealth is generally of so gradual a character as to leave no special points which the historian can take hold of; and this was notably the case with Saint John, which, after the first burst of activity caused by the arrival of the Loyalists, for some years must have progressed very slowly. In some remarks on Nova Scotia and New Brunswick, said to have been written by the surveyor-general of the former Province, which appear among the Transactions of the Massachusetts Historical Society for 1794, it is said of Saint John, " Its streets are regular and spacious; and there are many decent, well-built houses. It contains about one thousand inhabitants." This paper, which bears no date, must have been written about the year 1790.

In 1793 war broke out between Great Britain and France; a war which, with two short intermissions, was destined to last for two and twenty years. A provincial regiment was at once raised in New Brunswick, of which Gov. Carleton was colonel, and Beverly Robinson lieutenant-colonel. On the 6th May intelligence was received here of a French privateer of ten guns with 45 men cruising in the Bay of Fundy; and a night patrol was established. Capt. Robert Reed, with a party of "Independent Volunteers," took the first round of duty. Another guardhouse was ordered to be fitted up for the watch, and a double guard placed on Lower Cove Battery. This work was then considered a formidable one, its guns being eighteen-pounders, and it was believed no enemy's ship could pass it. It was proposed to fit out a vessel, and cruise after the Frenchman. A large privateer sloop was fitted out at Saint John, and sent out under Capt. Thomas; but the Frenchman prudently kept out of the way.

In May, 1794, occurred the highest freshet ever known in the Saint John. In June Prince Edward, Duke of Kent, the father of Queen Victoria, visited the Province. He left Halifax on the 14th, and sailed from Annapolis on the 16th in the "Zebra" sloop-of-war. At Saint John he was received by a captain's guard of the king's New Brunswick regiment.

Attended by Gov. Carleton, he hastened on to Fredericton, where he arrived on Saturday evening, the 21st. From the river-bank where he landed, the road was lined by the troops in garrison and by Capt. Jarvis's Fredericton militia; and the town was illuminated. Next morning, notwithstanding the sacred character of the day, royal salutes were fired, a levee held, addresses presented by his Majesty's counsel for the Province and the inhabitants of the county of York, and the king's New-Brunswick militia were inspected. Early on Monday morning the prince and Gov. Carleton embarked again, and, passing through the falls, reached Saint John at two, P.M. On Tuesday, the 24th, the prince inspected the batteries and the ordnance stores; and at threeheld, P.M., a levee at the house of Mr. Chipman, the solicitor-general, which was crowded with the chief citizens and the officers in garrison. His grandson, the Prince of Wales, was entertained in this same house. The Duke of Kent, who seems to have been in a great hurry, left Saint John in "The Zebra" the same evening, amid the salutes and cheers of the inhabitants, and the firing of guns from the batteries.

In 1795 there was considerable fear of French attacks, both in Saint John and Halifax; and the provincial regiment was ordered from Fredericton to Saint John. Privateer vessels, sailing under French colors, were at this time making havoc among the merchant vessels of New Brunswick and Nova Scotia. The house of assembly addressed the lieutenant-governor on the subject of procuring cruisers or guard-ships, to be stationed in the Bay of Fundy. Additional defences were also erected at Saint John, at the instance of the lieutenant-governor, which the house refused to vote money to pay for. William Campbell was in this year appointed mayor of Saint John, an office which he continued to hold for more than twenty years. In this year, also, a grist wind-mill was erected on King Square, on the lot on which the Hazen House now stands. The enterprise was abandoned in 1800.

In 1796 the commissioners under the fifth article of the Treaty of Ghent, to determine which was the true Saint Croix, were appointed. Ward Chipman of Saint John was appointed agent on the part of his Britannic Majesty, and E. Winslow secretary of the commission. In 1798 the commissioners gave their decision, which was that the Scoudac was the true Saint Croix of Champlain.

In 1799 the Duke of Kent, who had been in England for his health, returned to Nova Scotia; and the corporation of Saint John sent him an address of welcome. The people of New Brunswick this year also showed their patriotism by subscribing £3,085 sterling, as a voluntary contribution to the military chest for 1798.

Prior to the beginning of the nineteenth century, it was not unfrequent to see negro slaves advertised for sale in the "Royal Gazette." Finally the legality of slavery was tested before the Supreme Court. On Feb. 18, 1800, the Supreme Court divided equally on this question; the Chief Justice and Judge Upham holding slavery to be legal in the Province, and Judges Saunders and Allen considering slavery to be illegal. It was in this year that the first proposal was made of a survey for a canal, to connect the St. Lawrence and the Bay of Fundy; a work which is destined in a few years to be an accomplished fact, and of enormous benefit to Saint John.

In 1800 the war with France was going on with as much vigor as ever; and the 4th of July of that year a public fast was proclaimed in the Province on account of it. In 1801 most of the counties received grants to aid them in erecting court-houses and jails.

In this year the Duke of Kent interested himself regarding the construction of a road between Halifax and Quebec. The famous Saint John dog-tax act was also passed in this year, the money realized therefrom to be for the support of the poor. The roads of New Brunswick, about this time, seem to have been in a bad way; for in January, 1803, D. Campbell reported that there were not ten miles of road in the Province fit for a wheel carriage, except in the county of Sunbury.

In 1805 the public grammar school in Saint John was incorporated, and the College of New Brunswick established at Fredericton.

Early in January, 1806, the news of Nelson's great victory at Trafalgar reached Saint John, and caused great rejoicing. Admiral Collingwood's despatches were published in the " Gazette " of Jan. 13. A ball was held at Cody's coffee-house in honor of the event, which was attended, to use the language of the " Gazette," by a " great assembly of beauty and fashion." There were also celebrations at Norton and Kingston, attended by the inevitable dinner and the drinking of the usual loyal toasts.

In 1808 the good people of Saint John seem to have been under a good deal of anxiety with regard to the war with France; for in January of that year an order was passed that no vessel or boat should be allowed to leave the harbor of Saint John without the countersign. On Feb. 12 Gabriel G. Ludlow, the first mayor of Saint John, died, and was buried in Carleton. He had been president and commander-in-chief of the Province from the year 1803. In June Capt. Shore, with two companies of the New Brunswick Fencibles, was sent to garrison Sydney, C.B. Among the wonderful events of this year may be mentioned an accident which happened to the Saint Andrews packet "Speedy." While lying at anchor, a whale, or some other sea-monster, fouled itself in her cable, and actually dragged her from her anchorage for a distance of more than three miles, to the infinite consternation of those on board.

In June, 1809, the 101st Regiment, which had been in garrison at Saint John, was sent to the West Indies; and part of the New Brunswick Regiment was sent to Saint John to take its place. During the summer the troops were employed in making a road from Fredericton to Saint John. On Oct. 16, 1809, a negro wench named Nancy was advertised for sale in the "Royal Gazette," by Daniel Brown, and a good title guaranteed; so that, at that time, slavery was still deemed to exist in New Brunswick.

In 1811 every thing pointed to a war between Great Britain and the United States. The New Brunswick Fencibles were, on Feb. 18, gazetted as his Majesty's 104th Regiment, the first colonial regiment of the line. On Oct. 1 five commissioners of customs, for a special revenue inquiry, arrived at Saint John; and on the same day an order in council was passed, proclaiming Saint John a free port. On the 30th October the freedom of the city was granted to Lieut.-Col. McCarthy of the Royal Artillery, who was about to leave the Province.

In 1812 the long-impending war came. War was not formally declared by the United States against Great Britain until June 18, but the colonists had made preparations for it long before. A public fast was proclaimed in New Brunswick; but, while the people were praying, they were also sharpening their swords. On the 9th of March an act was passed appropriating the sum of £10,000 to his Majesty, in defence of the Province. This was a handsome donation, for the total revenue of New Brunswick at that period was only £6,000. On the same day an act was passed "to encourage the erection of a passage-boat, to be worked by steam, for facilitating the communication between the city of Saint John and Fredericton." This act gave certain persons the exclusive privilege of navigating the Saint John by steam for ten years.

United States privateers soon began to swarm on the coast, and the Saint John people went into privateering on their own account. A large number of men-of-war also cruised in the Bay of Fundy; so that between the arrival of prize vessels, and the excitement attending the news from the seat of war, matters were kept pretty lively in Saint John. The people on the borders of New Brunswick, on both sides of the line, took no part in the contest; and this wise neutrality, while it prevented useless bloodshed, also left no bitter memories after the war was over. Gen. Smyth, the administrator of the Province, on the 3d of July issued a proclamation forbidding any one under his command from offering any molestation to the United States people living on the frontier of New Brunswick, or interfering with their goods or their coasting-vessels. The war was not only very unpopular in Maine, but throughout the whole of New England. When the declaration of war reached Boston, all the vessels in port, except three, immediately hoisted their colors half-mast; and the people soon compelled the three to follow the example of the others. On the Canadian frontier, and on the sea, however, the conflict was maintained with vigor. Towards the close of this year, various defensive works were erected at Saint John, Fort Frederick was repaired and strengthened, and batteries erected on Partridge Island and other points; and a prominent pentagonal work was proposed to be erected at the mouth of the Nashwaak. A shocking occurrence happened on the 5th of December, 1812, which deeply concerned the people of Saint John. H. M. brig of war "Plumper," bound from Halifax to Saint John, was wrecked near Dipper Harbor, and upwards of fifty persons on board of her drowned. She was a twelve-gun brig, was commanded by Lieut. J. Bray, and had $70,000 in specie for Saint John. This was probably the most fatal shipwreck that ever took place in the Bay of Fundy.

There was at this time a demand for more troops in Western Canada; and accordingly the New Brunswick Regiment, the 104th, was ordered to march overland to Quebec. They left Saint John under the command of Major Drummond, on Feb. 11, 1813, the people helping them out as far as the roads were passable with sleighs. Beyond that, the journey was performed on snow-shoes. This march, considering the season of the year, and the character of the country traversed, must take its place among the greatest marches recorded in history. It is safe to say that such a march could not have been performed by any other men but the hardy forest pioneers of Northern America. The regiment reached Quebec as compact and perfect as when it left St. John, without losing a man. Arnold lost more than three hundred on the shorter route by the Kennebec, and during a mild season of the year; yet Arnold's march has been lauded as a wonderful proof of the vigor of the Continental troops in 1775, while this great march of the sons of the Loyalists is seldom mentioned.

The departure of the 104th Regiment left Saint John somewhat bare of troops, although their places were in part supplied by the second battalion of the Eighth Regiment, which remained there. In compliance with the wish for more arms, Sir George Prevost sent from Halifax ten twenty-four pounders for the batteries on Partridge Island, and one thousand stand of muskets, by the store-ship "Diligence;" but this vessel was driven ashore in a snow-storm on Beale's Island, to the westward of Machias. The vessel and what was saved of her cargo fell into the hands of the enemy. About this time a New-Brunswick fencible regiment was raised by Gen. Coffin for the defence of the Province; and considerable numbers of militia-men from Westmoreland and other counties were brought to Saint John to assist the regulars in garrison duty.

On Monday, the twenty-third day of May, 1814, the news arrived at Saint John of the entry of the allied sovereigns into Paris, and the abdication of Napoleon. Great rejoicings followed. An ox was roasted whole in King's Square, and the city was illuminated. The Treaty of Paris, signed on the 30th of the same month, brought the long period of war with France to a close. The war between Great Britain and the United States was brought to a close a few months later. The conclusion of this war brought a curious immigration to Saint John. Many of the black slaves in Maryland and Virginia had availed themselves of the presence of the British navy in Chesapeake Bay, and had taken refuge on board the English men-of-war. Three hundred of these emancipated slaves arrived at Saint John on the 8th June, 1815; and the people here were a good deal puzzled how to dispose of them. They were subsequently settled at Loch Lomond, where their descendants are still numerous.

News of the total defeat of Bonaparte at Waterloo was received at Saint John towards the close of July, and of course the people rejoiced as loyal citizens should. A patriotic fund was raised in all the colonies, as well as in the mother country, for the families of the slain and of the severely wounded in that great battle. The large sum of 1,500 pounds was subscribed in Saint John, the first sixteen names on one list opened here giving 470 pounds. A theatrical performance was given in the old theatre at the corner of Drury Lane and Union Street, which realized twenty pounds. That was the last time the building was used for theatrical purposes.

On Feb. 12, 1816, the first advertisement of a steamboat to be run between Saint John and Fredericton was published in the "Royal Gazette;" and on the 11th of April the steamboat "Gen. Smyth" was launched at Saint John. She was owned by J. Ward, R. Smith, H. Johnston, and P. Frazer; and a considerable degree of diligence seems to have been exhibited in fitting her out, for she arrived at Fredericton on her first trip on the 21st May.

On the 2d February, 1817, Gen. T. Carleton, who had been lieutenant-governor of the Province since its first inception, died in England at the age of eighty-one. Gen. Smyth became lieutenant-governor in his place. On the 19th February, the New-Brunswick Regiment, the famous 104th, was reduced. In this year a meeting was held in Saint John for the purpose of establishing a national school. This year the population of New Brunswick was estimated at thirty-five thousand. It was in this year also that the first brick house was erected in Saint John, — the building on the corner of Germain and Church Streets, now destroyed.

During the spring of 1818, the first pine logs were brought down the Saint John from above Grand Falls; and it was in this year that citizens of the United States first began to assert territorial claims on the Madawaska and Upper Saint John.

In June, 1819, about thirty-two hundred immigrants, mostly disbanded soldiers, landed in Saint John. An emigrant register office was established here in October of that year; and for some years after that time the number of immigrants who annually came to Saint John was large. It was the beginning of a period of great commercial prosperity, of abnormal growth, which well-nigh ended in utter ruin.

On the 26th March, 1820, the Bank of New Brunswick was established. This institution, after an interval of fifty-five years, still exists, with greatly increased capital and augmented prosperity; and its impregnable vaults saved many a man's fortune in the last great fire. The trade of Saint John was increasing so fast, that, in October of this same year, there were about a hundred square-rigged vessels in Saint John Harbor. In 1822 the first cargo of deals was sent to England.

In 1824 there was a great fire in Saint John, which destroyed much property. In this year, which was one of great inflation and supposititious prosperity, a steamer was started to ply between Saint John and Passamaquoddy. In this year the first census was taken, and the population of the Province was found to be 74,176. The population of Saint John County at this time was 12,907.

In March, 1826, a great and destructive fire took place in Indiantown, a suburb of Saint John. The year 1826 was a sickly one in Saint John, and, in a financial point of view, the most disastrous the city has ever known. Hundreds were ruined by the re-action in England after the speculative years 1824 and 1825; and much colonial timber was sold for less than it had cost to convey it across the Atlantic. It was long before Saint John recovered from the disasters of 1826. In 1827 steam navigation between Saint John and Digby was commenced, and has been continued to the present time. In December, 1828, the Court-House on King's Square was completed.

In October, 1834, cholera broke out in Saint John; and boats for Fredericton were ordered to stop at the short ferry for inspection. Nov. 8 there were 103 cases of cholera in this city, and had been 47 deaths. In this year a census of the province was taken, and the population of Saint John County ascertained to be 20,668.

In 1835 an act to incorporate the Saint John

Bridge Company was passed. The object was the erection of a bridge over the falls. The corporators named in the act were B. L. Peters, Ralph M. Jarvis, Nehemiah Merritt, John Robertson, James Peters, jun., James Hendricks, David Hatfield, Robert W. Crookshank, Robert Rankin, R. F. Hazen, E. L. Jarvis, Charles Simonds, E. B. Chandler, William Crane, Hugh Johnston, Thomas Wier, John W. Weldon, and Jedediah Slason. The capital stock of the company was to consist of £20,000.

On the 13th January, 1837, a great calamity befell Saint John, nearly the whole of the business part of the city being burned down. The number of houses destroyed was 115, and the damage to property was estimated at £250,000. On April 30 of the same year, steam navigation on the Saint John took a decided advance. The steamer "Novelty" reached Woodstock, being the first steamer that succeeded in ascending the Meductic Rapids. On May 20, the provincial banks all suspended specie payment, in sympathy with the money-panic which overwhelmed America at this time. On Aug. 7, the bridge structure over the falls, which the company above spoken of were erecting, fell, and killed seven persons. This year was signalized by troubles in Lower Canada; and, in consequence, the Forty-third Regiment was marched overland from Fredericton to Quebec, leaving the former place on the 16th December, and reaching their destination on the 28th December. The militia of York and Saint John Counties were called out at this time, and did garrison duty. On the 2d August, 1838, a dreadful calamity happened, by the upsetting of a boat in the falls, nineteen persons losing their lives. In this year the Saint John Mechanics' Institute was established; Beverly Robinson, Esq., being its first president.

The following year (1839) was memorable for the boundary disputes, bringing Great Britain and the United States to the verge of war. Saint John was intensely excited; but war, fortunately, was averted. In August another terribly destructive fire took place in Saint John, by which property to the value of £200,000 was destroyed. The people of this city became seriously alarmed; and at a special session of the legislature, held in September, an act for the better prevention of fires in Saint John was passed.

On the 27th of May, 1840, Sir John Harvey laid the foundation-stone of the Saint John Mechanics' Institute building; a structure inseparably connected with the social and educational history of the place. On the 23d of July of this year, the Right Hon. P. C. Thompson, the governor-general of Canada, arrived at Saint John from Halifax, attended by Sir John Harvey. He was received here with much consideration. The population of Saint John County was found to be 32,957. The population of the city proper was 19,281. The increase since the census of 1834 had been very large. On the 17th of March, 1841, there was another destructive fire in Saint John, at which four lives were lost. Public meetings were held about this time, to petition her Majesty against the removal of the duties on Baltic timber, by which colonial wood was protected. On the 17th of August of this year, the first battalion of the Saint John city militia, under the command of Col. Peters, was presented by his excellency the lieutenant-governor with a suit of colors. On Aug. 26, a calamitous fire broke out in the suburban town of Portland, which destroyed sixty houses. The damage was estimated at £30,000. Still the fire record of the year is not exhausted; for on Nov. 15 there was another frightful fire in St. John, which destroyed the new market-house, and the building in which the public offices were. Many incendiary attempts were made at this time, and the public mind was highly excited in consequence.

July 29, 1845, there was another great fire in Saint John, which destroyed forty buildings. On the 16th of October of that year, the foundation-stone of the cathedral was laid in Fredericton by Sir William Colebrooke. In this year the Saint John Gas-Light Company was incorporated; and, on the evening of the 18th of September of the same year, gas was turned on for the first time.

On the 27th of February, 1849, there was another great and destructive fire in Saint John,— on King Street and King Square,— and in the following month there was another great fire, in which about one hundred houses were burned. On the 12th of July of this year, riots with loss of life occurred in the city, growing out of religious differences. The 28th of July was the date of a public meeting held at Saint John, to consider the depressed state of the Province. At this meeting the colonial association was organized.

In 1851 another census of the Province was taken, by which it appeared that the population of Saint John was 22,745. Since that time its growth has been steady and substantial; in 1861 its population numbered 27,317, and in 1871, 28,805.

The reason of this apparent slowness of growth during the last decade is, that Saint John has in a measure overgrown its limits, and that any considerable increase hereafter can never take place in the city proper, its bounds being too circumscribed to admit of a large population. Portland, and the parishes of Lancaster and Simonds, now are increased by the overflowing of the population of Saint John. The population of Saint John County in 1871 was 52,120.

CHAPTER X.

THE GREAT FIRE.

The Origin unknown. — The Sudden Appearance of the Flames. — The Spread of the Calamity. — The Fire Department. — The Streets and Wharves destroyed. — The Public Buildings. — The Shipping. — The Churches. — Explosions, Deaths, Accidents, &c.

NOTHING is publicly known about the origin of the fire; and the circumstances connected with it are such as to indicate that the combustion began by accident in some hidden corner. Perhaps a spark borne by the wind from some chimney, perhaps a lucifer match carelessly let fall where the pressure of foot or wind would grind it into ignition, and possibly some lover of mischief or vicious wretch intentionally, set the fire which resulted so disastrously to the unoffending people. The ground facts upon which all the theories, speculations, and arguments must rest are simply these: viz., 1st, The fire began in a wooden building on York Point Slip. 2d, When discovered, it was burning rapidly in large bundles of hay. 3d, The breeze was so fresh and strong that the smallest fire in such a place would instantly leap into a conflagration. How rapid was the increase of the fire, may be understood when we state that within one hundred and thirty seconds after the alarm was sounded Engine No. 3 was throwing water upon the ignited buildings. Other engines followed immediately; but, before they could find a suitable location to play upon the flames, the conflagration by means of sparks and heat had spread to a score of wooden structures. "The Saint John Daily Telegraph," in its first edition published after the fire thus described the progress of the great calamity: —

"The fire was first discovered in a building owned by Mr. Fairweather on the south of York Point Slip, next to McLauchlan's boiler-shop; and to the latter building the flames had spread before the firemen had reached the scene. The engines arrived, and did their best to stop the flames; but all their efforts were in vain. Nothing could be done. The flames then spread to the various buildings on Hare's Wharf, which were also quickly consumed; and before the fire could be checked it broke out with a roar into Smyth Street, carrying every thing before it. From there the flames spread into Drury Lane and Mill Street, following that into Dock Street, taking both sides. Ere this, however, the rear of the

London House and adjacent buildings had been attacked by the fire.

" The Portland engine and firemen, and a Carleton engine, soon came to the relief of the city men.

" One engine had been stationed at the corner of Mill and Union Streets, while the men with branches were down on Union Street, opposite Drury Lane. The buildings were a mass of flames at the end of Smyth Street and Drury Lane; and, while the workers were vainly endeavoring to have the fire end there, a momentary gale took the flames across Union Street to the opposite houses, and then they receded; but their touch had been fatal, and in less than five minutes the erections were doomed to destruction. Both sides of the street were soon in the grasp of the devouring element; and the men lingered so long in their struggle to save the buildings that at last they were obliged to drop their branch-pipes, and run up the street, after which they dragged the hose after them. Another lot of men were working at the foot of Union Street, and by placing boards in front of their faces managed to battle with the flames until their clothing became singed.

" When it became evident that the business part of the city was in the greatest peril, there was a great rush to the Bank of New Brunswick and its vaults.

Bankers brought great heavy boxes of specie, and immense packages of notes, also great numbers of boxes of bonds, and bills of exchange, and office secretaries; many others besides bankers did so; and Mr. Schofield, who was in charge, kindly placed the use of the vaults at their disposal. The use of the cellars and other parts of the bank was also permitted. At that time the bank, which had taken most precautions against fire in regard to its front, was threatened in the rear; and whether it would be able to fight the enemy was doubtful.

"It was heart-rending to witness sick, infirm, and aged persons, being dragged through the streets in search of a place of safety, which it was very difficult to find. Women and children wept freely, and even full-grown men could not restrain their emotions. Streams of blood, the results of injuries, marked the faces of several men; and others had received bruises and been maimed in various ways. Many men and women might be seen, utterly exhausted with the fatigue and the heat, which became insufferable, dragging bedding, pieces of furniture, and other articles, through the streets; a vain task in many cases, as the new places of refuge sought out often proved as unsafe as those that were deserted.

"Queen and King Squares and other open spaces

were speedily piled with bedding, chairs, tables, and other valuables. Then women and children gathered to the same spots, partly to try and watch over their property, and partly because they knew no other places of safety. The burning of the Bell-Tower, the flight of cinders in all directions, and the danger of its falling on those who were near it, produced an unpleasant sensation on the square.

"It was somewhat disheartening to the band of workers to learn that a building on Main Street, a mile away, had caught fire from the cinders that were hurled away from the scene of the conflagration. This was totally unexpected, and the people were of course not prepared for it: so the flames went, no one being able to offer any resistance; and house after house was razed, while the occupants had only an opportunity of saving their effects.

"Proceeding along Smyth Street in a southerly direction, the fire soon reached Nelson Street, and then Robertson's Place; then extended to Robertson's Wharf, and then up the South Wharf. As it gained Nelson Street on the south, it there met the flames coming up that street; and the combination made a terrific heat, that could not be borne by those who were in the vicinity, attempting to save property: indeed, so rapidly were they overtaken that it was with difficulty many could get out any thing besides their books.

"Allied with the strong wind from the north-west, it did not take long for the entire wharf to be in a blaze.

"Half a dozen wood-boats were at the head of the market slip, and at the end of the wharves about the same number of schooners. Before the fire had assumed formidable shape on the North Wharf, the men on the vessels began to pour pails of water on the decks. The water was low just then, and something like this was necessary to extinguish the sparks that were continually showered down on them. One thing in their favor was, that the tide was rising; but the fire proved an earlier visitor, and those at the head of the slip were, in a quarter of an hour, on fire in so many places that it was impossible for each outbreak to receive attention.

"Before the vessels had been well on fire, the flames passed above their masts, forming a bridge of fire over the slip, that soon afforded a stepping-stone to the shops on South Wharf. Not one of these west of Ward Street was capable of withstanding the intense heat and sparks, all being of wood. They went down as if felled by a hurricane, the schooners in front having been hauled out to a place of safety. Many of the occupants of the stores were off helping their unfortunate brother merchants, and some arrived just in time to save their books; others were just enabled to witness the destruction of all their stock.

"Some of the embers lodged in the steeple of Trinity Church; and with nothing to save it — for the fire was so high as to be almost beyond reach — the fire was left to pursue its own way. As the news spread that some wooden houses in Horsfield Street, as well as others on Duke Street (near the Victoria Hotel), were on fire, thousands were alarmed. The cause of this was that the wind had carried to the rear buildings on these streets, large cinders which kindled a flame instantly.

"Fear gave way to terror as it was learned that this fire was spreading north, south, east, and west, — to Germain, Charlotte, Duke, and Horsfield Streets. Not an engine to be had, and every thing going down before the unrelenting fire. A building on Charlotte Street had hardly become a prey to the flames, when others on either side followed suit. In half an hour all but the Germain-street side of the square was in ashes.

"The Victoria Hotel and St. Andrew's Church were in great danger; and the hotel guests, as well as the employees, began to make preparations for seeking new quarters. But where they were to go, could

ACADEMY OF MUSIC.

VICTORIA HOTEL.

be more easily asked than answered. Should the house take fire, as it was quite evident it would, there would hardly be any safety on that street; and, as the destroying element was pursuing a south-west course, their only alternative was to seek refuge in the King's Square. Very little time was given them to collect their valuables; and, in the majority of cases, they had to leave with a scanty wardrobe. About the same time St. Andrew's Church took fire, and it did not stand long.

"Adjoining the church was the two-story brick building occupied as a tailor-shop in the lower story; and Beacon, Pioneer, and Siloam Lodges of Odd Fellows, as well as Millicete Encampment of that order, had the upper flat. Some of the members managed to get into the building, and save most of the regalia and paraphernalia, prior to that building being destroyed.

"The buildings at the southern corner of Dock and Union Streets, and on the opposite corner, caught almost simultaneously. To say that the fire raged fiercely here, would but too faintly describe the terrible manner in which it kept on, unheeding the streams of water directed upon it. The engine was obliged to shift its position from this quarter, the heat being most terrific. There was danger, too, of the hose being burned, and of all things the preservation of that was most essential. The engine was taken down Dock Street; but it seemed as if the fire did not wish to part company, and kept up a rapid pursuit. It also sped along the western part of Mill Street, crossing over to the opposite side, and darting with lightning-like rapidity upon Messrs. Rankine & Sons' biscuit-manufactory, then following onward towards North Street.

"From the South Wharf the flames entered into Ward Street, and extended to Peters's Wharf in a remarkably short space of time, carrying every thing before them. Then they proceeded to Water Street, and from thence soon made their way to the southern part of the Market Square, making a jump up to Prince William Street. At this stage a wooden house on Canterbury Street took the flames, and the Church-street buildings were soon imperilled. Then the flames advanced to Princess and King Streets, and on Germain Street, in front of Trinity Church, began to take the fire very rapidly.

"The Academy of Music, a splendid building, was also destroyed. The two stores were occupied, and the Knights of Pythias had a hall in the front up stairs. A great many of the actors who have been playing under Mr. Nannary's engagement lost portions of their wardrobe, and all the scenery was burned. When the fire had reached the Market

Square, and had obtained a strong hold on the many fine buildings thereon situated, several explosions were heard coming from one of the hardware-stores. They caused a general scattering of the people about, and the reports reached as far up as the Court House.

"The fire entered King Street on the western side (from Germain and Canterbury Streets); extended northerly on Charlotte Street, to the Saint John Hotel, burning the Trinity School in its course; went up the south side of King's Square, and levelled to the ground the Lyceum, destroying the marble-works of Mr. S. P. Osgood and Messrs. Milligan; proceeded to Mr. Robertson's stable, across to Saint Malachi's Hall, up Leinster Street, and then back to King Street east; down nearly to Pitt Street from there; and by our latest advices it threatens to proceed to the bank on Crown Street, but will not pass to the northern side of King Street east. All buildings south of King Street have been burned, the exceptions being rare.

"In the other part of the city the conflagration was stopped about North Street, having extended as far up Union Street as Messrs. J. & T. Robinson's. The Bank of British North America was saved; the police office and station opposite were burned.

"At an early part of the day the electric telegraph office was burnt down, and its valuable batteries and apparatus destroyed. The office is now established at the Intercolonial Railway Station. Some of its wires are cut off; and last evening the operators were mainly employed in answering messages of inquiry as to the safety of relatives and friends, or transmitting in very general terms the tragic story of deaths and disasters.

"A great quantity of the goods saved fell into the hands of thieves, who hung around like vultures, eager to avail themselves of any opportunity that afforded, to carry off what they could lay their hands on. Policeman Ring discovered two men in the act of dividing a lot of clothing and other articles which they had carried from a house, and stopped them in short order.

"The Ballast Wharf is covered with thousands of people, anxious to escape by water; so is the railway track, and grounds around the track between the Ballast Wharf and Courtenay Bay.

"The office in Carleton was used last night for the reception and transmission of mails. The evening mails were made up and sent off from there on time. This arrangement is only temporary, and the postmaster expects to have a city office provided to-day.

"The following newspaper offices, with their plant and stock, were completely swept away: 'The Freeman,' 'The Evening Globe,' 'The Daily Telegraph,' 'The Daily News,' 'The Watchman,' 'The Religious Intelligencer.' The 'Globe,' 'Telegraph,' 'News,' 'Intelligencer,' and 'Watchman' had job-offices attached.

"Messrs. Chubb & Co. lost their large job-office, book-bindery, &c.; Messrs. McMillan lost their job-office building, &c.; Mr. Knodell lost his job-office; Mr. Roger Hunter lost his job-office.

"The following persons are reported to have lost their lives in the fire: Benjamin Williams, Germain Street; Harold Gilbert, near Victoria Hotel; William McNeill, of James Adams & Co.'s establishment; Garret Cotter, of Mr. James S. May's establishment; Hugh McGovern, of Straight Shore. Two men whose names are unknown are reported run over and killed. The body of an unknown man was found on Prince William Street at four o'clock this morning.

"There were many persons hurt; accidents were quite common, and we regret to say in particular among the brave firemen.

"During the entire day, teams of every description could be seen loaded with household effects; while others less fortunate carried their little all in their arms, — removing the goods to places where they might obtain temporary shelter, for a permanent abiding-place was an impossibility. A few unoccupied houses in Portland were quickly taken; and those who were fortunate enough to possess vacant apartments in the city were besieged with applicants for the rooms. It was hard in all cases to refuse the urgent appeals from the unfortunate people; and there were frequent cases of occupants of houses overcrowding themselves in order to afford accommodations to the distressed.

"It was Mr. John H. Parks, one of the directors, who had the presence of mind and the energy to rescue three ladies from the Old Ladies' Home. He got a carriage in due time, got the ladies into a tugboat, and landed them safely in Carleton. Their deliverance from death was, under God, due to him; and the hearts of the ladies are filled with joy and gratitude.

"Mrs. Trepagle had left the Home to assist her sisters, Mrs. Reed, and another lady sister. They all perished together. Mrs. Reed was the mother of the ex-mayor, Thomas Reed, Esq.

"The following are among the list of public buildings, &c., burnt: —

"Post Office, Bank of New Brunswick, City Building, Custom House; Maritime Bank Building, in which are the bank, that of Montreal and Nova Scotia, office School Trustees, &c.; Bank of Nova

Scotia Building; Academy of Music, in which was the Knights of Pythias Hall; Victoria Hotel; Odd Fellows' Hall; No. 1 Engine House; Orange Hall, King Street; Temperance Hall, King Street, east; Dramatic Lyceum; Victoria School House; Temple of Honor, Wiggin's Building; Barnes Hotel; the Royal Hotel; Saint John Hotel; Acadia Hotel; the Brunswick House; Bay View Hotel; International Hotel; Wiggin's Orphan Asylum.

"The churches burnt are Trinity; Saint Andrew's Church, Germain Street; Methodist, Germain Street; Baptist Church, Germain Street; Christian Church, Duke Street; Saint James Church; Leinster-street Baptist; the Centenary; Carmarthen-street Mission (Methodist); Saint David's Church; Reformed Presbyterian Church; Sheffield-street Mission House."

CHAPTER XI.

SCENES ATTENDING THE CONFLAGRATION.

Similarity to the Fire in London.— The Description of that Calamity applied to this. — Scenes of Confusion. — Acts of Heroism. — Effect of the Fire upon Men's Natural Dispositions. — Thieves. — Deaths by Fire. — Sheltering a Homeless People. — All Things Common.

THE afternoon and evening of that awful day presented scenes of confusion such as few cities have seen since the great fire in London, in 1666, which this disaster so much resembled. It is rather surprising to find that the territory burned over in Saint John was one-half as large as that covered by the great conflagration in London, and that proportionately the fire in Saint John becomes by far the greatest desolation. How similar were the scenes, and how much unchanged human nature is, will be instructively apparent when we compare the descriptions of the destruction in London, with the annihilation in Saint John. In the volume published in London in 1722, containing an account of the Great

Plague in London, by Daniel Defoe, an account of the fire is added, wherein the event is described in a manner so applicable to this, that it will have a double interest here; and we insert it with that view.

"A raging east wind fomented it to an incredible degree, and in a moment raised the fire from the bottom to the tops of the houses, and scattered prodigious flakes in all places, which mounted high in the air, as if heaven and earth were threatened with the same conflagration. The fury soon became insuperable against the arts of men, and the power of engines; and beside the dismal scenes of flames, ruin, and desolation, there appeared the most killing sight, in the distracted looks of the citizens, the wailings of miserable women, the cries of poor children and decrepit old people, with all the marks of confusion and despair. No man, that had the sense of human miseries, could unconcernedly behold the dismal ravage and destruction.

"The fire got the mastery, and burnt dreadfully by the force of the wind; it spread quickly, and went on with such force and rage, overturning all so furiously, that the whole city was brought into jeopardy and desolation. There was a tumultuous hurrying about the streets toward the places that burned, and more tumultuous hurrying upon the spirits of those that sat still, and had only the notice of the ear of the strange and quick spreading of the fire. Now goods were moved hastily from the lower parts of the city; and the people began to retire and draw upward. Yet some hopes were retained that the fire would be extinguished, especially by those who lived in remote parts: they could scarce imagine that the fire a mile distant could reach their houses. All means to stop it proved ineffectual; and the wind was so high that flakes of fire and burning matter were carried across several streets, and spread the conflagration everywhere.

"But the evening drew on; and now the fire was more visible and dreadful. Instead of the black curtains of the night that used to spread over the city, now the curtains were yellow; the smoke that arose from the burning part seemed like so much flame in the night, which being blown upon the other parts by the wind, the whole city, at some distance, seemed to be on fire. Now hope began to sink, and a general consternation seized upon the spirits of the people. Little sleep was taken in London during that night. Some were at work to quench the fire, others endeavored to stop its course by pulling down houses; but all to no purpose. If it were a little allayed or put to a stand in some places, it quickly recruited and recovered its force ; it leaped and mounted, and made the more furious onset, drove back all opposers. Some were on their knees, in the night, pouring out tears before the Lord, interceding for poor London in the day of its calamity; yet none could prevail to reverse the doom which had gone forth against the city. The fire had received its commission, and all attempts to hinder it were in vain. . . .

"Then, then, the city did shake, indeed! and the inhabitants did tremble. They flew away in great amazement from their houses, lest the flames should devour them. Rattle! rattle! rattle! was the noise which the fire struck upon the ear round about, as if there had been a thousand iron chariots beating upon the stones; and, if you turned your eyes to the opening of the streets where the fire was come, you might see in some places whole streets at once in flames, that issued forth as if they had so many forges from the opposite windows, and which, folding together, united in one great volume throughout the whole street; and then you might see the houses tumble, tumble, tumble, from one end of the street to another, with a great crash, leaving the foundations open to the view of the heavens.

"Fearfulness and terror surprised all the citizens of London; men were in a miserable hurry. Full of distraction and confusion, they had not the command of their own thoughts to reflect and inquire what was fit and proper to be done. It would have grieved the heart of an unconcerned person to have seen the rueful looks, the pale cheeks, tears trickling down from the eyes (when the greatness of sorrow and amazement could give leave for such a vent), the smiting of the breast, the wringing of hands; to hear the sighs and groans, the doleful and weeping speeches of the distressed citizens, when they were bringing forth their wives (some from their child-bed) and their little ones (some from their sick-beds) out of their houses, and sending them into the fields with their goods. . . . The streets were crowded with people and carts to carry what goods they could get out. They who were most active, and had most money to pay carriage at exorbitant prices, saved much: the rest lost all. Carts, drays, coaches, and horses, as many as could have entrance into the city, were laden; and any money was given for help, — five, ten, twenty, thirty pounds, for a cart to bear forth to the fields some choice things which were ready to be consumed; and some of the countrymen had the conscience to accept the prices which the citizens offered in their extremity. Casks of wine and oil and other commodities were tumbled along; and the owners shoved as much as they could toward the gates. Every one became a porter to himself; and scarcely a back, either of man or woman, but had a burden on it in the streets. It was very melancholy to see such throngs of poor citizens coming in and going forth from the unburnt parts, heavily laden with portions of their goods, but more heavy with grief and sorrow of heart, so that it is wonderful they did not quite sink down under their burdens."

How surprisingly accurate is that description when applied to the great fire in Saint John, will be seen by reading the following extract from the Saint John "Globe" of July 12, which contained an excellent account of the whole destruction:—

"The scene as viewed from the heights of Carleton, where the situation could be taken in at one view, was magnificent and saddening. Before the spectator was a vast sea of flame, through which the ruined and broken walls and windowless gables gaped staring and pitiful; while here and there stood out some noble edifice like the Wiggin's Orphan Asylum, silent, massive, but succumbing at last to the fiery furnace that raged around it. The clouds of smoke filled the whole heavens, and blackened the sky with their horrid forms. Even amid these harrowing sights and sounds prevailing, one scene of beauty stood out grandly magnificent. That old landmark of bygone years, the Bell-Tower,— the subject of newspaper ridicule and individual satire,— became enveloped in flame. When denuded of its outer covering, the timbers showed a burning beauty beyond description. It had been built solidly, and offered long resistance to its overpowering foe, — the foe of whom it had sounded so many an alarm of coming danger, — but now struggled helplessly and unaided in its embrace; and, when corner-post and cross-tie and studding burned with a clear white brilliancy, it appeared as if inwrapped in a vast illumination. If in life it was plain, in death it showed forth beautiful. In the front lay the harbor slumbering peacefully (for as the night wore away the wind died out), but lighted up with the red glare of the burning city; whilst every mast and spar, shroud and line, of the tall ships stood doubly distinct from the red glare behind. How powerless indeed seemed man in a contest with one of the great elements of nature! how vain his works, how defenceless his condition!

"It required, however, personal contact with the burning districts to realize the awful horrors of the scene. When the houses around Queen Square were on fire, and the goods placed on the square were ablaze, a perfect sea of fire rolled around the spectator, escape from which appeared to be impossible. In the vicinity of the gas-house and around its high fences, bedding, furniture, and household effects were piled up in immense masses; while grief-stricken groups silently stood around, or, yielding to their emotions, screamed in terror at the circumstances in which they were placed. Death is said to be the great leveller, but for the moment fire took its place; and rich and poor were placed in the same circumstances, were subject to the same privations, and involved in the same ruin. People fled by, bravely struggling to save some trunk or bundle which the pursuing heat compelled them to drop, or which some living spark soon set fire in their hands. Some, despairing of saving any thing, came out of their houses, and locked the doors, and left all their goods to the fate which soon overtook them.

"Men and women, overcome by fatigue and suffering from hunger and thirst, turned into alleys and by-ways, and slept until some friendly hand aroused them from the danger into which they were falling. In the throes of that awful agony which only woman feels, on the public street, a woman gave birth to a child; and the wall of fire followed up all, driving the unfortunate sufferers from street to street, until they took refuge on the very edge of the sea, such as could get into boats or scows or steamboats being taken to a place of safety. It was a night of anxiety, of terror, of horrors: yet the morning sun rose upon a scene of great beauty. . . . The scene on the second morning after the fire, as the sun came up from the east, was one of extreme misery. The tall chimneys looming up in the gray of the morning were slowly gilded by the long level rays thrown parallel to the plane of the horizon; and this added to their grim wretchedness, making them a mockery of brightness when contrasted with the wreck of which they were so conspicuous a part. Scarcely a soul was seen on the desolate streets; but here and there amid the ruins was some solitary figure digging amid the still heated *débris* of a dwelling, in search perhaps of some long-cherished treasure now, alas! gone forever."

From three o'clock in the afternoon, when the old Bell-Tower trembled with the shock of the alarm, until the early dawn of the next day, there was a confused hurrying to and fro, and a continuous rattle of carts and wagons hastening to the windward of the fire with the precious relics of two thousand homes. Many a load of valuables was moved from Dock Street and from its vicinity to Princess Street, then again taken away to Sydney Street, and at last burned after another remove to Main Street. Men stowed away all the property they possessed in the house of some friend far removed from the conflagration, and confidently went to the work of helping their neighbors do the same thing; when, lo! the next hour, when they sought the place on some errand, they saw only flames, ruins, coals, ashes.

One gentleman had been at work saving his goods,

and in his haste had torn his clothing; so, when the goods were safely deposited in the stable attached to a friend's dwelling, he thought he would go around to his house, and get another coat. Imagine his surprise when he found his way blocked while several streets away from his house, and when he was told by an acquaintance that his house had been burned more than an hour, and his family could probably be found in the old burying-ground, or in the fields the other side of the bay.

Others carried away from their dwellings large bundles of goods upon their backs, and reached a place of safety, only to find that they had been carrying a bonfire which had half consumed their cargo.

There were almost innumerable instances of heroism and self-sacrifice, — too many by far to be individually recorded; and any attempt to make their names historical would be successful only in belittling the whole matter, inasmuch as the number known to any one writer would be very insignificant when compared with the whole. Little boys, in absence of father or employer, performed surprising feats in saving the families, the stock in trade, or the books of account. Small girls led their blind parents, with thorough presence of mind, through the hurricanes and showers of fire, shielding their charge by methods mature men might have overlooked. There were wives whose husbands, and daughters whose fathers, were sick in bed, or crippled, but who, with a show of strength born of desperation, took the invalids bodily in their arms, and hastened with them to a place of safety. There were firemen, who, in their zeal to save human lives and their neighbors' property, clambered upon the dizzy edges of roofs and towers, and held their position until they seemed to be standing in a lake of flame. No fault was ever found with the heroic men of the Fire Department who battled with that calamity. Although their efficient chief, who for so many years had directed their movements, was absent from the city, yet so thorough was their discipline, and so earnest was their desire to be of service, that all their work was done with most commendable promptness and precision. But what could four steam fire-engines do against the whirlwinds of flame which found such combustible material on which to feed? Certain it is, however, that had not the firemen fought so bravely, and had not the engines worked so successfully, there would not have been a place of refuge left in Saint John or the adjacent city of Portland.

How such a dire calamity develops and strengthens the tendencies of human nature! Like the camps and sieges of war, the excitement and the abrogation of civil law in such a time call out the best or the worst features of human character. During the progress of that disaster there were exhibitions of affecting self-sacrifice, of martyr-like bravery, by men who had been estimated by the community as selfish, morose, and unkind. Enemies, whose social contests had been long and bitter, when touched by the fire vied with each other in doing for one another deeds of the noblest kindness; and they will never quarrel again. Women who hated each other, and were for years estranged by the tongues of foolish gossip, sat together by the tombs that night, and in mutual woe became mutual friends. Men left their property they might have saved, and hastened to the assistance of the aged and the infirm; and in countless ways did the people perform for each other acts of charity and friendship.

In the other direction the development was not so marked; but there were men who stole that night who had never been known to steal before. They may have cheated children, and may have taken little advantages of innocent friends in order to get a penny more than they had honestly earned; but the devils that chafed within had been kept hid from the public gaze until this resistless opportunity came. Thieves there were in almost every street; and many valuable bales and packages wrongfully found their way into by-nooks, caves of the mountains, and obscure dwellings, which afterwards were discovered and returned by the officers of the law. In that dark interval, when the statutes of the land were held in abeyance, and the few policemen could not enforce the simplest ordinance, the good men became better, and the bad men worse; seemingly reversing the statement of Shakespeare, that

"One touch of nature makes the whole world kin."

For here the touch of the law had kept them kin, and it was the touch of natural freedom that made them enemies. But the disposition to rob and steal was not so prevalent or so malicious as that which was developed in many large fires in other continental cities. There were several attempts by incendiaries to kindle the houses which remained; but they were not so persistent as they were in Chicago and Quebec.

One old lady, so aged and infirm that she had long been assisted and cared for by the kindness of friends, was not willing to be saved alone. Her sister, who had been her companion for threescore years, was in danger; and she felt that she must go and warn her. The sister lived near by, and the old lady started briskly to her aid. She would not leave her infirm relative to die alone. Beyond this nothing is known of them. One old lady who resided in the same place wandered away, and was burned in the street, as already related in tracing the steps of David Tournay. But how these two aged sisters clung together, or how they called for help, and prayed for deliverance, men will never know; for the fiendish flames came and howled and danced, the whirlwinds growled, the smoke darkened the windows, and the great tide of fire rolled on and ingulfed them. Like Saul and Jonathan, they "were lovely and pleasant in their lives, and in their death they were not divided."

Others there were to whom death came that night; but how, or just the hour, or where, their weeping friends cannot tell. Of the score or more who were victims in the calamity, and whose names are known, there are but a few whose death was seen, and its full details known.

There was an uncertainty connected with the movements of almost every person; and no one could safely calculate upon meeting their friends even at an appointed place. The frightened refugees sought the first shelter which was offered them, some going to the homes of friends, some going into the fields, some on board of the vessels, and some fleeing far into the country. The people whose houses were untouched — and how few they were! — opened their doors to all who came, until bedchambers, halls, drawing-rooms, kitchens, and cellars were crowded with people and their hastily deposited property. They had ever been known as an hospitable people; but here was an extra call upon their sympathy and regard, which made the few who escaped with their property doubly generous, although there appears no long roll of contributors to the relief fund by the people of Saint John and the towns which environ it. Yet no one in all the swollen list of givers from abroad made more generous donations than did the people of the stricken community: they literally divided with each other. Every place where a bed could be placed was occupied; and again and again were the relays of visitors invited to the family tables. Mistresses became kitchen-maids, servants became hosts; and for a while the homes that were left were honest examples of a community of brethren of the apostolic order, wherein all things were common. Yet there were many who could not even then find shelter, so scarce were the accommodations when every door was opened.

CHAPTER XII.

AFTER THE FIRE.

The Ruins. — Obliteration of Streets. — Appearance of the Squares. — Exodus of the People. — Establishment of Business Quarters. — Absence of Food. — Danger of Starvation.

THE return of the sun on the morning which succeeded the fire was a dismal one indeed to the houseless people, although to the rest of the world it was as bright and fair as usual. The site of the city was covered with ruins of all heights and shapes; some standing as firm as the rock on which they were founded, while some toppled and wavered, ready to come crashing to the ground on the slightest occasion. Great heaps of living coals showed where piles of lumber or high buildings had been; and from myriads of indescribable mounds and crags of iron, brick, stone, and mortar, little puffs of smoke curled upward about tall chimneys, and united in the great cloud which hung overhead. The oldest inhabitant could not for a time locate the streets, so thickly covered with rubbish and ashes was the whole area of two hundred acres. At the wharves only the burnt stumps of piles remained, to show the line where vessels had so often deposited their cargoes. At the custom-house and post-office, only an imposing front of stone remained, with window-apertures, marred and cracked with the heat.

The sites of great warehouses, old churches, and costly residences, were lost in the general ruin; and, for a long time after the heat had so far subsided as to permit passage, it was difficult to find the corners of streets, or tell without measurement just where any certain house had stood. Such buildings as the Victoria Hotel, Orphan Asylum, and schoolhouses — grand even in ruin — were soon recognized; and, with them as landmarks, the bewildered citizens groped to the hearthstones they had so hopefully left for the store or the shop on the previous day.

Ruin, ruin, everywhere! All that was valuable was gone. As if in derision, the fire had left lucifer matches unburned in smoking heaps of ashes; and huge supplies of coal in cargoes of hundreds of tons were untouched, while the hotel or church they were purchased to warm was beyond the need of any more heat. The whole peninsula was left in all its natural deformity, save where the rocks had been hewn and blasted to make passable streets. A city must be founded anew upon these barren ledges.

VICTORIA HOTEL.   PRINCE WM STREET, IN RUINS.

It was a sad sight. Even the stranger shed a silent tear as he wandered over unrecognizable masses of *débris*, and realized in a vague manner how the owners of those remains must feel. It was like looking upon the face of an unknown corpse. There was the evidence of past life, the certainty of there having been a death-struggle, and the probability that the dead had loving friends somewhere, who were weeping for him, and would not be comforted.

Like veterans which singly have escaped the terrific conflicts of battle, the Hazen House, the court-house and jail, and the engine-house stood, scarred, begrimed, and alone; living reminders of the rage and destruction which had passed by them, leaving all but them prostrate and ghastly in unsightly distortion.

The collection of furniture, merchandise, crockery, glass-ware, carpets, trunks, and clothing, which had been hastily deposited in King's Square and the old burying-ground, began to move away, as destinations were secured for them by the owners. Lawyers secured apartments in retail stores; physicians opened offices in rear kitchens; while merchants accepted the first stable, loft, shed, dwelling, or shop that they could secure, and whatever was saved of the stocks in trade was advertised for sale from the strangest of corners, and the most obscure of streets and alleys. People set up housekeeping in rooms scarce large enough for a bed; and all kinds of trades were carried on in back yards and house-cellars. Every thing which could be called a shelter, and hired for money, was at once taken; and rents went up to fabulous rates.

Many of the houseless people who could not find shelter in the city sought quarters in the country; and every available conveyance was brought into requisition to convey them to the farmhouses where they had secured accommodations. Yet this exodus left many in the city unprovided for, who blocked the halls and chambers of public and private business, and who were only given shelter at last, by means of tents and shanties hastily pitched on the squares and vacant lots.

There were thousands of people in the city, or rather on the ruins of the city, that morning, who had lost every thing, and had no reason for telling where their dinner was to come from. It was an appalling spectacle, for to the horrors of the fire were now added the apprehensions of starvation. There was not food enough in the city, left by the fire, to keep the people three days; and of course that was in the hands of a few. The many saw before them severe and immediate suffering.

CHAPTER XIII.

EXTENT OF THE CALAMITY.

Estimated Loss. — Great Extent of the Destruction in Proportion to the Size of the City. — Names of the Owners of Buildings. — Names of Occupants. — Business Firms burned out. — Roster of Losers by Streets. — The Effect on the Working Classes. — Summary of the Property destroyed.

ALTHOUGH the city of Saint John covered so large an area, yet, as we have already stated, it was not such a wealthy city as Chicago, Boston, or Montreal; and hence the destruction, when stated in money, does not reach so large a sum as that which would have been lost in the burning of so large a territory in either of them. The loss of property in Saint John would not probably exceed thirteen millions of dollars, although some of the citizens place the estimate much higher. About five millions of dollars' worth of property was insured in sound companies. That insured in local mutual insurance companies was nearly all a useless investment, on account of the universal loss. The names of the companies having losses in Saint John, and other information concerning it, will be found in a subsequent chapter.

We give below the list of owners of the buildings destroyed, and, as far as possible, the occupants of them at the time of the fire, according to the roster prepared by the Saint John "Daily News" of July 9, 1877: —

On North Market Slip. — Heirs Donald McLauchlin: by Daniel McLauchlin, boiler-maker. George Sidney Smith: by H. H. Fairweather, store-room (this is where the fire made its first appearance). Heirs Robert L. Hazen: by R. P. and W. F. Starr, coal-sheds. George W. Gerow: by W. A. Spence, hay and feed (this building was set on fire after the great conflagration).

On North Street. — James Lawton: by J. F. Lawton, saws; Edward J. Wetmore, flock manufacturer. Property belonging to James Tyzick. William Kievenear: by self. William Kievenear: by Michael McIntyre. James Costigan: by self. John Howe: by Joseph Gannalo. John Howe: by Robert Hays.

On Smyth Street. — George Moore: by self. Heirs P. McManus: by Margaret McManus. P. McCourt: by Mrs. Mary Horton. Patrick McDevitt: by self. Thomas Sheenan: by self. Peter Bone: by self. E. McLeod (assignee J. C. Brown): by James

EXTENT OF THE CALAMITY. 181

Domville; J. C. Brown, commission-merchant. Heirs Charles Brown: by R. P. and W. F. Starr, merchandise. Margaret S. Robertson: by A. T. Clark, commission-merchant; W. N. E. Webb, cordage. Margaret S. Robertson: by George Snider, commission-merchant. Margaret S. Robertson: by L. McMann & Sons, importers. Margaret S. Robertson: by D. D. Robertson. M. S. Robertson: by R. P. McGivern, coal-shed. Margaret S. Robertson: by J. L. Dunn & Co., iron.

On Drury Lane. — Ann Leonard: by Johanna O'Regan. Heirs John Hinsborough: by Patrick McLaughlin. John Allen: by Thomas McAnnulty. William County: by self. Thomas Morrow: by Mrs. Daniel O'Neal. John Donovan: by self. Heirs H. Graham: by Mary Graham. Heirs Thomas Daley: by Mary Daley. Heirs H. Graham: by John Cronin. Heirs Helen O'Leary: by P. O'Leary. Thomas Hounhan: by self. Edward Mullin: by Denis Purtle. John Holland: by self. Catherine Healy: by self. Margaret McCarron's property. Edward Mullin: by self. Heirs John Bryden: by Catherine Bryden; Bryden Brothers & Co., biscuit-makers.

On Mill Street. — Mrs. Ann Carleton and heirs Thomas Quantance: by M. McCallum, liquors. William Finn: by John McDougall, cabinet-maker.

Robert Grace: by Joseph Isaac, tobaccos. John Lloyd: by Mrs. C. Carty. John Lloyd: by W. H. Gibbons, coals. Robert Grace: by self. Heirs John Frost: by Charles O'Hara, hair-dressing saloon. Heirs E. Lawrence: by Thomas Chapman. Thomas A. Rankine: by Thomas Rankine & Sons, cake manufactory. Thomas A. and Alexander Rankine: by Donald McDougall; M. V. Paddock, drugs. John Bellony and heir John Cotter: by Anthony Cain, groceries and liquors; Stephen Power, groceries and liquors. Thomas A. Peters: by L. McGill, shoe store. Thomas A. Peters: by John Haggerty. Ann Leonard: by James O'Brien. A. G. Kearns: by Thomas Marsfield. John Allen: by self. J. S. Brittain: by self. James Morrow: by self. John Ryan: by self. Edward Hayes: by self.

On Georges Street. — Heirs Peter Sinclair: by Mrs. E. Sinclair. Thomas A. and Alexander Rankine (new three-story brick building belonging to factory). Michael Burk: by self. S. R. Foster: by self, nail-factory. Michael Duneen: by self. Margaret Sullivan: by self.

On Hare's Wharf. — Coal-sheds owned by Margaret Hare, leased by James Domville & Co., and sub-let to Lloyd and others.

On Robertson Place. — Mary Allan Almon: by John W. Nicholson, commission-merchant. D. D. Robertson occupied offices and warehouse.

On Fire-Proof Alley. — Heirs of Benjamin Smith: by J. S. Johnston & Co. William Carvill: by George Carvill, iron-merchant.

On North Market Wharf. — Eliza Robertson: by Frederick Godard, provisions; John M. Taylor, flour, &c.; Hatfield & Gregory, provisions; J. & W. F. Harrison, flour, &c. George F. Smith: by self. John Kirk: by John Littlejohn, liquors. Heirs of McLaughlin estate: by D. J. McLaughlin. J. V. Thurgar: by Thurgar & Russel, liquors. Conrad J. Henrick: by White & Titus, provisions. Hannah A. Bates: by James Domville & Co. R. P. McGivern: by self, I. & F. Burpee & Co., and William Beals. H. W. Frith and Diocesan Church Society: by White & Slipp, flour-dealers; C. H. Hilyard, liquors. Heirs of John Duncan: by Erb & Bowman, flour, &c. Heirs of George Bonsall: by L. H. Waterhouse, coals; Stephenson & McLean, commission-merchants.

On Nelson Street. — Jane Inches: by Maxwell, Elliott & Bradley, blacksmiths. James Lawton and Joseph Stone's property. W. H. Brown: by self. James Lawton: by James Whelpley. Charles Lawton: by self. Eliza Robertson: by Barbour Brothers and others. Heirs of Benjamin Smith: by Kinnear Brothers. John Fitzpatrick: by self and John Risk. Heirs D. J. McLaughlin: by A. W. Marsters. Bela

R. Lawrence: by Fred Fitzpatrick. Fred Fitzpatrick: by self and Joseph Bullock, kerosene oil. J. D. & George H. Lawrence's property. Mrs. William Hammond: by Ed. Lantalùm & Co., junk. Berton Brothers' property. George Carvill: by self. Edward T. B. Lawton and Benjamin Lawton: occupied by Benjamin Lawton, boat-builder. William Scovil: by Flint, Dearborn, & Co., spice-mill. Geo. Carvill: occupied as a storage-yard.

On Dock Street. — John McSweeney: by John Bellony, residence and picture-store; A. J. Talbert, dry goods; William Purchase, watchmaker. John O'Gorman: occupied by self as a grocery and liquor store. John McSweeney: occupied by John Mullin, groceries and liquors. Heirs of B. Ferguson: by Stephens & Figgures, groceries and liquors. Johanna R. Ritchie's property. Heirs F. W. Hatheway: by G. M. Burns; Thomas L. Bourke, groceries and liquors; John Coholan, provisions. Heirs William Hammond: by Thomas Nash, soda-water; Francis Collins, commission-merchant; Lee & Logan, groceries and liquors. James Dever: by Daniel Patton, liquors; Simeon Jones and J. N. Wilson, liquors. Heirs John Stanton: by J. Donovan, boots and shoes; Michael Binnington, liquors. Henry Melick, heir John Melick: by W. H. Thorne & Co., hardware. Robert Robertson: by Thomas M. Reed, drugs; Mullin Brothers, clothing; Hugh McCafferty, liquors. Heirs Hugh Johnson: by Thomas Lunney, clothing; Brown & Nugent, liquors. Thomas Parks: by E. M. Merritt, groceries and liquors. Heirs W. A. Robertson: by J. W. & M. Clementson, crockery-ware. Heirs Thomas Parks: by Thomas B. Buxton, liquors. W. F. Butt: by A. G. Kearns, groceries and liquors. Otis Small: by Small & Hatheway, steamboat agents; E. E. Brewster, agent Prescott Brewing Company. J. W. & G. H. Lawrence: by John Currie, confectioner; Charles Watts, liquors. Trustees Varley School: by Michael Kavanagh, liquors. Richard Grace, two buildings: by McDonald & Hatfield, clothing; and Stephen Welsh. S. J. & W. D. Berton: by Berton Brothers, wholesale grocers. Heirs Elijah Baker: by William Martin, clothing. Daniel Monchan: by self as boot-store. Joshua A. Corkery: by B. Cotter, clothing. John Gallivan: by Daniel Coughlan, clothing.

On Market Square. By W. W. McFeeters, clothing; C. R. Ray, dry goods; P. J. Quinn, dry goods; Kerr & Scott. J. M. Walker: by Lewis & Allingham, hardware. Heirs John Wilmot: by Richard Thompson, "Sheffield House." Daniel & Boyd: by owners as wholesale dry goods; Joseph Barnes & Co., retail dry goods. Heirs Thomas Merritt: by A. C. Smith, drugs; W. W. Jordan, dry goods. John McManus: occupied by self, clothing.

On South Wharf. — Heirs H. W. Wilson: by F. Tufts, provisions; Oliver Emery, provisions. Heirs Thomas Gilbert: by Gilbert Bent, flour, &c. R. & G. Barbour: by Barbour Brothers. George S. DeForest: by self, provisions. William Scovil: by George Morrison, jun., provisions. H. & J. Gilbert: by Andrew Malcolm, groceries. George C. Wiggins: by Griffin Brothers, fish. James E. Masters: by Masters & Patterson, fish, &c. James Trueman: by self, provisions. Heirs I. L. Bedell: by W. I. Whiting, provisions; Samuel T. Strang, provisions. J. H. Allen: by self, provisions; Thomas Gorman, provisions. James & Robert Reed: by Thomas Boyne; W. Lorrimer, provisions; George L. Partelow, liquors. Heirs Thomas Merritt: by C. A. Clark, provisions; J. C. Ferguson, provisions. Heirs Benjamin Smith: by William Rising, provisions.

On Ward Street. — Heirs Benjamin Smith: by John M. Stafford, liquors. Heirs Benjamin Smith: by Richard Coughlan, liquors. W. W. & C. G. Turnbull: old buildings taken by them while their new building was being erected. Wm. B. Frith: storage and coal sheds. Properties belonging to Knox & Thompson and heirs of John Walker & Co. W. B. Smith's property. B. S. H. & J. S. Gilbert: by Charles J. Partelow, liquors. George S. DeForest: by William Black, ship-chandler. Bela R.

Lawrence: by Gilbert Bent as storage-rooms. Mrs. Catherine McNamara: by self. William Breeze's bonded warehouse. Moses Lawrence: by Schofield & Beer, grain, &c. William M. B. Frith: by George McKean, merchandise. William M. B. Frith: by J. W. Frith, ship-chandler. William M. B. Frith: by P. McCormack, clothing. John Mitchell: by owner, ship-carving. William Meneally: by self. Gallagher and Young's cooperage. Azor W. T. Betts: by John Corbett, block-maker.

On Johnson's Wharf. — Stephen S. Hall and C. H. Fairweather: by Hall & Fairweather, storage. John Wishart: by self. Heirs John Walker: by Robert Carleton, blockmaker; William McFee, blacksmith. W. A. Robertson: by self, storage.

On Disbrow's Wharf. — John and William Magee: by Jones & Cassely, riggers.

On St. John Street. — Sarah A. and Jane Tisdale: by James McFarlane; Arthur P. Tippet, fruit and groceries; Jas. Kennedy, provisions. Bela R. Lawrence: by C. M. Bostwick, provisions. William B. Jack: by Thomas McAvity & Sons, brass-founders. B. S. H. & J. S. Gilbert: by Thomas McAvity & Sons. W. W. Turnbull: by Troop & McLauchlan, ship-chandlers. Allen Brothers, property. Property of James Harris & Co. James Ferrie: by self, grocery and liquors. George Carvell: by John Evans, liquors. Heirs John Walker: by William Stanton, liquors. Heirs John Walker: by Charles Ring, liquors. Heirs John Walker: by John Melick, ship-brokerage. City Corporation: by harbor-master. Magee Brothers' property. Henry Brennan: by self, saloon. Charles Merritt: by C. E. Scammell & Co., ship-chandlers; George Thomas, merchandise; Joseph Prichard & Son, iron and cordage. Charles Merritt: by John Regan. Charles Merritt: by T. McCarthy, coal, &c. W. A. Robertson: by R. Robertson & Son, ship-chandlers. J. & R. Reed, by owners; J. L. Woodworth, agent Mispeck Mills. City Corporation, as fish-market. Mrs. Louisa Hanford: by Mrs. Catherine James. Mrs. Louisa Hanford: by W. Pike, workshops. George McLeod and Alexander Keith: by Hevenor & Co., coppersmiths. George McLeod and Alexander Keith, storage-sheds. George McLeod and Alexander Keith: by George McLeod. City Corporation: storage. Heirs William McKay: by Wills & Rubins, blacksmiths. James E. Holstead and Mrs. Louisa Hanford: by James E. Holstead. Norris Best and Mrs. Louisa Hanford: by N. Best, iron-merchant. J. & R. Reed: by D. V. Roberts, ship-chandler. Henry Vaughan: by self; S. Leonard & Co., groceries. Heirs of George L. Lovitt: by J. Donaldson. Augustus Quick, and Driscoll Brothers. Archibald Rowan:

by self, plumbing. Unoccupied property owned by Messrs. C. Merritt and George and H. Chubb. Bank of New Brunswick: by John Runciman, brass-founder. Bank of New Brunswick: by James Dyall, plumbing. Thomas Furlong: by owner, liquors; John D. Devoe, liquors. Heirs E. Stephens: by Adam Young, foundry warehouse. Stephen Whittaker: by James Moulson, groceries. Heirs Richard Sands: by Andrew Buist, liquors; John Horn, liquors; M. A. Finn, liquors; and J. W. Potts. Heirs William Parks: by J. & J. Hegan. Heirs Andrew Hastings: by George Robertson, groceries. Charles and John Patton, groceries and liquors. Heirs J. M. Robertson: by James T. Kirk, clothing.

On Prince William Street.—Ed. Sears: by Andrew Johnston, tailoring. City Corporation: police station. Henry McCullough: by H. & H. A. McCullough, and Watts & Turner, dry goods. President and directors of Maritime Bank: by Maritime Bank, Bank of Montreal, Bank of Nova Scotia, Board of School Trustees, Board of Trade, Stock Exchange; agency Dun, Wiman, & Co. Heirs John Gillis: by Magee Brothers, dry goods; John McSweeney & Co., shoe-store. Buildings owned by Mrs. John Kinnear: Hon. Isaac Burpee. Heirs John Ennis, heirs Noah Disbrow: all rebuilding after previous fire. Heirs Samuel Nichols: by Fairall & Smith, dry goods. John Armstrong:

by James Manson & Co., dry goods. L. H. Vaughan: by Barnes & Co., printers. J. L. Dunn: by E. Peiler & Brothers, music-dealers; James S. May, clothing; R. H. B. Tennant, shirt-maker. John Anderson: by Joseph H. Valpey, shoe-store; John Mitchell, jun., shoe store. Heirs Samuel Nichols: by Robert Stevenson, shoe-store; Ed. Lawton, drugs. J. & A. McMillan: by owners as book-store and printing-establishment. Heirs of J. M. Walker: by Eastern Express Company; S. Jones & Co., brokers; Sheraton & Skinner, carpets. Fred. A. Wiggins: by M. Francis & Sons, shoe store; Z. G. Gabel, India-rubber goods; John R. Vaughan, shoe-store. City Corporation: City Building. Heirs Jane Boyd: by William Elder, printer; Moses Michaels, tobacconist. Property of Morris Robinson and Bank of Nova Scotia. Maria S. Bayard: insurance-office. A. B. Barnes: by self as a hotel. Heirs George L. Lovitt: by O. S. Lovitt; James T. Magee, tinsmith. Hugh Davidson: by Thomas Lunney; Alfred Mills, chronometers. Nathan Green: by self as tobacco-store; and Samuel Corbett, cabinet-maker. Susan and Phœbe Purdy: by Susan Purdy. Mrs. John McIntyre: by W. H. Olive, agency. Patrick McArdle: by self, liquors; J. J. Mullin, clothing; Charles Bailie, fishing-rods. William Cotter: by Doody & Toole, plumbing. William Cotter: by self, meat-store. Heirs Francis

Ferguson: by A. R. Ferguson. Thomas F. Raymond: by owner, as hotel "Royal;" Michael Blackhall, livery-stable. Thomas McAvity: by James Griffin. Heirs Thomas Pettingill: by Charles H. Hay. Heirs James Pettingill: by O. S. Pettingill. Heirs Ed. Finnegan: by Henry Finnegan; Solomon Hartt, tobacconist. Robert S. Hyke: by self, as hotel "International." John Foster: by owner, groceries and liquors. John McCoskery: by Charles A. McCoskery, groceries and liquors. John McCoskery: by Mrs. Lordly as boarding-house. Moses Lawrence: by William Hawker, drugs. Charles King: by David Churchill, fancy goods. George A. Freeze: by George Scott. Robert Pengilly: by Thomas Pengilly, drugs. Heirs Thomas Reed: by John Richards, liquors. Heirs William McFadden: by James A. Burns. C. E. Robinson: by self, ship-brokerage. C. E. Harding: by self. James Milligan and Joggins Coal Mining Association, coal-sheds. City Corporation: by M. May. Heirs H. Chubb: by William Kirk. Heirs H. Chubb: by Jacob Weiscoff, liquors. Heirs H. Chubb: by Peter Garvin. W. H. Hatheway: by self. William Blizzard: by self. Heirs William McKay: by A. Brims & Co., brewers. Rev. Wm. Scovil: by W. H. Scovil. J. J. Kaye: by M. Wallace. City Corporation: by John Howlahan. Dominion of Canada: Custom House. Trustee Hanford estate: D. Bridgeo, boarding-house. Trustee Hanford estate: J. Hammond, boots and shoes; D. Coughlan, clothing. Patrick Morrisey: by self, liquors. William Finn: by self; A. J. H. Bartsch. Ann Thomas: by Mrs. Bridget Cain, fruit, &c.; Thomas Gunn, clothing. John Tilton: by Robert Wetsel, saloon; Messrs. Gould, dyers. Henry Vaughan, and heirs Simonds & Vaughan: by Stewart & White, commission-merchants. Ellis & Armstrong: by owners, printers; Adam Young, warerooms. Charles Merritt: by St. John Building Society, News Room, Stadacona Insurance Company; Wilson, Gilmour, & Co. Charles Merritt: by John Ross, liquors. Charles Merritt: by W. H. Sinnott, law-office. Charlotte Gibbons: by George Sparrow, saloon. James D. Lewin and Bank of New Brunswick: by Bank of New Brunswick. Dominion of Canada: Post Office. Heirs H. Chubb: by George and James Chubb, printers and stationers. Heirs Ambrose Perkins: by W. A. Hayward, crockeryware. Heirs William Major: by William Major, hair-dressing saloon. Heirs J. M. Walker: by George Philps, banker. Richard S. and J. S. Bois DeVeber: by owners, wholesale dry goods. Jessie H. Nickerson: by H. K. Tufts, shoe-store. Alexander Jardine: by A. Jardine & Co., groceries; Samuel Hayward & Co., hardware. Heirs Richard Sands: by Wisdom & Fish, rubber-belting and gas-fitting; James B. Cameron & Co., oil-lamps; T. W. Angling, "Freeman" office; Steves Brothers, general merchandise. John Hegan: by J. & J. Hegan, dry goods. Heirs John Hastings: by J. J. Hegan and Beard & Venning, dry goods. Robert Douglas: by M. Farrall, clothing. Heirs Benjamin Longmair: by Robert Marshall, insurance; P. C. Redmond, clothing; Mrs. John Benson, millinery; Roger Hunter, printer. Daniel & Boyd: by owners.

On Canterbury Street. — Wm. G. Lawton: occupied by owner, dry goods. John Vassie: occupied by owner, dry goods. A. G. Bowes: by Bowes and Evans, tinsmiths. James O'Connor: R. J. Ritchie, agent, not occupied. Heirs W. H. Owens: by Geo. Flinn, saloon. Sarah Owens: by George A. Noble, shoemaker. A. R. Wetmore: by McKillop & Johnston, printers. Thomas R. Jones; by self, as factory. James Walker: by N. B. Paper Co. Willis & Mott: by owners as "Daily News" office and paper-collar factory. North British & Mercantile Insurance Co.: by H. Jack, company's agent, and Everitt & Butler, wholesale dry goods. Thomas R. Jones: T. R. Jones & Co., wholesale dry goods. Thomas R. Jones: by W. H. Thorne & Co., hardware. George V. Nowlin: by B. Brannan, liquors. George Moore: by owner, tinsmith. Heirs D. J. McLaughlin: by Henry Conroy & Son, hair-dressers.

On Germain Street. — Heirs John Ward: W. F. Butt & Co., clothing; Thomas White, confectionery. Heirs John Ward: Thomas Campbell, gas-fitter. Heirs W. Tisdale: by A. Gilmour, clothing. James E. White: by S. R. Knowles, trunks; R. B. Emerson, stoves. N. B. Masonic Hall Company: by James Sweeney. N. B. Masonic Hall Company: by C. E. Burnham & Co., upholsterers. N. B. Masonic Hall Company: by E. McNicoll, Messrs. Belyea & Knowles. Rector and Wardens Trinity Church: Trinity Church. John A. Anderson: by Ann Lyons, old furniture. D. J. McLaughlin: by Mary Ann Armstrong. D. J. McLaughlin: by William & James Notman, photographers. Edward Sears, by self. W. Tremain Gard, goldsmith. Jane Brown, millinery. Edward Sears: by W. T. Gard; G. Caldwell, dentist. Trustees Wesleyan Methodist Church: by Rev. R. Roberts. Trustees Wesleyan Methodist Church: church. Trustees Saint John Grammar School: schoolhouse. Trustees Saint John Grammar School: by Richard Welch, tailor. Trustees Saint Andrew Church: church. Victoria Hotel Company: hotel. Property of Otis Small and Moses Lawrence. Heirs Edwin Bayard: by Mrs. Edwin Bayard. H. R. Ranney: by Mrs. Wesley Thompson. John McMillan: by James McMillan. John McMillan: by John McMillan. Heirs Robertson Bayard: by Dr. James

A. McAllister. Heirs Samuel Seeds: by Mrs. John McGrath. Heirs Samuel Seeds: by Mrs. Seeds. Heirs Robert Parker, barn. Trustees Home for the Aged: Home for the Aged. Trustees Germain-street Baptist Church: by Rev. Mr. Carey. Trustees Germain-street Baptist Church: church. John H. Harding: by self. John H. Harding: by Charles E. Turnbull. John Chaloner: by self. Mrs. Duncan Robertson: by self. Heirs William Hammond: by Mrs. Hammond. Heirs William Hammond (two houses): by William Wilson. William Thomas: by self. W. C. Perley: by self. Charles Philips: by self. Heirs G. E. S. Keator: by William Lewis, blacksmith. James Miller: by R. Bent, groceries. James Miller: by self. Caleb Larkins: by A. J. Devine. Heirs Donald Cameron: by Mrs. B. A. Cameron. William J. Stevens: by O. D. Wetmore. George Hutchinson, jun.: by self. Property belonging to heirs B. Robinson. Heirs A. Balloch: by W. B. Lyon. Mrs. Samuel Seeds: by Robert Ritchie, groceries. Heirs Samuel Seeds: by C. K. Cameron. F. W. Climo: by Mrs. Mary Crane. Charles R. Ray: by self. James R. Ruel: by self. Mrs. H. M. Johnson: by J. M. C. Fiske. Heirs Thomas Parks: by Rev. H. Daniel; J. R. McFarlane, tallow-chandler. Heirs Thomas Parks: by Charles Edwards. Heirs Edward Ketchum: by E. E. Kenney, pianos. Heirs

R. Bayard: by John Friel. Heirs Lauchlan Donaldson: by Dr. J. E. Griffith. Heirs Lauchlan Donaldson: by Mrs. Mary Keator. William Bayard: by Dr. William Bayard. Alexander Sime: by self. H. U. Miller: by self. Joseph Bullock: by self; Dr. A. F. McAvenny. James Lawton: by self. William Davidson: by self. Academy of Music Company: Academy of Music; A. T. Bustin, pianofortes. William Breeze: by self; Miss Philips, hair-jewelry; Samuel Tufts, groceries. J. C. Hatheway: by self; William Irvine & Brothers, groceries. Heirs Henry Hennigar: R. J. Moffatt; Joseph E. Arrowsmith, meat and vegetables. George V. Nowlin: by Benjamin Williams. George V. Nowlin: by Miss Kate Reid; William Bruckhop. George V. Nowlin: by Richard O'Brien, liquors; W. E. Blanchard, sewing-machines. Heirs Daniel Leavitt: by J. D. Underhill; George Hutchinson, watchmaker. James H. Peters: John S. Climo, photographer. James H. Peters: by Charles H. Hall, sewing-machines. Trustees Mrs. Alexander: by John Leitch & Co., commission agency. James H. Peters: by Hatchings & Co., bedding, &c. James H. Peters: by Lordly, Howe, & Co., furniture. Robert Robertson: by Dr. A. M. Ring; Charles K. Cameron, millinery; Hamilton, Lomburg, & Co., commission agents. Heirs D. J. McLaughlan: by H. Brockington, tailoring; John

EXTENT OF THE CALAMITY. 197

Guthrie, hack and livery stable. S. K. Foster: by self; Pugsley and Bradley, dentists. S. K. Foster: by Samuel Nixon; Thomas H. Keohan, millinery and pictures. S. K. Foster: by James P. Hanington, drugs; Thomas B. Colpitts, photography; W. K. Crawford, book-store.

On Charlotte Street. — Houses owned by Charles Merritt, John Holden, James Vernon, Dr. McLaren, Dr. John Berryman, Mary L. Wheeler, Patrick Doherty, James Mason, Mrs. T. L. Coughlan, Samuel Corbett, Samuel Hayward, Mary A. and heirs Samuel Crawford, Eliza Chapman, Johannah Dacey and heirs Timothy Dacey, James Devoe, Thomas Welly, John Farren, heirs Benjamin Longmore, heirs Francis McAvenny, heirs William Potts, C. E. Harding, Pugsley, Crawford and Pugsley, William Breeze, R. P. McGivern, James Vernon, Agnes Stewart (two houses), John Marvin, Samuel Smith, John Watson, Charlotte Stevens, Thomas McAvity (two), William McDermott, Alexander and heirs Robert Jardine, Maritime Sewing Machine Company, Alexander McDermott, John Fisher, sen., James McGivern, Dominion of Canada, John Sandall, J. D. McAvity, H. Duffell, Mary and heirs Peter Fleming (two), Michael Flood, Kate Mulherrin, Nicholas Powers or Denis Lawlor, Peter Besnard, jun., William McDermott, H. Maxwell (three), James A.

Harding, James Robinson, Paul Daley, Currie and Holman, William White, W. H. Harrison, John Fielders, William McAuley, Jane Murray, Eliza McLaughlin, Louisa Hanford, John D. Devoe (three), Nancy Hazen, Ann D. Thomson, James Williams, William Davidson, Mary Farley, Mrs. Frederick James and others, Peter Besnard, sen., Peter Besnard, George Stockton, John Lawson, John Nugent, Daniel Mullin, Rev. A. Wood, James H. Pullen, Elena Clarahue, John Berryman (three), J. O. Miller, F. J. Cochrane, James Langell, Corporation Trinity Church (three), Gideon Prescott (three), James Guthrie and G. Hevenor, George Williams, John D. Gaynor (two), William Hillman, John Winters (two), James Rodgers, Daniel E. Leach, Peter Besnard, William M. Ward, Corporation Trinity Church, occupied by George Hayward (hotel), Robert McAndrews, groceries; George Sparrow, saloon; J. J. Johnston, clothing, Fulton Beverly (two).

On Sydney Street. — Buildings owned by Dr. Travers, W. J. B. Marter (two), T. C. Humbert, John McBrine, Right Reverend Bishop Sweeney (St. Malachi's Hall), George V. Nowlin (two), Ed. McAleer, E. Kinsman, Trustees Reformed Presbyterian Church (church), W. S. Marvin, William Davidson, John Anderson, Susan Dobson, William Mcneally, George

EXTENT OF THE CALAMITY. 199

J. Coster, Robert Gregory, Right Reverend Bishop Sweeny (Temperance Hall), Board of School Trustees (Victoria Schoolhouse), Michael Flood, John R. Armstrong, William Wedderburn, Norris Best, Henry Thomas, John Murray, James Knox, William Burnes (two), Robert McKay, E. M. S. Stewart (three), William Vassie, Thomas W. Peters, E. L. Perking, R. Rolston, Sarah McRory, John Carney, Ellen Mooney, Coldwell Howard, James Lemon, Sarah Taylor, Elizabeth Robbins (two), J. D. Vanwart, Ann Wane (two), Dominion of Canada (several properties for military stores, &c.), John McAnulty, Alexander McDermott, Mary Clark and heirs, John Clark, C. Longstroth, Alexander Kearns, D. J. McLaughlan and others, Henry Jack and others, R. W. Crookshanks, E. L. Perkins, Charles Hillan, S. K. F. James, Margaret Maloney, W. J. Morrison, Michael McAlear (two), Stephen J. Lauckner, James Milligan (two), Christian Brothers, John Gray, Trustees St. David's Church (church), E. Richey, Rebecca Schooler and heirs, David Marshall, L. S. Currie, James Vernon (two), William D. Aitkin, Robert McIntyre and Co., James L. Taylor.

On Horsfield Street. — James H. Pullen, Mrs. W. McKay (two), Peter Besnard (two), John Lowe (two), Ellen McAvenny, John Nugent (two), Sophia McLean, Mary Durant, Thomas Beddell, Catherine

Noyes, M. Perry, Knox and Thompson, William Breeze.

On Harding Street. — Robert Carleton, Mary Donahey, Sarah Gillice (two), John Wilson (two), Mary, Richard, and Neil Morrison, George Henderson, James O'Connor (three), William McDermott (two), heirs J. W. Young (two).

On Pagan Place. — Joseph Sulis, Louisa Donald, Mrs. Emma Allison, A. L. Palmer, Moses Lawrence (two), Robert Leonard, Charles S. Taylor, Stephen G. Blizard.

On St. Andrew's Street. — Thomas W. Peters (two), Robert Gaskin, H. Ahlbone, John Kee (two), James Gilmour, James Ritchey, John Ritchey, James Sterling (two), John Wishart, Margaret Suffren, E. Woodley, John McCaffery, Robert Wetsell.

On Carmarthen Street. — Building owned by Ann Cronin, Elizabeth and Samuel Gardner, heirs Aaron Eaton (three), H. A. Austin, George E. King, Charles Barnes, Mary A. Ward, E. E. Lockhart, James Adams (three), John D. Lormer, Samuel Ferguson (two), George P. Johnston and others (three), Hugh Bell, Catherine Bonnell, James Hill (two), W. D. Carron, James Muldon, Saint John Gas Light Company (gas works), Trustees Methodist Church (church), Trustees Protestant Orphan Asylum (orphan asylum), Margaret O'Neil (two),

James McKinney, James McCrouchford (two), Mary Ann Pointer, Daniel Smith, John Kirk (two), Samuel Dunham (two), Alexander Steen, Seth Scribner, Daniel Doyle, Mary Doyle, John Kirkpatrick, Esq., Smith, Hugh S. Normansell, Jane Carson, Catherine Nagle, Richard Evans, John Richey, Thomas Rankine, Thomas Doyle, John Wilson, Charles McLean, W. P. Dole, Joseph Henderson, H. Henderson, Rev. J. R. Narraway, Andrew Kenney, L. H. Waterhouse, Agnes E. Prouse, William Nixon, Daniel Driscoll, Robert Wetsell, George Sparrow and J. S. Richardson, William Finley.

On Wentworth Street. — Buildings belonging to E. E. Lockhart, Thomas Dobson, George Sparrow, George Blatch, Cornelius Sparrow (two), John W. Fleming and others, Henry Whiteside, John Fitzpatrick, Henry Coffey, M. Barnes, C. Flaherty, C. E. Sulis, B. P. Price (three), James Moulson and others (two), John A. Anderson, B. McDermott, R. P. Emerson, J. T. Barnes, George Doherty (two), C. Cathers (two), Alexander Steen, William Hill (two), Knox and Thompson (four), John Carr.

On Main Street. — John E. Turnbull (four), John Woodley, James G. Jordan, Alexander Steen (two), James Tole, James O'Brien, William Bowden, William Coxetter and Michael Tucker, Thomas M. Reed, Sarah L. Collins (two), Daniel McDermott, P. Vanhorn, James Mahoney (three), James Moulson, Jane Halcrow, Lawrence Markee, George J. Sulis (two), William Lewis, John and Robert Magee, Troop & Co. (Vinegar Works), J. W. Nicholson, George R. Bent (two), A. L. Rawlins, D. Knight, F. Mahoney, Edward Thurmott, William McKinney, Archibald Dibblee, George V. Thomas, John Guthrie, Mary Ann Ratcliff, James McKinney, O. V. Troop, Rector and Wardens Saint James Church (church), C. Langstroth, Andrew Armstrong.

On Britain Street. — Building owned by Sarah McFadden, Jane Barbour, John Collins, D. J. Schurman, John Scott, Henry Spears, Thomas Miller, Thomas McCullough, Thomas Crozier, James Price, William J. Colson, P. McGonnagle, C. Larkins, H. W. Purdy, E. Murray, heirs D. Hatfield, James McAvity, William Furlong, John Abbott, John Bartlett, Albert Peters, George Garraty, B. Coxetter, E. Thompson, Margaret McPartland, Fay Stewart, Daniel Jordan (two), William Ennis, James Nicholson, Robert Barbour, Albert Betts, H. W. Purdy, Charles Merritt (three), George W. Belyea, J. J. Jardine, James Gorman, J. Moore (two), Lawrence McMann (two), James Peckthall, F. M. Hancock, C. J. Ward, Mrs. James Bell, W. H. Hatheway, John Hutchinson, Peter Besnard, sen. (three), Robert Johnston (two), J. Hayes, Neil Hoyt, Nicholas Carroll, M. Barnes, Heirs L. H. DeVeber (two), F. Pheasant, Andrew Doyle, Robert Dalton, W. J. Pratt, D. Robinson, W. A. Magee, S. McGarvey, Margaret McPartland, Bridget Murphy, Thomas Bissett, Bridget Farren, J. George, Edward Duffy, J. E. Turnbull (two), E. Thompson (two), John Moran (two), John Crowley, W. H. Quinn (three), Francis Williams (two), F. M. Hancock, John Wishart, David J. Schuerman, Mary McCurdy, H. Maxwell and Son, G. Blizard, Thomas Robinson.

On Saint James Street. — Thomas M. Reed, O. Cline, Richard Cline, James Kemp, John Bridges, W. I. Whiting, J. McLarren, E. Thompson, Mrs. Alex. Coughlan, William Leahy, Samuel Rutherford, John Doody, John Sherrard, John Knowles, John Sears (three), Cornelius Cain, William Furlong (two), Bridget Murphy, John Watson, Thomas Viall, George Young, James Ellis, E. L. Perkins (two), William Simpson, Alice McKean, Patrick McGonagle, M. Burk, P. Ferrie, Mrs. Thomas Hanlon, Samuel Fisher, Eliza Wilson, John Wilson, jun., J. and A. Campbell, Daniel Sullivan, Robert Holmes, Cornelius Moriarty, John Runciman, Robert J. Coldwell, W. Casey, Board of School Trustees (schoolhouse), Rev. William Scovil, John Fisher, John Cain, Rev. William Scovil, and Trustees of Wiggin's Orphan Asylum (asylum), Jeremiah Drake, William Duffell, Thomas

White, Thomas Pike, William Furlong, F. P. Robinson, John Winters, James Price, William Gilfillan, Louisa Oglesby, Martha Ray, Jane White (two), William Russell, Mrs. David Millar, heirs Thomas King, P. Condon, James Aykroyd, David Stewart, Patrick Ferrie, Charles Osburn, Elizabeth Spence, Rev. M. Ritchey, Thomas Kedey, William Lewis (three), Michael Flood, John Wishart, John S. Mullin, John Littler, Michael Flood, heirs Daniel Hatfield, heirs F. Dibblee, Purdy heirs, B. Coxetter, Thomas G. Merritt, heirs Richard Sands, Caleb Larkins, Thomas F. Raymond, Mrs. Clementson, D. J. Schurman, Thomas Littlejohn, Charles Sinclair, John Callahan.

On Pitt Street. — Buildings owned by Silas H. Brown, Henry Lawlor, James' Cummings, Francis Jordan, Rebecca Fisher, Ed. R. Fisher, D. S. Robinson, James Hewett, C. Lawton (two), and several smaller buildings.

On Sheffield Street. — Buildings owned by Gilbert estate, Matthew Thompson (two), James Carr, E. Vanhorn, James Brown, heirs Ged. McKelvie (two), John A. Anderson, Robert Robertson, Margaret Hennigar, Joseph Kimpson, Ferguson & Rankine (two), Young Men's Christian Association, Michael McVane, (two), Robert Conniff, John Kirk, Alex. Harvey, Jane Wasson, Mrs. P. Riley, James Henry Anthony,

John McCabe (two), John Woodburn, C. O'Keeffe, Richard McCluskey, John Fisher, Alexander McDermott, Purves & Moore, J. Drake, E. Magee, John Porter, Rector and Wardens Saint James Church, Stephen and James Oakes, Samuel Dunham, Mary Ann Pointer, Catherine O'Neal (two), Michael McVane, Daniel Smith, Joseph McCullough, McKelvie heirs, Trustees Methodist Church, David Dodge and Elizabeth Nixon, Lewis Wheaton, George Anning, Joseph Sulis, James Vanhorn.

On Queen Square, north side. — E. L. Jewett, Thomas Furlong, Isaac Woodward, John Boyd, George B. Cushing, Robert Crookshanks, A. L. Palmer, James Manson (two).

On Queen Square, south side. — W. B. Smith, heirs Charles Brown, John Horn, J. W. Barnes, D. Robertson (two), Mrs. Charles Brown and heirs of Charles Brown, John Stewart, F. Tufts, John Tucker, H. Jack.

On Queen Street. — John Foster, Richard Longman, Margaret Oliver, Thomas P. Davis, H. Hawkins, Jessie Day, Mrs. Alex. Dalsall, J. H. Harding, James U. Thomas, Joseph Sulis, George Riley and heirs, Robert Riley (two), Jeremiah O'Connell, William Davis and heirs, John McNichol, Mary Bersay, John R. McFarlane, James McCart (two), Ed. Edgson, Mrs. Jane McPherson, James Thomas and heirs, John

Thomas, Hugh Kelly, Samuel Benterell, John Hamilton, Margaret Homer, heirs John Roberts, George S. Fisher, Robert Turner, John McBrine (two), Richard Cassidy (two), John Kerr, Thomas Jordan, D. S. Kerr, John Pettingill, C. Flood (two), George Suffren, Charles E. Raymond, John Fitzpatrick, James Gallaghar, George Johnson Nixon, A. Quirk, heirs R. Bayard, R. J. Leonard, G. F. Soley (two), Alex. Steen, Hugh Carswell, Mrs. John Milledge, Hugh S. Normansall, heirs John Whitney, John Wilson, jun., John Wilson (two), Margaret and heirs Joseph Hanley (two), Thomas Doyle, Andrew Evans, Robert Marshall, William Black, F. M. Hancock, Alex. McKelvey, William Pike (two), heirs D. J. McLaughlin, J. McFarlane, Thomas McAvity, jun. Robert Hickson, M. Frances, D. Brown, Mary Crothers and heirs John Crothers, Ann Thomas, Andrew Keohan, Mary Williams, John Scallon (two), Simeon Leonard.

On Mecklenburg Street. — James Hutchinson and heirs Joseph Stephenson (two), Richard Longmaid, H. Vaughan (two), John Vassie, Charles McLean, heirs James Whitney, Margaret Hillman, C. McIver, heirs Charles Whitney, John Dyers, Mary Dockrill, W. M. Jordan, James Emerson, James McNichol, heirs Joseph Atkins, Mary Ann McLean, F. L. Lewin, T. W. Seeds, Benjamin Dodge, John Ennis,

John Dick, James Woodstock, Phebe Bookhout, Martin Burns, Edward Purchase, Thomas Dobson, Ann Atkins, James Knox, Francis Gallagher, Matthew Steen, William Causey, George V. Nowlin, Andrew Armstrong, W. McVay, William McKeel, heirs Aaron Eaton, John Magee, William Magee, J. W. Nicholson.

On Duke Street. — P. McArdle, Peter Flanagan, Mrs. Francis Ferguson (two), Joseph Bell, John McSorley (three), heirs R. Bayard (two), A. Blain, Peter Besnard (two), Mrs. William Livingston, Mrs. W. Frazer, John Marven, Samuel Tufts, Jeremiah Shannon, O. Bailey, trustees Madras School, Corbett, Seely and Besnard, R. W. Crookshank, Susan Stephenson, Bernard Brannan (two), Robert Thomson (two), Samuel Gardner, Andrew Gilmour, Rev. William Scovil, S. K. Brundage, Joseph Henderson, H. Henderson, William H. Yandall, William McBay, J. Wilkins, sen., J. Wilkins, jun., William Francis, James Adams, Mrs. Gilchrist, James Saunders, Sarah Whitney, Sarah Partelow, Edward Purchase (two), Robert S. Jones, George Sparrow, Mary Ann McLean (two), M. Morrison, Charlotte Jones, Michael Burns, P. Bushfan, George Sparrow, William Wright, heirs William Melody, Margaret Hartness, E. Burnside, Howard D. Troop, John Marven, John Cook, James Adams, Sarah Ferguson, heirs Edward Brundage (two), Clara and heirs Thomas Kent, William Stephens, Jacob Seely, trustees Christian Church (church), John Wishart, L. H. Waterhouse, James Milligan, Sarah Jane Ferguson, George A. Thompson, John Richards, W. F. Butt, Arthur Daniel (two), heirs Daniel Culbert, James Vernon, Mrs. Earley, Peter Besnard, sen., Sarah Gillice, Mrs. William Livingston, J. O'Connell, Peter Dearness, Peter Besnard, sen., heirs Michael McGuirk (two), James Reed (two), Ann Jane Ritchie, George Stockford, Caroline Wood, Hugh Davidson, Susan Chittick (two), James and Robert Reed.

On Orange Street. — William Meneally, John Smith, Andrew Gray, M. Hennigar (two), O. D. Wetmore, Andrew Kinney (two), Chas. H. Wright, James Adams, W. R. McKenzie, D. G. McKenzie, W. E. Vroom, Stephen J. and heirs George King, Howard D. Troop, C. W. Weldon, A. C. Smith, R. R. Sneden, E. J. Berteaux, Joseph Prichard (four), Jane Cook, James McLean, Catherine Allen, Thomas Johnston, Henry Lawlor, B. Murphy, James E. Whittaker, J. R. Woodburn, Z. G. Gabel, James Estey, Charles Drury, Emma J. Daley, John Sweeny, J. W. Hall, George McLeod, J. Albert Venning, Robert Blair, Margaret Sinnott, heirs Robert McAfee, heirs William Bailey, James Morrison, heirs Thomas P. Williams.

On Princess Street. — Alexander Barnhill, W. J. Ritchie (Ritchie's Building), E. Thompson, Robert Grace, P. Bradley, J. C. Hatheway, M.D., Edward Sears, Patrick Fitzpatrick, William Burtis, Andrew Buist, James Hunter, Knox & Thompson, John Burk, J. H. Lee, B. Lester Peters and heirs B. Peters, Thomas Rodgers, John Anderson (two), John Murphy, B. Bustin, heirs John Mason, G. Bent, Margaret Hunter, John Nugent, Mary Craig, James H. Bartlett, Mrs. David Miller, Thomas Miller, James Bustin, Frederick Dorman, heirs Thomas P. Williams, O. Doherty, Adam Young, C. E. Robinson, J. H. Scammell, John Healey, John Gardner, Mrs. Mary A. and E. E. Lockhart (two), Ann and heirs of George A. Lockhart, R. W. Thorne, H. Williams, W. Sandall, Robert McAndrews, James Robinson, Susan and heirs J. Johnston, Ann Hamilton and heirs Clara Dean, William Fogg, Mary Ann Ellsworth, J. V. Troop, Simeon Jones, Alexander Lockhart, trustees Centenary Church (parsonage), W. C. Drury, Thomas A. Godsoe, J. W. Scammell, Thomas D. Henderson, G. W. Whitney, A. D. Wilson, Mrs. Ellen Smith, John Dougherty, Charles Patton, trustees Joshua S. Turner, Thomas Bustin, P. Halpin, Sidney B. Paterson, Barbara Clark, W. C. Godsoe, James Truman, J. V. Troop, trustees Centenary Church (church), James Leitch, Edward Willis,

Joseph Miller, Robert Law, George Thomas, Charles Watters (judge), Benjamin Lowe, H. A. Hatheway (two), Harriet Truman, W. Walton, George Matthews (two), S. A. Dixon, E. M. Merritt, Michael Thompson, Alexander McL. Stavely, H. S. Gregory, Helen York and Capt. Thomas York, John Anderson, James Sullivan, Michael Thompson, George F. Thompson, John J. Munroe, John E. Ganong, T. Gray Merritt, Jane Woods, John Burke, Mrs. James Drake, George C. Wiggins, W. H. Hayward, M. N. Powers, Catherine and heirs Michael Donnolly, Frederick A. Wiggins.

On Leinster Street. — Francis Cassidy, James Miligan, Lydia Gardner (two), Joseph Edgar, John Roop, George V. Nowlin, Mrs. Wallace and George W. Masters, Mrs. Samuel Bustin, Alexander McL. Seely and trustees of Baptist Church (church), Jane Rutherford, H. L. Frances, Mary Murray, Francis McDevitt, trustees Varley School, Mrs. E. Lunt and heirs Enoch Lunt, Joseph Lunt, George V. Nowlin (two), A. W. Masters, George V. Nowlin and Silas H. Brown, James Sullivan, Mrs. Lydia J. Calhoun, Joseph Read, W. H. and D. Hayward, A. H. Eaton, John Corr, E. K. Foster, John Gallagher, Denis Sullivan, heirs William Bailey, Francis Hewitt (two), John Roop (two), George W. Masters, G. V. Nowlin, Charles H. Dearborn, G. Merritt, Gilbert Murdoch, Thomas C. Humbert, John McBrine.

On Church Street. — George A. Knodell, M. Thompson, George Pattison, Thomas S. Wetmore, James H. Peters, Mrs. Jane Disbrow, Ellen Mahoney, Edward Maher, Archibald Bowes, Robert T. Clinch and heirs E. Barlow.

On King's Square, south side. — Charles M. Bostwick, Charles Merritt, Trustees Irish Friendly Society (lyceum), heirs B. Ansley, James and Robert Milligan, C. A. Robertson.

On King Street. — Mrs. John Gillis and heirs John Gillis: occupied by J. K. Storey and Co., dry goods. James Manson: by self, dry goods. Robert T. Clinch and heirs E. Barlow: by James Adams & Co., dry goods, and E. Sharp & Co., dry goods. D. J. McLaughlin and heirs Daniel McLaughlin: by H. R. Smith, bookstore; John Mullin, boots and shoes; J. R. Woodburn, photography. Stephen E. Whittaker: by J. H. Russell, hotel; W. Della Torre & Co., fancy goods; George Stewart, jun., drugs. James E. Whittaker: by Bardsley Brothers, hat-store; Salmon & Cameron, photographers; Scott & Binning; W. J. McGovern, hats and caps. George Barker: by J. D. Lawlor, sewing-machines; I. J. D. Landry, pianos. Mrs. George Taylor: by F. S. Skinner, groceries; Percival & Purchase, fancy goods; W. C. Gibson, fancy goods. John Dougherty: by E. Moore, J. L. Thorne, and John Kerr. The other owners on this street burnt out were heirs of William Melick, Mrs. John Hay, John Fisher, William Kennedy, Corporation of Trinity Church, Thomas Hale (two), J. S. Hall, C. Flood, Samuel Schofield, Thomas Seely, Ann Howe, John Mitchell, Mary Piddler, William Peters, Heirs H. Chubb, Joseph Nichols. James R. Ruel and Robert Light: by C. & E. Everett, hatters. Mrs. Charles C. McDonald (three): by Adams & Saunders, boots and shoes; L. L. Sharpe, watchmaker; W. Waterbury, hardware; James McConnell, boots and shoes. Joseph W. Hall (two): by H. Kirkpatrick. W. H. Scovil: by P. Sharkey & Son, clothing. Robert T. Clinch and heirs E. Barlow: by electric telegraph office.

On Union Street. — Brown estate, Peter and John Campbell, Daniel Donovan, Mrs. Lantalum (two), J. W. Hall (two), John Gallivan, John McSweeney (three), heirs D. McLaughlin, Charles Lawton, Senator Dever, J. Fred. Lawton, L. Burns, J. Hegan, John Lloyd, Hare heirs, Mrs. John Bryden, John Higgins, W. Wilson, A. Yeats & Sons (three), J. and T. Robinson (two).

In the foregoing list, the reader will observe the great number of dwellings owned by single individuals; and when he recalls the fact, that, in seven cases out of ten, their homes were all they could claim as their own, he will begin to comprehend how

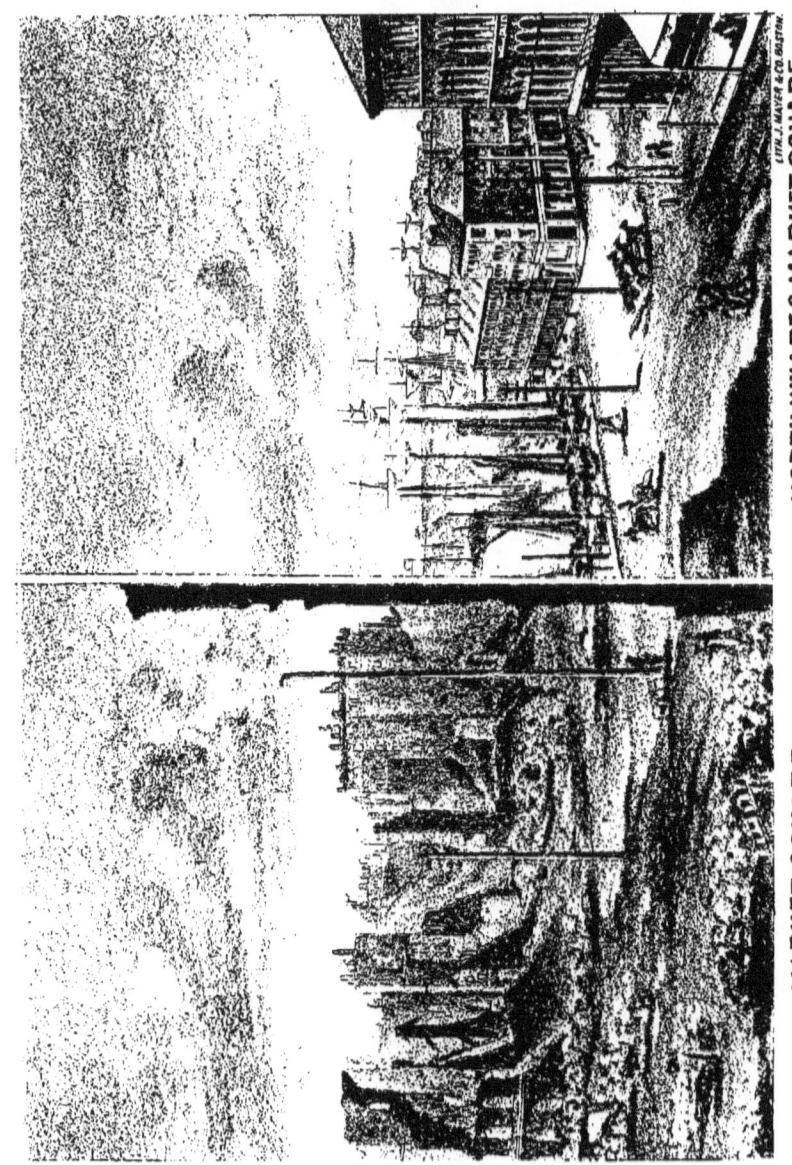

great was the loss to the working classes of Saint John.

The whole area over which the fire extended is stated by the best authority at 290 acres, of which 83 acres were in Queen's, 73 in Duke's, 95 in Sydney, and 39 in King's Wards. This estimate cannot be more than ten acres from the truth one way or the other, and may be accepted as being as nearly correct as can be given without an actual re-survey of the ground. The number of streets and squares over which the fire extended, and which were totally or partially destroyed by it, was 39, — Britain, Carmarthen, Church, Drury Lane, Georges, Harding, King Square, Leinster, Market Square, Mill, North, Pagan Place, Princess, Queen Square, Robertson Place, Smyth, St. Andrews, Ward, Wentworth, Canterbury, Charlotte, Dock, Duke, Germain, Horsfield, King, Main, Mecklenburg, Nelson, Orange, Pitt, Prince William, Queen Street, Sheffield, Sydney, St. James, Water, North Wharf, South Wharf.

Twenty-one streets were utterly destroyed, not one house being left throughout their whole extent. The remainder, with the exception of King and Pitt Streets, had in no case more than a block left; and in most only two or three houses escaped the flames. The total length of the streets destroyed was about ten miles.

The following is an estimate of the number of persons who resided in the burnt district, based on the census of 1871: Queen's Ward, 5,483; Duke's Ward, 4,678; Sydney Ward, 2,530; King's Ward, 1,500; Total 14,191.

The number of families burnt out is estimated at 2,780, and the dwellings consumed at 2,000.

The following is a list of the number of establishments in the several lines of business designated, which were destroyed by the fire: Manufacturers, 20; architects, 4; auctioneers, 7; bakers, 11; banks, 5; bankers, private, 4; barristers, 80; blacksmiths, 10; block and pump makers, 8; boarding-houses, 55; boat-builders, 5; book-binders, 5; book-stores, 7; boot and shoe makers, 38; boot and shoe stores, 14; brass-founders, 6; builders, 27; cabinet-makers, 9; clothiers, 29; commission-merchants, 93; confectioners, 6; dentists, 9; druggists, 8; dry goods (wholesale), 14; dry goods (retail), 22; dining and oyster saloons, 10; flour-dealers, 32; fruit dealers, 7; grocers (wholesale), 40; grocers (retail), 102; gas-fitters and plumbers, 9; hairdressers, 13; hardware stores, 8; hotels, 14; insurance-agents, 29; iron-merchants, 8; liquor-dealers (wholesale), 27; liquor-dealers (retail), 116; livery stables, 8; lumber-merchants, 12; marble-works, 6; merchant-tailors, 36; newspapers, 7; painters, 13; photographers, 6;

physicians and surgeons, 15; printers (job-work), 10; riggers, 7; sailmakers, 5; ship-chandlers, 14; ship-smiths, 8; stove-dealers, 8; tobacconists, 7; undertakers, 4; watchmakers and jewellers, 12.

The above forms a pretty long list, and will give some idea of what the mere losses in stocks must have been, exclusive of buildings. We must confess ourselves without data at present to estimate these losses accurately. No average can be struck among establishments which vary so much in character and extent; and there is no means at present of summing up the individual losses, for even the insurance-agents, with all the appliances at their command, have not yet got through their work, and many were not insured at all.

The loss of public buildings was severe. Three theatres were destroyed; viz., the Academy of Music, Dramatic Lyceum, Dock-street Opera House.

The number of places of public worship destroyed was 13, divided among the denominations as follows: 4 Baptist, 3 Presbyterian, 3 Methodist, 2 Episcopal, 1 Christian.

The other buildings of a public character were the Custom House, Savings Bank, Post Office, City Building, Wiggins Orphan Institution, Victoria School, Temperance Hall, Home for the Aged, Protestant Orphan Asylum, Deaf and Dumb Institution,

St. Malachi's Hall, R. C. Temperance Hall, Grammar School building, Varley School, National School building, besides a large number of other school-buildings throughout the city.

CHAPTER XIV.

THE DEAD AND WOUNDED.

The Number of Deaths unknown. — Eighteen suddenly killed. — Deaths in the Hospital. — Mention of Individual Cases. — Accidental burning. — The List of the Injured. — The Dependent Families.

THE number of deaths reported by the local press was astonishingly small in view of the extreme danger which threatened the whole people; and there may have been several deaths which would not become known until months or years of absence confirmed the suspicion. A writer in the Saint John "Globe" gave an account of the dead and wounded, which was as nearly complete as such an account could well be. He said that eighteen persons, at least, died sudden deaths in connection with the fire. Out of these only eight were taken to the deadhouse, and only two inquests were held; the coroner deeming it unnecessary to hold an inquiry in the other cases. Among the first to be killed were Garret Cotter and Peter McGovern, who were killed by the cornice falling off Adams's building. Cotter was a young man, a cutter by trade, working in Mr. J. S. May's. He lived in Crown Street with his widowed mother, his father having been killed many years ago on the railway. Peter McGovern was an old man, and lived with his family on the Straight Shore. In the Reed House on Main Street, Lower Cove, three ladies were burned to death. These were Mrs. Reed, mother of ex-Mayor Reed, and the Misses Clark, Mr. Reed's aunts. Mr. John E. Turnbull and others made desperate efforts to save the ladies; but all attempts were unavailing. Their bodies were never recovered. Capt. William Firth, the well-known ship-chandler, also met his death in the flames. His remains were found in Prince William Street, near Barnes's Hotel. He left a wife and family. Mr. Samuel Corbett, cabinet-maker, on Prince William Street, is among the missing, and there is no doubt whatever that he met a horrible death. Mr. Joseph Bell, painter, cannot be found; and he, too, has become another victim to the terrible disaster. He was a married man. Two persons were drowned in the harbor while endeavoring to save their property in boats; the bottom of the craft breaking, and the boat filling. So great was the excitement, that, although the boat was only a few yards from the vessels in the stream, both of its occupants had sunk before any effort was made to rescue them. These were James Kemp and Thomas Holmes. Kemp was a young man of about twenty-one years, and was clerk in Mr. Michael Farrel's clothing-store, Prince William Street. He leaves a wife and one child. Thomas Holmes was a lad of about seventeen years of age, and lived with his mother on Harding Street. Another victim was Timothy O'Leary, an old man who kept an apple-stand at the foot of Dock Street, and whose body was never found. There is no question, however, but that he was burned in Drury Lane. He leaves a wife. Mrs. Coholan, wife of William Coholan, Smyth Street, also perished in the flames. Her body was never found. Mrs. Bradley, who lived on Princess Street, also met her death on this never-to-be-forgotten night. Some human bones were found on the door-step of her house, and it is thought that these were what remained of her. A young man named Richard Thomas was burned. His remains were found in the ruins of R. O'Brien's tavern on Germain Street. He was formerly a clerk in Fitzpatrick's warehouse, Nelson Street. A young man, Robert Fox, belonging to the Marsh Road, is known to have perished in the flames.

Two men have been killed by the walls since the day of the fire. The first accident occurred on Friday afternoon, 22d inst., and was caused by the premature explosion of a blast while the post-office walls were being thrown down. The victim was an old man named John A. Anderson. He was standing on his property on Germain Street, almost two hundred yards away from where the explosion took place, when the flying bricks struck and fatally injured him. He was taken to the Public Hospital, where he died shortly afterwards. The second victim was George Gallagher. He was killed on Tuesday, 4th inst., on Water Street, a portion of a wall that enclosed the vault in Messrs. DeVeber's store having fallen on him, and inflicted injuries which resulted fatally a few hours afterward in the hospital. He was a man of about fifty-five years of age, and lived with his family in Mr. Thomas McPherson's house on Sewell Street. John Ross, a tailor, who was badly burned during the fire, died in the Public Hospital. There are one or two others that are missing since the fire, and it is supposed they have perished in the flames.

There are a number of persons missing, whose friends believe they were killed or burned; but, as there is an uncertainty about it, we omit their names, lest some of them should return to their friends, and claim to be alive, notwithstanding their death had become a matter of history.

The number of injured ones could not be safely

estimated, as there were hosts of people more or less injured by the heat, the crumbling walls, or by falling from roofs and windows.

At the hospital a large number of persons received medical treatment. Many of them had only sustained slight injuries, and the physician in charge did not have time to record their names on his books. There were several others who received severe injuries, but soon recovered. Indeed, with but one or two exceptions, they were soon able to leave the building. The names of those who stayed at the hospital for any time were Daniel Dooley, John Ross, Patrick Brady, William Coxetter, William Donahoe, Helen Davidson, Bayard Thompson, Walker Lamb (who was injured by an explosion at the post-office), Andrew Donovan, Michael Barrett, William Porter, Jeremiah Sullivan, Thomas Sullivan, Richard Powers, John Anderson, and George Gallagher. The two last were the only persons whose injuries resulted fatally.

Lieut. Joseph Ewing, who sustained severe injuries by the explosion at the post-office walls, was for a while confined to his house. His injuries consisted of bruises on the head, back, and legs.

There were many women and little children dependent upon the earnings of the deceased and the injured, who were thus doubly afflicted, having lost every thing they possessed, together with every possible means of obtaining more. Sad, sad, sad, must have been those hearts, when they sat in the ashes of their homes, and wept for the dead.

CHAPTER XV.

PUBLIC BUILDINGS AND SHIPPING.

Description of the Public Buildings. — Trinity Church. — Germain-street Baptist Church. — Other Church Edifices destroyed. — City Hall. — The Custom House. — The Post Office. — Public Halls. — Academy of Music. — Temperance Halls. — Masonic Hall. — Hotels. — Gas Works. — Shipping destroyed.

WHAT an enormous task the people have before them in restoring the city of Saint John to its original condition, especially in replacing its public buildings, banks, and commercial structures, will be better understood after reading the description of those destroyed, as given by the writer mentioned in the last chapter. There were many imposing and richly decorated edifices, which were the pride and ornament of the city and Province.

Trinity Church (Episcopal) was not only the first church destroyed by the fire, but was also the oldest church in the city, and a memorial of the Loyalist colony which founded the city. Its corner-stone was laid by the first colonial bishop in 1788; and the church was opened on Christmas Day, 1791. The material was of wood throughout, and the edifice had undergone a great many alterations in its construction. The spire with its clock was a noted city mark. The building had seating room for 1,000 persons: it was situated about 75 feet from the Germain-street front of its lot, which continued up to Charlotte Street, on which end was a large building belonging to the church, and used as a schoolhouse and sabbath school. An especial interest centred in old Trinity, not only on account of its associations, but as being the custodian of the royal arms, which, with the bell and organ, were removed into it at the time of erection, from the old church on Germain Street. Rev. Mr. Brigstocke is rector. The royal arms and the communion plate were saved from the fire, principally through the exertions of Capt. Frank Hazen; and the arms had been saved from a fire in New York and Boston before coming to St. John. The church was insured for $20,000; the Sunday school building, for $3,000; the organ, for $1,000.

St. James Church (Episcopal) was situated on Main Street, between Sydney and Carmarthen Streets. It was built of wood, in the Gothic style of architecture, in the year 1851, and could seat about 500 persons. The cost of construction was

$3,000. A schoolhouse was also in connection with the church, and was situated in the rear. Rev. William Armstrong was rector from the time it was built.

Germain-street Baptist Church faced on Germain Street on the corner of Queen Street. It was a beautiful brick building, in the Gothic style of architecture, and was erected in 1865. The inside was tastefully and richly finished, and the edifice was one of the finest churches that Saint John contained. Its seating capacity was 700, and the original cost $21,000. When repaired after a destructive fire a few years ago, it was greatly improved. Rev. G. M. W. Carey is pastor.

The Christian Church, a small wooden structure, was located on Duke Street, near Sydney. It was built in 1854, at a cost of $5,000, and had seating-room for 450 persons. The congregation was not a very wealthy one; and, until within the last few years, was the only church in Saint John of that particular branch of the Baptist denomination. Elder George Garraty has been officiating minister for the last eleven years. It was insured for $3,500.

Leinster-street Baptist Church was built in 1864, at a cost of $12,000. This church also contributed towards forming one of those modestly beautiful and tastefully adorned places of worship which were a credit to the city. It was built of wood, and could give accommodation to 600 persons. Rev. J. D. Pope was pastor.

St. Andrew's Church, Presbyterian, was a wooden edifice, occupying the lot next adjoining that of the Victoria Hotel on Germain Street. The venerable Dr. Burns, who for many years ministered in this church, when on his death-bed in Edinburgh, exclaimed, in reference to the Victoria, " Dear me! St. Andrew's Church, which once towered far above all on that street, is now itself overshadowed by a mammoth tavern!" It was built in 1816; was first opened for service in May, 1817, by the above-mentioned clergyman. A very fine organ was put into it in 1868, which cost $1,600. The building seated 1,000 persons. The Rev. William Mitchell, lately of Montreal, was pastor. The church was insured for $6,000.

St. David's Church, Presbyterian, was located on Sydney Street. It was a fine wooden edifice, capable of seating 1,000 persons, and was somewhat different from other city churches in its internal arrangement, being of circular form. It was built in 1848, and cost $12,000. Rev. Dr. Waters was the pastor.

The Reformed Presbyterian Church was built in 1850, at a cost of about $6,000. It was a wooden structure, located at the corner of Sydney and Princess Streets. The church was in connection with the Reformed Presbyterian Synod of Ireland. Although the congregation has been organized for the last thirty-six years, they have never had any other pastor than the Rev. Alexander McLeod Stavely.

Germain-street Wesleyan Methodist Church, built in 1808, and afterwards altered to its recent enlarged size, was situated on Germain Street, corner Horsfield Street. It was a wooden structure, with seating-room for 900 persons. The entire cost of the building was about $26,000. It was insured for $8,000. In the rear, and accessible from Horsfield Street, were a schoolroom, vestry, and class-rooms.

The Centenary Methodist Episcopal Church was one of the most commodious places of worship in the Province, giving seating-room to 1,200 people. It was erected of wood in 1839, on one of the most elevated portions of the city; and, in the fall of its tower, the mariner and harbor pilot lost one of the best-known landmarks in the city, and the Wesleyan Methodist denomination one of their most valuable church properties. Recently extensive alterations and repairs were made upon it. It was partially insured. Rev. Howard D. Sprague was pastor.

The Carmarthen-street Mission House was also

swept away. The congregation worshipping there had commenced a new church.

A mission-house on Sheffield Street, erected a year and a half ago by the Young Men's Christian Association, may be counted among the church property.

While the Catholic Church did not lose heavily in a financial point of view, it lost buildings whose historical associations rendered them dear to the people of that denomination. St. Malachi's Hall, or as it has long been called, "the old chapel," was the first Catholic church built in Saint John. It was over sixty years of age. Up to 1855 it was the only Catholic church in the city. In that year the cathedral was opened for divine service. St. Malachi's was afterwards converted into a public hall and schoolhouse. The large hall had been used for temperance meetings, school exhibitions, bazaars, &c. The upper portion has been used for schools. A few years ago an ell was added to the building. Temperance and religious societies met there, and it was utilized for many purposes. The building was insured for $9,000.

The old Temperance Hall on Sydney Street was built about 1845, when the temperance movement was at its height, by the Total Abstinence Relief Society. It was owned by the Catholic Church, and has been used as a schoolhouse. It was insured for $4,000.

PUBLIC BUILDINGS AND SHIPPING.   229

The dwelling-house on Sydney Street, opposite Orange, also belonged to the church. It was occupied as a residence. It originally cost $8,000. There was $3,000 insurance on it. It is a remarkable fact that the policy expired at noon on the day of the fire.

The post-office, of which Saint John was proud, was without an equal in point of beauty in the Maritime Provinces. The dimensions were fifty feet front on Prince William Street, and extending back to Water Street ninety feet. The architecture was a combination of the various orders of which the style denominated "modern" consists. On each side of and over the entrances were sixteen red polished Bay of Fundy granite columns, of surpassing beauty; excepting these, the building was entirely composed of gray sandstone, the whole material being the product of native quarries. The building rose three stories above Prince William Street, and four stories above Water Street, with a mansard roof, surmounted by a graceful clock-tower, which rose to an altitude of one hundred feet above Prince William Street, and one hundred and thirty feet above Water Street, and from which an exquisite view of the bay and city surroundings was obtainable. This superb structure, which was an ornament to the city, as well as an honor to its projectors, was erected by the Dominion Government at a cost of $150,000, and was first opened to public use in June, 1876. When under the full control of the fire, it presented a magnificent spectacle.

Next to the Post-Office, the Custom-House was the most important and valuable property owned in the city by the Dominion Government. It had a solidly built three-story granite front on Prince William Street, two hundred and fifty feet long, by ninety-two feet deep towards Water Street, which face was built of brick four stories high. It was well adapted for its particular purpose, and compared favorably with any similar building in America. In it were the offices of the customs, inland revenue, marine and fishery department, emigration agent, government engineer, shipping office, penitentiary office, gas inspector, and weights and measures. A storm signal-station gave warning to those interested, of the approach of a storm; there was also a signal-station on the roof, which repeated the signals given on Partridge Island of "vessels in sight," "pilot wanted," "ship in distress," &c.; and from the roof also a very fine view of the harbor and scenery could be secured. The building was erected in 1842, by the late John Walker, Esq., at a cost of $120,000. The wharf in rear of the Custom-House, of which one was adjunct to the other, costing $40,000, was badly damaged besides. The combustible nature of a great portion

POST OFFICE.

REED'S POINT.

of the goods warehoused in the building tended to make its destruction most complete.

The savings bank on the corner of Canterbury and Princess Streets was two stories high, built of white freestone, and was as tasteful a specimen of the ornate style of architecture as Saint John possessed. It was not very large, but admirably answered the purpose of its erection; and was built in 1859, at a cost of $20,000, by the directors of the savings bank under provincial control, and transmitted to the Canadian Government in 1867, who thoroughly reconstructed the edifice.

The Dominion Government, which never insured its property, lost by the fire about $400,000.

The City Corporation was a heavy loser by the fire. Over $60,000 worth of buildings were burned, and these were about half insured. The City Hall was a handsome stone building, which cost $23,000 when purchased from the Commercial Bank. Considerable money has since been spent on it in repairs. It contained the offices of the mayor, common clerk, chamberlain, water and sewerage commissioners, clerk to the assessors, city engineer, and superintendent of streets. It was insured for $15,000. The police court and station on Chipman's Hill was insured for $2,000. The station was a substantial brick building; the police-court was a wooden structure.

GREAT FIRE IN SAINT JOHN.

Located on Prince William Street, and next adjoining the post-office, stood the old Bank of New Brunswick, which was incorporated in 1820. This building had been in existence for over fifty years, being built in 1826, and had passed on to a period of existence later than was attained to by any of its founders. The whole of it was devoted to the exclusive use of the bank. The structure was of stone, with massive columns of the Ionic order.

At the time it was destroyed, it contained over $30,000,000.

The building of the Maritime Bank, on Chipman's Hill, adjoining the Western Union Telegraph Office, had a beautifully cut gray freestone front, supported by a granite basement, and topped with a Mansard roof. It was four stories high. Besides the office of the Maritime Bank, it contained the offices of the Bank of Nova Scotia, the Bank of Montreal, the Secretary of the Board of School Trustees, Dun, Wyman, & Co.'s mercantile agency, and the Board of Trade; also the offices of Z. Ring, W. H. Purdy, and G. Fred. Ring. It was built in 1873, at a cost of $60,000.

The Bank of Nova Scotia was opposite the Bank of New Brunswick on Prince William Street. This corporation had only just purchased the edifice known as "Cushing's Building," at a cost of $15,-000. The structure was a plain brick, three stories high, and was being put under through renovation and repairs at the time of the fire. It had then received a mastic coating on the front. The office of the bank at time of the fire was in the Maritime Bank Building.

The Academy of Music, situated on Germain Street, between Princess and Duke. The Academy was a building which the citizens of Saint John were justified in regarding with pride. The original intention was the erection of a building that would cost about $20,000; but after the act was passed, incorporating the Saint John Academy of Music Company, with a capital of $20,000, it was subsequently amended, and the capital stock increased to $30,000. The gentlemen most energetic in promoting the scheme were Drs. Keator and Carritte, and Messrs. J. W. Beard, Simeon Jones, John Boyd, John Magee, H. D. Troop, Hon. T. R. Jones, John Guthrie, J. W. Nicholson, T. B. Buxton, J. V. Thurgar, F. P. Robinson, J. R. Armstrong, and others. The exterior of the building was composed of brick; and the dimensions were 200 x 50 feet 10 inches. The front was 65 feet high from the sidewalk to the top of the ornamental work rising above the cornice, and was divided into three floors — the first being 15, the second 13, and the third 18 feet. The finish was Italian in its general style; and the main wall of the front was covered with a red mastic, which, with the brown sandstone trimming, made a very pleasing effect to the eye. The main entrance door, 13 x 17 feet, was surmounted by a bust of Shakespeare. The doors were of solid walnut, weighing about 1,600 pounds. The seating-capacity of the Academy was 1,300, but it would hold 1,500. The first floor, or parquette, was furnished with opera chairs. The number of chairs was 540. The balcony, or first gallery, would seat about 400 persons. The second gallery had a separate entrance and ticket-office. Three proscenium boxes, one above the other, on each side of the stage, accommodated five persons each. The cost of erection was over $50,000, on which there was an insurance of only $12,000. The last chosen Board of Directors was as follows: Dr. Ring, President; Messrs. Dr. Steeves, John Boyd, John Guthrie, and James I. Fellows; J. R. Armstrong, Secretary.

The Dramatic Lyceum was a building on the south side of King's Square. It was erected some twenty years ago by Mr. J. W. Lanergan, who was determined to furnish a suitable place for theatrical representations.

The "Opera House" had its location on Dock

Street. It was built by Otis Small, Esq., in 1871, and was eighty-three feet front, and three stories high above Dock Street, which was equal to five stories in the rear. The front was covered with mastic, and showed Gothic windows. The lower floor was occupied as stores; and the whole of the upper portion was thrown into a high and spacious hall, with roof supported by arches resting on columns, on which the galleries also rested. The sittings would accommodate about a thousand persons.

The Victoria Hotel was situated on the corner of Germain and Duke Streets, and was a magnificent square structure of brick, covered with mastic; was five stories high above the basement, covered over 10,000 square feet of ground, and was acknowledged to be the finest hotel in the Dominion, both in its extent and equipment. The edifice was principally in the Italian style of architecture. The basement was of dressed granite. Porticos were attached over the Germain and Duke Street entrances: these two facings, with their pediment window-caps and the heavy projecting cornice, gave the exterior a fine and imposing effect, while the great height of the building made it tower up conspicuously over all surrounding objects. The building's capacity allowed accommodation for over 300 guests, and its management required the services of 200 employees during the summer season. The hall was 40 x 20 feet, and the vestibule 20 x 15 feet, the floors of which were inlaid with marble. The dining-room, 40 x 60 feet, was elaborately elegant, and could seat 200 persons. The public parlor, on the second floor, was 19 x 100 feet; and private parlors with bed-rooms attached were numerous; while all the rooms were large, airy, and magnificently furnished, and fitted with all modern acquisitions of hotel luxury. The sleeping-apartments included 232 rooms, irrespective of private suites of chambers. The whole number of guest-rooms was 200. Water was introduced into every room. A steam elevator gave conveyance from one floor to the other; and the building was heated by steam throughout, the rooms being provided with grates also. The whole cost of the building was $165,000, and the furnishing about $65,000. The former was insured for $70,000, and the latter for $30,000.

The Royal Hotel was situated on Prince William Street, directly opposite the Custom House, and was formerly known as Stubbs' Hotel. It was a three-story wooden building, and a popular resort for strangers.

Barnes' Hotel was a large three-story brick building, with mastic front.

Saint John Hotel was situated on the corner of

King and Charlotte Streets, and in former times was the " Victoria " of the city, — the centre for all important gatherings, the colonial governor's headquarters when he visited Saint John, the scene of festivities, balls, and official dinners. The Masonic Order held lodge-meetings therein.

Among the other hotels destroyed were the Bay View, Acadia Hotel, Fisher House, Gordon House, Isbister House, Boston House, and other lesser establishments.

The Wiggins Orphan Asylum was a splendid edifice on St. James Street, erected through the munificence of Stephen Wiggins, Esq., at a very heavy cost. It had been in operation only a brief period.

The Protestant Orphan Asylum was a brick building, situated on the corner of Carmarthen and Britain Streets.

The Masonic fraternity occupied the front portion of the upper story of a building on Princess Street, where there were two lodge-rooms and several ante-rooms, whilst the encampments of Knights Templars and the bodies of the Ancient and Accepted Scottish Rite had their ante-rooms, armories, &c., on the story below. For nearly twenty-one years this building was the headquarters of Freemasonry in New Brunswick, the craft having previously held its meetings in Marshall's Building, corner Princess and Charlotte Streets, which also fell a victim to the fire. On Sept. 24, 1856, the late Grand Master Keith of Halifax, then Provincial Grand Master of Nova Scotia and New Brunswick, dedicated the hall to Freemasonry.

Not a thing in the room was saved. All the valuable treasures were burned. The societies burned out were, —

Albion Lodge; Saint John Lodge; Hibernia Lodge; Union Lodge of Portland; New Brunswick Lodge; Leinster Lodge; Carleton Royal Arch Chapter; New Brunswick Royal Arch Chapter; Saint John's Council Royal and Select Masters; New Brunswick Council Royal and Select Masters; Moore Conclave Knights R. C. of Rome and Constantine; Encampment of Saint John, Knights Templars; Union De Molay Encampment, Knights Templars; Harington Lodge of Perfection, A. & A. Rite; Harington Chapter, Rose Croix, A. & A. Rite; The Royal Order of Scotland; New Brunswick Consistory S. P. R. S., 32°.

The Grand Lodge of New Brunswick was also a heavy loser, as its valuables, together with all of the books, — and there were many rare and curious ones, — were destroyed. Indeed, so complete was the destruction, that not even a copy of the proceedings of Grand Lodge was to be found.

PUBLIC BUILDINGS AND SHIPPING.

The buildings in which the following societies held their meetings were also destroyed; viz., Sons of Temperance, United Temperance Association, Good Templars, Knights of Pythias, Temple of Honor, Orange Lodges, Irish Friendly Society, Shipwrights' Union, and the Odd Fellows; the latter having an encampment and three lodges burned out, and their furniture, organs, regalia, &c., destroyed.

The gas-works and wharves were destroyed, with a loss that cannot safely be estimated, as the property was of such a nature that more or less of it was saved, although the necessary loss was very great.

The vessels destroyed were those lying in the Market Slip. They were unable to move out; and their owners were obliged to stand by and see the earnings of a lifetime swept away in a moment. The vessels burned were, —

The schooner "Angie Russell," 25 tons, hailing from Canning, N.S. She had discharged a cargo of fish. Owned and commanded by Capt. Boylan.

The schooner "Brill," 74 tons, owned by the McSherry estate, Saint John. She had on board the balance of a cargo from Boston for Fredericton.

The schooner "Brilliant" was a fishing-vessel of 18 tons, owned and commanded by Capt. Patch of Campobello.

The schooner "Bear River," 37 tons, was owned in

Bear River, N.S., by Capt. Winchester and others. She had an outward bound cargo.

The schooner "Ella P.," 23 tons, hailing from Barrington, N.S., and owned and commanded by Capt. Thurber, had a cargo of fish.

The schooner "Eliza Jane," 27 tons, hailing from Bay Shore, N.S., had a cargo of salt. Vessel owned and commanded by Capt. Bent.

The schooner "L. L. Wadsworth," of Westport, N.S., was a little fishing-schooner of 12 tons, owned by Capt. Brown, and was loaded with fish.

The schooner "Lily," of Weymouth, N.S., was of 8 tons register; was owned and commanded by Capt. Israel.

The schooner "Martha Rowan," 25 tons, belonging to Westport, had a cargo of codfish. Capt. Peters was master and owner.

The schooner "Parrot," 27 tons, hailed from Saint George, N.B., and was commanded by Capt. Hutton. She had a full cargo, including a piano.

The schooner "Star," 13 tons, Capt. Benson, hailed from Westport, and had a cargo of fish.

The wood-boat "Burnett," 46 tons, Capt. Reed; wood-boat "Linda," 26 tons; wood-boat "Messenger," 33 tons; wood-boat "President," 46 tons, Capt. Orchard, were all loaded with cord-wood.

Four scows — two of them owned by Mr. Raynes

of Fairville, and two by Mr. Joseph Armstrong — were also destroyed.

The schooner "Justice," of Westport, was badly burned, but was hauled out in time to prevent total destruction.

The schooner "George Calhoun," lying in Walker's Slip, had her mainmast burned. Other vessels also received slight damage.

The total value of vessels and cargoes was about $40,000.

CHAPTER XVI.

FRIENDS IN NEED.

First Assurances of Help. — The Liberality of the People. — Telegrams from Cities in America and Europe. — Returning Past Kindnesses. — The Behavior of the Recipients. — List of Contributors. — The Amounts given and received. — How Chicago, Boston, and London responded. — Other Cities and Towns.

THE generous and hearty manner in which the cities of England, the United States, and the Dominion, hurried forward supplies for the suffering people of Saint John will never cease to awaken thankfulness in the hearts of the recipients, and will serve to bind the English-speaking people of the earth closer in bonds of Christian fellowship. For when the half-clad, starving people, actually without food for another meal, could see no way out of the pit of despair into which they had so suddenly fallen, and when homeless ones wandered about their heaps of ashes, half longing for death, then, almost as soon as the wires told that a fire was raging, the kind-hearted people in distant countries and states sent words of sympathy, accompanied, as all true sympathy is accompanied, with remittances of money, food, and clothing. Oh, it was a grand and noble exhibition of human kindness! It was noble because it came from honest, sincere friends. It was grand because such acts toward such a deserving people show the latent power which rests in union of states and nations, and bring nearer that great day when the sympathy of the world will be all the insurance men will need. North, South, East, and West sent messages of good cheer, bidding the saddened populace to take courage, for help was at hand. It would be utterly impossible to mention in a book of this size all the acts of kindness done by strangers, or to enumerate the names of donors. It was so universal, so spontaneous, that we can only outline it. Would that all those messages of love could be written in letters of living light, so high and so conspicuous that all nations could read them, and profit thereby! From the noblest sovereign which England ever had, from titled lords, members of Parliament, members of Congress, mayors of cities, and numerous individuals, came the despatches showing that the industrious, peaceful citizens of that city had friends all over the world, who were thinking of them, and desired to help them. These notifications and queries were sent to the lieutenant-governor, to the mayor, to the chief engineer, to the chief of police, to the United States consul, to members of the city government, to well-known merchants, to ship-owners, and to many others; and, as no one had been at that early hour selected to receive the unexpected contributions, the shipment of supplies was made to a vast number of different persons. Thus did Saint John find a fitting return for her great liberality and charity when Chicago, Boston, Quebec, and many other cities were in a like extremity.

We insert here a number of the messages verbatim, in order to convey to the reader a more correct idea of that outburst of sympathy than any language but their own could convey.

Her Majesty Queen Victoria sent the following, which was received by the people with marked feelings of thankfulness and respect: —

I am commanded by the Queen to express the great sorrow with which she has heard of the terrible calamity that has befallen the city of Saint John, and her Majesty's sympathy for the sufferers.

A. MacKenzie.

Fredericton, June 21.
To Mayor Earle.

Relief committees organized; propose sending special train, with provisions to-night: will wire you when train leaves.

E. L. WETMORE, *Chairman.*

PORTLAND, ME., June 21.

To the Mayor of Saint John.

Shall forward you on behalf of our citizens, by this evening's steamer, all the cooked provisions and hard bread we could gather. Please telegraph me what you need most, — whether provision, blankets, and the like, or money,

M. M. BUTLER, *Mayor.*

TORONTO, June 21.

To the President of the Board of Trade.

At a meeting of the Commercial Exchange to-day, the following resolution was proposed and carried: moved by W. H. Howland, and seconded by Mr. Worts, "That the members of this association desire to express their earnest and heartfelt sympathy with the people of Saint John, who have suffered from the disastrous fire in their city, and express their willingness to aid and assist the ruined and homeless sufferers by that calamity." You are hereby authorized to draw upon me at sight for $600, to be distributed for the benefit of the destitute sufferers. ROBERT SPRATT,

NEW YORK, June 21.

To C. U. HANFORD.

The "Flamborough's" sailing is postponed till the 26th for supplies. Notify the merchants. The freight is uncharged.

A. E. OUTERBRIDGE.

TORONTO, June 21.

To PRESIDENT OF THE BOARD OF TRADE.

Draw at sight for $1,000, probably more to follow, in aid of the suffering.

A. M. SMITH, *President Board Trade.*

OTTAWA, June 21.

To MAYOR EARLE.

Tents from Halifax and Quebec have been ordered at once. The Halifax train to-night is ordered to wait for them, so as to have them in Saint John to-morrow morning. Application for assistance will be considered by the government immediately, and I will wire you to-morrow morning. This is an unprecedented calamity for New Brunswick, which is painful to think of. Wire for any thing you think I can do for you.

ISAAC BURPEE.

MONTREAL, June 21.

To THE MAYOR OF ST. JOHN.

You will have received by this time a message from the mayor of Montreal, informing you that a train-load of provisions leaves Montreal this evening, and will be pushed through by every possible exertion, so as to arrive at Saint John at the earliest possible moment. The contents of the train will be delivered on your order, and I have given directions that delivery is to be made at whatever hour of the night it may arrive. Mr. Luttrell will advise you of the probable arrival of the train; and, if you will give the necessary orders for its delivery, the contents will be distributed the moment the train arrives.   C. J. BRYDGES.

MONTREAL, June 21.
To S. Z. EARLE, *Mayor*.

Relief committee forwarded to you to-night, will be in Saint John to-morrow night, special train of provisions: —

1,000 barrels flour, 100 barrels beef, 100 barrels pork, 150 barrels corn-meal, 150 barrels oatmeal, and a car-load each of bread and biscuit. This is to be distributed by your relief committee.

J. L. BEAUDRY, *Mayor*.

MANCHESTER, ENG., June 21.
To DANIEL & BOYD, ST. JOHN.

Draw on us for one hundred pounds for relief of sufferers.   Much sympathy,   McLAREN.

MANCHESTER, ENG., June 21.
To DANIEL & BOYD, ST. JOHN.

Sorry for your calamity. Can I do any thing for you?   ORAM.

To KINNEAR BROTHERS. COGNAC, FRANCE.

Subscribe two hundred dollars to relief fund.

GEORGE SAYER & CO.

DR. BAYARD. LONDON, *via* HALIFAX, June 22.

Deep sympathy with you and all sufferers. Draw on me in New York for $250 to relieve distress according to your judgment.

JOHN T. LORD.

W. C. WATSON, ST. JOHN. PICTOU, N.S., June 22.

New Caledonia Club sympathizes with their friends and your city in your awful calamity, and send to your care, by to-day's express, provisions and clothing for the destitute. The town sends to-morrow. DANIEL T. HISLOP.

Five barrels of flour were received by Mr. S. T. King from James A. Lee, Calais, Me., for the sufferers. They were handed over to the Relief Committee.

Houlton's contribution was a good one. Mr. John McMaster of that place, who was in town, left $250 in cash with Rev. Dr. Maclise, and $60.60 in goods from the people of Houlton, for Saint John's suffering citizens.

R. S. Mackintosh, produce-merchant, writing to J. S. Turner, made the following offer: " Use $50 in any way you think advisable to relieve the sufferers."

BATHURST, June 23.

Bathurst will forward contribution to your relief committee; $400 were subscribed at meeting last evening; first instalment by to-day's train.

K. F. BURNS.

TORONTO, June 23.

TO MAYOR SAINT JOHN.

Let me know certain, to-night, what you most need in new clothing, household goods, or any thing that this city can supply to help you, and there will be immediate response. Outside many subscriptions.

DAVID COWAN, *Chairman of Citizens.*

BOWMANSVILLE, ONT., June 23.

TO MAYOR OF SAINT JOHN.

Our company will send fifty bedsteads and chairs for benefit of sufferers: will they be of any benefit?

F. F. MACARTHUR,
Manager Upper Canada Furniture Co.

DETROIT, MICH., June 23.

HON. S. L. TILLEY, *Lieut.-Gov. of New Brunswick.*

National Division S. of T., North America, in annual assembly, extends you and citizens of Saint John assurance of sincere sympathy in this hour of trial,

and in event of funds being necessary for relief of distress, draw on National Division for $300 as a first instalment.   Louis Wagner, *M. W. P.*
     Samuel W. Hodges, *M. W. Scribe.*

               Chicago, June 23.
To Mayor Earle.

 The Produce Exchange of the city has deposited with the Bank of Montreal to your credit $1,000.
    John C. Cowles, *Secretary and Treasurer.*

               Chicago, June 23.
To Dr. Earle, *Mayor.*

 The committee of the Board of Trade have collected from members over $5,000, and now at your credit with Bank of Montreal. We are collecting.
       W. Richardson, *Chairman.*

               London, June 22.
To His Honor Gov. Tilley.

 Please cable immediately, whether fire caused great distress among poor; whether circumstances, sufferers, and extent of calamity, render assistance abroad necessary.   Rose.

            Bangor, Me., June 23.
Park A. Melville, *Daily Telegraph.*

 Let me know, soon as possible, what is most needed by the Knights of Pythias burned out.
    A. F. Snow, *D. D. Grand Chancellor,*
       Norembega Lodge, K. of P.

MONCTON, June 23.

To WILLIAM ELDER.

At a meeting of the employees of the mechanical department of the railway in Moncton on Saturday, they voted unanimously to give one day's pay to the sufferers by the late fire in Saint John.

MONTREAL, June 25.

To JOHN BOYD.

St. Andrew's Church, Church of Scotland, collected impromptu yesterday over $250 for the sufferers. We think of sending it chiefly in made-up clothing. Can you suggest any thing better? Would you undertake distribution among most necessitous?

ANDREW McLEAN,
REV. GAVIN LAING.

BOSTON, June 25.

To J. E. IRVINE, *President Y. M. C. A.*

We send clothing for distribution among sufferers; draw on us also for $100.

GEORGE A. MINER,
President Boston Y. M. C. A.

TORONTO, June 25.

To STEWART & WHITE.

Would 100 good common bedsteads be accepted from us for the deserving poor? Grand Trunk carry free. Answer. R. HAY & CO.

GLASGOW, June 25.

DANIEL & BOYD, *St. John, N.B.*

Deep sympathy. Lord provost calls meeting Thursday, to give it expression.

WILLIAM MCLAREN & SONS, *Glasgow.*

BOSTON, June 25.

TO GEORGE E. SNIDER, SAINT JOHN.

I start for Saint John this afternoon, on board United States revenue cutter "Gallatin," in charge of supplies from Boston Relief Committee. Hope to arrive to-morrow or Wednesday morning. Inform mayor. STANTUM BLAKE.

Mr. Snider also received from Hill and Berry, Fredericton, $100 for the relief fund.

TORONTO, June 25.

TO THE MAYOR OF SAINT JOHN.

Please inquire of the Knights of Pythias if they require relief, and if so to what extent, from their brethren in Ontario; and tell them to communicate with DR. JOHN S. KING,
Grand Chancellor for Ontario.

EASTPORT, June 25.

TO THE MAYOR OF SAINT JOHN.

Please accept for sufferers of fire, from Boynton High School, Eastport, $2.38.

Hundreds of like messages crowded the wires, of

which a partial summary is added, although it includes but a small proportion of the whole number received.

Charlottetown sent word that she would raise $6,000, and advised the mayor that $400 were sent by mail.

D. S. Babcock, president of the Stonington and Providence lines, offered free transportation from New York to Boston, of all supplies for the sufferers.

A. H. Chandler telegraphed that Dorchester would send $250 more per Monday's express.

The Chicago Clearing House Associated Banks telegraphed they gave $1,000; the Chicago Produce Exchange, $1,000; and the Chicago Board of Trade $5,000.

Annapolis Royal subscribed $1,242, and more was coming; Amherst sent $1,100 worth of provisions; St. Andrews, N.B., forwarded $400, with offers of clothing; Sackville sent 25 barrels of potatoes, and 15 lots of other provisions.

The treasurer of the counties of Leeds and Grenville, Brockville, sent $200.

The mayor of Bath, Me., said, Draw for $1,000, contributed by the citizens, and asked how $300 additional should be expended.

The mayor of Sarnia, Ont., sent word to draw on him at sight for $50, the contribution of Huron Lodge, No. 10, K. of P.

The mayor of Brookville, N.S., said, Draw for $500, and the mayor of Brantford for $1,000.

William Cummings & Son, of Truro, sent a case and parcel of clothing, &c.

A bale of blankets was said to be on the way from D. McInnes & Co., Montreal.

J. F. Power & Co., Montreal, sent 50 barrels of flour.

Canning, N.S., sent a check for $271.90; the Union Bank of Prince Edward Island, $5,000; and the Amherst relief fund, $500 on account.

Notice was received that the following had been sent, *viâ* the Intercolonial R.R., from the military district stores at Quebec: 372 circular tents, 7 marquee hospital tents, 1,247 gray blankets, 442 valises, and a lot of tent poles, pins, &c.

Joseph Robinson telegraphed John Boyd that Toronto donated $70,000.

W. C. Finlay, Hamilton Board of Trade, sent the mayor $1,000 cash.

Treasurer of Union Stock Yards, Chicago, Ill., sent mayor $1,200.

James Goldie, Guelph, authorized Rev. Mr. Mitchell to draw on him for $100 to assist homeless.

Imperial Insurance Company, London, authorized mayor and W. Elder to draw at sight for £500.

Malden, of Pembroke, Ont., authorized draft for $300.

Mayor Prince of Boston telegraphed to Mayor Earle to draw immediately for $5,000.

Isaac Burpee telegraphed to the mayor that the Dominion Government would advance $20,000 for food and clothing.

T. Williams, accoutant railway, Prince Edward Island, telegraphed mayor that the railway employees had raised $700 for sufferers of Saint John. "Draw immediately."

F. B. Edgecombe, Fredericton, telegraphed to the mayor that Fredericton had sent a further gift of two car-loads of cooked provisions and 700 loaves, and second load would be sent at once.

Brown, collector, North Sydney, telegraphed that S. T. Robinson of Toronto Coal Co. offered 150 tons coal.

E. A. Barnard, Calais and St. Stephen, telegraphed Samuel T. King that he had forwarded two barrels of good hams to him for the sufferers.

A. J. Drexel, treasurer, Philadelphia, telegraphed to the mayor to draw at once for $3,000. "More coming."

Mayor Waller, Ottawa, telegraphed to mayor to draw for $2,000.

Angus Morrison, mayor of Toronto, telegraphed mayor to draw from ten to twenty thousand dollars, as needed, and that his council would meet forthwith to make a grant. According to Joseph Robinson's telegram to John Boyd, the grant made was $70,000.

Collector Bowen, Sydney, C.B., requested the mayor to draw $400 through Bank of Nova Scotia.

John B. McLean, New York, offered assistance, and asked what was most needed.

Thus they came from all directions and in all forms, as will be more fully seen by consulting the list which we print at the end of this chapter. The cities of Chicago and Boston were especially generous, the latter sending $50,000; and their contributions, together with all the offerings from the United States, were received with especial thankfulness by the people. A resolution passed by the Episcopal Synod of Fredericton very fittingly expressed the feeling of the citizens of the Provinces, and will serve as an illustration:—

"*Resolved*, That the Lord Bishop of Fredericton, together with the clergy and lay members of the Church of England, now in synod assembled, desire to place on record an expression of their warmest sympathy with those who have suffered from the late disastrous fire in the city of Saint John. They deeply regret the loss incurred by their fellow-churchmen in the parishes of Trinity and St. James, by the destruction of their churches, and especially that of Trinity Church, one of the oldest in this diocese. The members of this synod desire also to acknowledge with deep gratitude to Almighty God, the comparatively small loss of life, and the prompt and generous aid to the relief of the sufferers from various cities in this Dominion, as well as from England and elsewhere, and pre-eminently from so many portions of the United States."

The people of Chicago could not forget the kindness of their brothers in Saint John, and were aroused to action by such paragraphs as this in their daily papers: —

"Our friends of Saint John, N.B., are in sore trouble. A fire more ruinous to their city than the great fire was to Chicago, because a far greater proportion of it is in ashes, has left thousands of them within sight of actual starvation. When Chicago was burned, the citizens of Saint John contributed *ten thousand dollars* to feed and shelter our scorched and scattered people. If we fail to return that money, with interest, and with the addition also of a thank-offering to God for our own restored prosperity, we are not the people they took us to be, when, in our sore distress, they sent us their generous gift."

The inhabitants of Boston, too, remembered Saint John's proffered liberality, and returned it in a manner becoming an honest and generous community. The following item in a Saint John paper tells in what manner Boston responded to the call for aid: —

"The American revenue cutter 'Gallatin' arrived

here yesterday afternoon, on her second trip, with supplies for the sufferers by the late fire, from Boston, Mass. The 'Gallatin' came to anchor off Reed's Point about four o'clock, where she was boarded by the harbor-master, and brought into the wharf that is used by the 'Empress.' As soon as she was securely moored to the wharf, the large number of people who had gathered together to witness her arrival gave three ringing cheers for 'the steamer "Gallatin" and our kind friends in Boston.' Shortly after her arrival, Mayor Earle, accompanied by some of the relief committee, were actively at work conveying the stores to the Rink, where they will be added to the common store."

The interest awakened in London by the great calamity was exceedingly complimentary to both cities, — the one for deserving, and the other for unselfish bestowing. A statement appeared in the London papers, June 28, signed by the Honorable Secretary and Honorable Cashier, as follows : —

"The Lord Mayor, in view of the recent calamitous fire at Saint John, N.B., by which disaster, according to official advices just received, 12,000 people have become destitute, and property of the value of $12,000,000 has been destroyed, and at the request of an influential deputation, will be glad to receive at the Mansion House funds in aid of the sufferers.

"The following bankers will also receive subscriptions: viz., Messrs. Glyn, Mills, & Co., bankers to the fund; Messrs. Williams, Deacon, & Co.; the London and Westminster Bank, the Union Bank of London, the Bank of Montreal, and the Bank of British North America.

"The distribution of the fund will be intrusted to the lieutenant-governor of New Brunswick, the mayor of Saint John, and the president of the Board of Trade, with power to associate any other gentlemen to aid them in their work."

And over two thousand pounds was at the same time acknowledged.

We give here the entire list of contributions received up to July 9, following the fire, which includes about one-half of the actual subscriptions, the balance of which was probably forwarded afterwards.

The following are the sums received in the order of their receipt: —

Sons of Temperance, Detroit, $300; Halifax, $10,000; Halifax boy, $1.08; Fredericton, $8,000; Philadelphia Maritime Exchange, $2,000; Boston, $5,000; J. H. Rogers, Boston, $100; Chicago Union Stock Yards, $1,200; Dominion Government, $20,000; Sarnia, Ontario, $1,000; Whitby, Ontario, $200; London, Ontario, $5,000; Amherst, $1,000; Parrsboro', $100; Boston Felt Roofing Co., $100; Imperial Fire Insurance Co., $2,433.35; F. Mehan, $5; E. Williston, Miramichi, $50; Bank British

260 GREAT FIRE IN SAINT JOHN.

North America, $2,433.35; Chicago Clearing House, $1,000; Bathurst, $400; Brantford, Ontario, $1,000; Sarnia, $50; Bath, Me., $1,300; Brockville (Midland counties), $200; Dorchester, $200; Stonington and Providence Line Steamers, $500; St. Andrews, $400; Charlottetown, $6,000; Lawrence, Mass., $465; Portland, Me., $2,000; Moncton, $200; Amherst, $500; Peterboro', Ontario, $200; Boston, $5,000; Dorchester, $410; Sayer & Co., $200; Toronto, $20,000; Chicago Produce Exchange, $1,000; Chicago Board of Trade, $5,000; Augusta, Me., $1,000; Canning, N.S., $279.90; Yarmouth, N.S., $1,500; Brookville, N.S., $5.23; Annapolis, $500; Bell of Dublin, $186.56; Clark, Dodge, & Co., New York, $237.19; Mrs. M. D. Smith, Ipswich, $25; Sherbrooke, Quebec, $1,000; St. Andrews, $150; N. W. Rice & Co., Boston, $100; Gorham Bradshaw, $100; John Hawson, $5; R. S. MacIntosh, $50; St. George, $200; John C. Johnston, $250; Sackville, $235; Newcastle and Douglastown, $900; Galt, Ontario, $500; Guelph, Ontario, $1,000; North Sydney, C.B., $400; Canada Screw Co., Dundas, Ontario, $200; Boynton High School, Eastport, $2.38; D. J. Odell, $10; Hallowell, Me., $500; Accident Insurance Co. of Canada, $200; Windsor, N. S., $3,000; Woodstock, $200; City of Lewiston, $500; Digby, $700; Aberfoye, Ontario, $200; Bangor, $7,000; Summerside, P.E.I., $1,500; B. Beveridge, & Sons, Andover, $100; Bridgetown, $206; Liverpool, N.S.$, 700; Truro public meeting, $2,000; Palmer & Embury, $50; Brantford, $500; New York, $2,000; W. C. B. & G. H. F. Customs, Ottawa, $2; Philadelphia, $2,000; St. Thomas, Ontario, $500; Bowmansville, $300; Canada Life Insurance Company, $500; New Haven Chamber of Commerce, $823.76; Archibald, New York, $2,000; Capt. W. G. Grear, Pictou, $50; Carleton County Council, $1,000;

Caledonia Club, San Francisco, $500; R. J. Uniacke, $36.20; Customs House, Ottawa, $150; Richibucto, $410; G. S. Nutting, Newton, Mass., $1; Londonderry, N.S., $15; J. Beder, New York, $4; Edward Armstrong, New York, $5; Fuller & Fuller, Chicago, $50; Peterboro', Ontario, $1,000; William Garringe, Chicago, $4.25; I. O. O. F., Memphis, $300; St. Catherine's, $500; Methodist Congregation, Woodstock, $30; Congregational S. S., Weymouth, $20; Ignatius Sargent, Machias, Me., $25; M. E. Church, Lincoln, Me., $5; Congregational Church, Malden, Mass., $15.16; Bucksport, Me., $300; Paris, $300; Hamilton, Ontario, $10,000; Newcastle and Douglastown, $100; Maritime Association, New York, $1,000; Municipality of Clark, $400; C. C. Hamilton, Cornwallis, $5; Edward Todd & Co., $25; Moncton, $1,100; Brockville, Ontario, $500; New Glasgow, N.S., $1,000; Rosemond Woollen Co., Quebec, $50; Kingston, Ontario, $1,584; Spring Hill Mines, N.S., $200; Albert Mines, $115; Westmoreland Coal Co., Philadelphia, $100; Glasgow, Scotland, $9,733.40; Pictou, $1,000; Welland, Ontario, $100; S. Jackson, Sheffield, Eng., $250; North British and Mercantile Insurance Co., $2,433.35; Bridgetown, N.S., $131.19; J. W. Campbell, Chicago, $50; St. James Church, Orilla, Ontario, $20; Annapolis, N.S., $54; Rev. James McLean, Londonderry, N.S., $2; R. J. Flanagan, Newcastle, $5; J. P. Taites, Sussex, $8; Commercial Union Assurance Co., $2,500; John McDonald, Toronto, $400; B. F. Thurlow, $85; Port Hope, $600; Stock Exchange, New York, $772.50; Gloucester, Mass., $100; Board of Trade, Buffalo, $332.68; Buffalo public school children, $1,000; Bay Side, St. Andrews, $50; Raymond Percy, Yarmouth, $1; Departmental Staff, Ottawa, $1,000; Clerks House of Commons, Ottawa, $150; Port Hope, Ontario, $300; Council of York County,

Ontario, $3,000; Ayr, Ontario, $200; Detroit, Mich., 1,000 Eliot National Bank, $647; Citizens' Hose Co., St. Catherine's, Ontario, $200; Shediac Comedy Club, $11; Stonington M. E. Church, $20; Salem, Mass., $700; New York (per British Consul), $3,500; Rev. Canon Carmody, Windsor, $10; Port La Tour, $40; Bridgetown, N.S., $56.73; Judge Wilkins, Nova Scotia, $80; Dalhousie, $200; Dover, Me., $592.75; Yarmouth, N.S., $700; New Bedford, Mass., $200; a friend, Grand Rapids, Mich., $1; Windsor, N.S., $350; Church of England, Lime Rock, Conn., $24; Chicago Clearing House, $1,000; Guysboro', N.S., $121; Manchester, Eng., $3,660; Liverpool, N.S., $819.27; Burt & Henshaw, Boston, $850; Maritime Association, New York, $4,400; Lord Mayor of Dublin, $86.67; Philadelphia, $2,000; J. H. Sternburg, New York, $25; Grace Church, Detroit, Mich., $97.42; Knox Church, Hamilton. $100; City of Hamilton (additional), $3,500; Maritime Association of New York, per A. C. Smith, $1,000; Liverpool, N.S., $819.27; Capt. Borgan, now at Chatham, $5; Erastus Titus, Baltimore, $261.97; Chicago, $10,000; Hon. Judge Keator, Ottawa, Ill., $50; San Francisco, Cal., $3,000; Officers, non-commissioned officers, and men in garrison, Halifax, through Gen. O'Grady Haly, $522.21; Alfred McKay, International Mines, Cape Breton, $100; Campbellton, Restigouche, per W. Mott, $147; Baie Verte, Restigouche, $50; A. Matthew, N.Y., $100; Norwich, Ontario, 100; Mongaup Valley, N.Y., per Rev. Wm. Ferrie, formerly of St. David's Church, $33.30; Peel County, Ontario, $1,000; F. H. Smith & Co., per E. G. Dunn, $25; Boston Theatre, per Mayor Prince, $886.03; Priest, Page, & Co., "Howe Scale Co.," $250; County of Wentworth, Ontario, $1,000; Chicago Board of Trade, $274.10; Lieut. Clements, Annapolis, $20; Clifton, Ontario, $300; Dominion Organ Co.,

Bowmansville, $102; Port La Tour, $8.27; Bank of Montreal, Newcastle, $100; Peterboro', Ontario, $124; Glasgow, Scotland, $4,880; Grey County Council, Ontario, $500; Garrison at Halifax, $42.50; Belfast, Ireland, $524; River John, Pictou Co., N.S., $381.50; James L. Bowman, Brownsville, Penn., $25; Waterloo, Ontario, Council, $200; St. Andrews, $100; Hiram Walker & Sons, London, Ontario, $200; Hillsborough, $60; Bank B.N. America, San Francisco, $2,600; Attleboro', Mass., $15; Arichat, C.B., $367; Philadelphia, $1,500; Clinton, Ontario, Masonic service, $53; Rogers Hill, Pictou, $40.36; Windsor, $207.32; a friend, Mount Vernon, Io., $1; Port Hope, Ontario, $134.20; Eldon, Ontario, Council, $500; Messrs. H. Andrews & Co., of Belfast, Ireland, £5; Messrs. James Scott & Co., Cork, Ireland, £10; Messrs. J. Lewenz & Co., London, £50 sterling; Messrs. Hiland, Chessman, & Co., Boston, $25 gold; through the Mayor of Charlottetown, the results of a meeting and subscriptions at Lot 34, St. Peter's Road, $55.50; Miss Logan, Orilla, Ontario, $10; Wentworth, N.S., Presbyterian Church, $3; Stewiacke, N. S., per F. H. Holesworth, $40; Petrolia, Ontario, per Mayor Kerby, $200.

THE SUPPLIES.

Burnham & Morrill, 10 cases beef; Sackville, supplies; Petitcodiac, box goods; Milltown, Saint Stephen, cooked provisions; Fletcher & Co., Portland, Me., provisions; Wetmore Bros., London, 20 barrels oil; E. Herritt, Petitcodiac, provisions; Toronto Coal Co., 250 tons of coal; Fredericton, two cars of cooked provisions; Peter Mitchell, Montreal, one case goods; J. T. Lewis & Co., Portland, Me., 1 case clothing; J. W. M. Kinnear & Co., Halifax, 5 barrels flour; Halifax, 1,025 blankets; Scotch bakery, Saint John, 250 loaves bread; Portsmouth, N.H., box clothing; A. Heney, New York, 100 barrels meal; Montreal, 1 train-load provisions; Quebec, supplies; Wilson Packing Co., Chicago, 50 cases beef; Halifax, quantity supplies; E. A. Barnard & Son, Calais, 2 barrels hams; Saint Stephen and Milltown, 1 case produce; Moncton, quantity bread; Upper Canada Furniture Co., 50 bedsteads; Lawrencetown, 29 packages supplies; Halifax, 1,500 blankets; Sussex, case provisions; Boston, supplies per cutter "Gallatin;" Hampton, lot supplies; Yarmouth, N.S., supplies; Amherst, N.S., supplies; Sackville, N. S., provisions; William Cummins & Sons, Truro, supplies; P. McInnes & Co., 100 blankets; J. F. Power & Co., Halifax, 50 barrels flour; Amherst, supplies; per "Argus" from Halifax, 16,100 pounds pork, 6,552 pounds beef, 3,100 pounds chocolate, 580 pounds tea; Fredericton Ladies' Committee, donation; Mrs. Sheriff Temple, Fredericton, case clothing; Deering, Milliken, & Co., Portland, 2 cases blankets; North Sydney, load coal; F. O. Leavitt, one tent; G. W. True & Co., Portland, 10 barrels flour and meal; Leath & Gore, 16 boxes soap; Halifax, supplies; Thompson & Bligh, Halifax, goods; Burns & Murray, Halifax, goods; S. H. & J. Moss, 2 cases clothing; Jennings & Co., cases clothing ; B. H. Calkin, clothes; Unitarian Parish, Portsmouth, N.H., clothes; Christian Temperance Union, Moncton, 3 cases clothing; Bangor, supplies; Salem, supplies; Windsor, N.S., supplies; Londonderry, supplies; Portland, Me., supplies; Adam Darling, Montreal, supplies; M. L. Paul, supplies; Thomas P. Beals, Portland, supplies; Montreal, supplies; Boston, goods; Cowdrey & Co., Boston, provisions; Saint Andrews, supplies; J. W. Jones, Lawrencetown, N.S., supplies; Connell and Hay, Woodstock, 200 barrels potatoes; J. & C. Harris, Moncton, supplies; Stock Yard, Chicago, provisions; Toronto, supplies; Kentville, N.S., supplies; Upper Clarence, N. S., supplies; James O'Brien & Co., clothing; Digby, N. S., clothing; New Haven United Workers, clothing; Hillsboro', supplies; Charlottetown, second-hand clothing; Fredericton, 5 cases clothing; Halifax, 50 stoves; Norcross, Miller, & Co., Boston, clothing; Portland, Me., clothes; Harvey, Albert Co., supplies; Thurston, Hall, & Co., Cambridgeport, Mass., 50 barrels flour and meal; Bridgetown, N.S., clothing; Woodstock, supplies; Annapolis, N.S., clothing; McLean & Blaikie, Great Village, N.S., supplies; R. Adams, Pollet River, N.B., bedding and clothing; Fredericton, supplies; Howe Spring Bed Co., New York, 50 bedsteads, 75 chairs, &c.; Alberton, P.E.I., supplies; Yarmouth, N.S., supplies; Young Men's Christian Association, Boston, supplies; Portland, Me., clothing; Montreal, supplies; Wilson Packing Co., Chicago, cooked provisions; Quebec, supplies; Montreal, supplies; Shediac, supplies; Unitarian Society, Dedham, Mass., supplies; Boston, supplies; Portland, Me., supplies; Quincy, Ill., 50 barrels flour; Saint Andrews, clothing; Saratoga, N.Y., supplies; Billings & Wetmore, supplies; Waterman Bros., 20 barrels oil; Pierce & Co., furniture; Montreal, supplies; Toronto, supplies; Upper Canada Furniture Co., Bowmansville, Ontario, furniture; Andover, one car provisions; Charlottetown, supplies; Salem, Mass., supplies; Fredericton, supplies; Prince Edward Island, supplies; Ottawa Ladies Committee, supplies; Toronto, supplies; Harry Piper, supplies; Galbraith, Christie, & Co., Toronto, supplies; A. Woodcock, Toronto, supplies; Christie, Bond, & Co., Toronto, supplies; Portland, Me., supplies; Wolfville, N. S., supplies; Montreal, 20 packages clothing; W. F. Johns & Co., Gananoque, Ont., supplies; Truro, supplies; Salem, Mass., Young Men's Christian Association, supplies; C. J. Stewart, Amherst, supplies; Thurston

& Cameron, supplies; Fredericton, through Sheriff Temple, 3 cases clothing and bedding; Campbellton, clothing; Kingston, Ont., 2 cases clothing; Charlottetown, P.E.I., per A. A. Macdonald, clothing; William Avard, Botsford, Westmoreland Co , 1 barrel pork; Quincy, Ill., 50 barrels meal; J. P. Coates, clothing; Philadelphia Maritime Exchange, clothing; Montreal, 1 barrel and 4 cases clothing; Union Stock Yard and Transit Co., Chicago, 90 barrels pork, 75 barrels flour, 25 barrels cornmeal, from the business men, banks, and Stock Yard Co.; James Stewart & Co's foundry, Hamilton, Ont., 6 cooking stoves and furniture; Halifax, N. S., 4 cases clothing and 2 barrels beef, 80 mattresses and 300 pillows; Lockport, N.S., 2 cases clothing and bedding; Port Medway, N.S., 1 case clothing; Bayfield, N.S., clothing; Mahone Bay, C.B., lot clothing; Stewiacke, N.S., box clothing; J. D. & J. W. Eaton, Salem, Mass., box of new blankets; Carter & Co., Elora, Ont., 5 barrels flour; Montreal Relief Association, 1 bale, 1 case, and 10 parcels clothing.

To show how scattered were the recipients of these gifts, as well as to show the confidence the public placed in the merchants of Saint John, we annex the statement of receipts for distribution made by one firm.

SENT TO MESSRS. DANIEL AND BOYD FOR DISTRIBUTION.

W. W. Turnbull, Esq., Saint John, $200; G. W. Vamvart, Esq., Woodstock, $100; Daniel Hawkesworth, Esq., Digby, $20; B. Rosamond, Esq., Ontario, $50; Messrs. Loeb & Co., New York, $50; Messrs. James McLaren & Nep., Manchester, £100 sterling; Messrs. Marshall & Aston, Manchester, £50 sterling.

SENT TO JOHN BOYD, ESQ., FOR DISTRIBUTION.

James H. Moran, Esq., Saint John, $100; Hon. Isaac Burpee, Minister Customs, Saint John, $100; Thomas Furlong, Esq., $50; Canada Life Assurance Co., $500; Thomas Nelson & Sons, Edinburgh, £50 sterling, through Dr. Rand, for teachers. Clothing from Saint Andrew's Church, Montreal, by Rev. Gavin Long, value $280; George Sloane, Esq., New York, $50 U.S. currency.

CHAPTER XVII.

ADMINISTRATION OF RELIEF.

The First Distribution. — The Random Applications. — The Danger from Impostors. — The First Organization. — Ineffectiveness of Original Plan. — The Great Number of Applicants. — How they were supplied. — The Introduction of the Chicago System. — The New Committee. — The Tents and Barracks. — Independent Shanties. — How Assistance could be obtained.

WHEN the first packages of provisions and clothing came, the persons to whom they were forwarded distributed them to the foremost comers who seemed in need; and by this random method many suffering ones were at first supplied with the necessaries of life. But as the call for succor became more urgent, and the influx of supplies more abundant, the necessity for some central efficient system became forcibly apparent. So long as each consignee of money and supplies distributed them as he saw fit, without taking the pains to make inquiries in regard to the needs of the applicants, many persons received vastly more than they needed, many were given supplies the same day by various different donors, and many deserving ones who happened to be unacquainted with the place, or the person in charge, went without altogether. The generous gifts of the sympathizing people were unequally bestowed, and often given to unworthy and dishonest applicants. Yet in the first hours of the public distress it was impossible to adopt any general plan of distribution which would answer the purpose. But when the first and most pressing calls had been supplied by individuals, a meeting of the citizens was held, and a committee appointed to take charge of the whole matter of receiving and distributing the gifts from abroad. The executive committee of that body consisted of the following gentlemen: A. C. Smith, chairman; W. H. Tuck, C. N. Skinner, E. McLeod, Harris Allen, J. A. Harding, Harry Leonard, F. A. King, J. H. Parks. L. R. Harrison was afterwards appointed secretary.

The committee for the receipt and distribution of supplies: John Magee, A. C. Watson, T. Furlong, W. H. Frith, Rev. J. Hartt, Rev. Dr. Maclise, Rev. Mr. Macrae.

The finance committee: C. H. Fairweather, George S. DeForest, W. H. Tuck.

The labors of this committee were exceedingly arduous. They were overrun with applications for help, and nearly overwhelmed by a hungry crowd of needy men, women, and children. They did the best they could, and, with a fortitude and patience wonderful to behold, worked and talked from the early hours of the morning until late at night, visiting those who could not come, and cooking at the rink for those who had no facilities of their own for preparing food: yet irregularities and impostors crept in. The great skating-rink which they selected as their headquarters became the focus for all the thousands who needed hats, coats, shoes, flour, bacon, salt, sugar, coffee, or meat; and with that vast army joined all the indigent population of the outlying districts, who with lies on their lips, and huge baskets on their arms, begged in piteous terms for a morsel (?) of bread for their horridly burned and starving (?) families.

The methods and amount of work done appear by the following paragraph from a daily paper: —

" From seven o'clock until eleven o'clock the rink was thronged with applicants for food, armed with tickets from the committee or prominent citizens. A careful estimate of the family and single tickets shows that from seventeen thousand to twenty thousand persons were supplied with substantial food. In addition to this, about three hundred were fed in the rink, receiving three substantial meals. Tea and

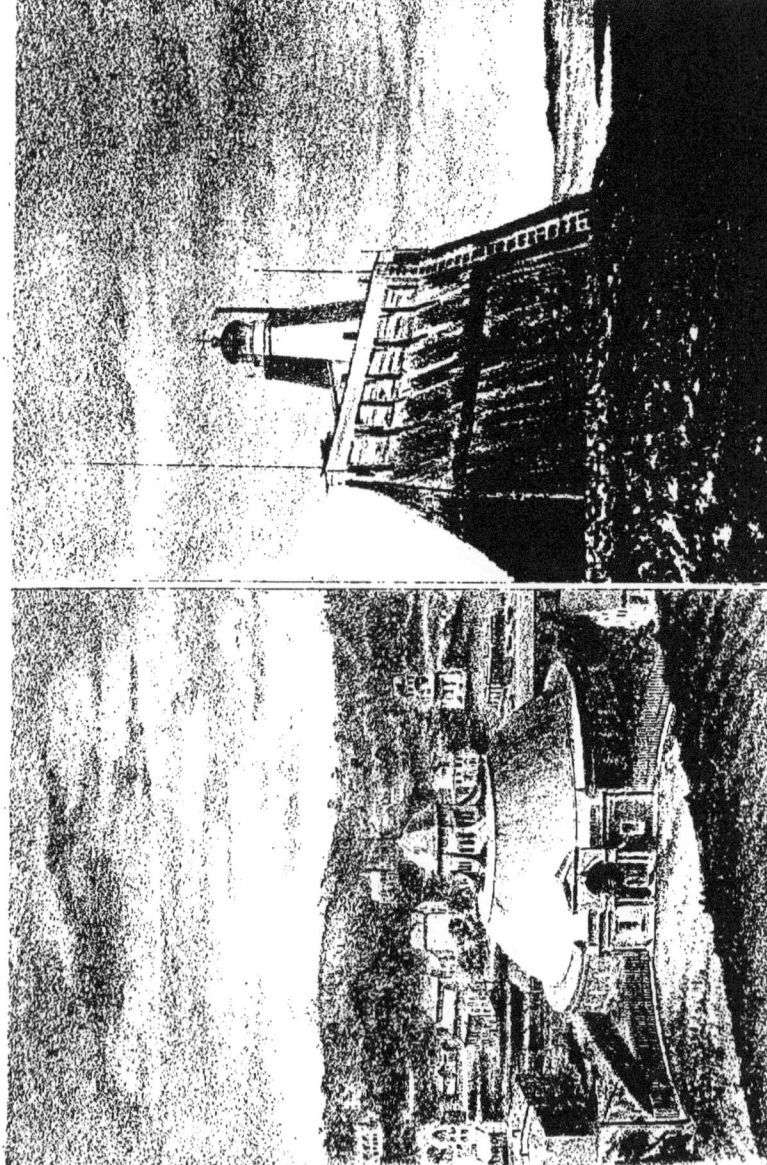

coffee are given out at every meal, and meat twice a day.

"Each holder of a ticket for food is admitted through the main entrance, and is at once directed to the circular counter in the middle of the rink. One of the clerks in waiting receives the ticket, and issues supplies in proportion to the number of mouths to be fed."

The arrival of the Rev. C. G. Truesdale of Chicago, who was chairman of the Chicago Relief Committee, and who was sent out by that city to assist the people of Saint John and to advise the merchants of his own city as to the kind of contributions most needed, changed the whole proceedings, and brought the work into a still more systematic form. Under his superintendence, the Relief Association was re-organized, and the following committees appointed:—

BOARD OF DIRECTORS.

Mayor S. Z. Earle, president; W. H. Tuck, Recorder, vice-president; James A. Harding (high sheriff), Attorney-Gen. King, James Reynolds, William Magee, A. Chipman Smith, C. N. Skinner, Harris Allan, John H. Parks, E. McLeod, F. A. King, H. J. Leonard, Gen. Warner, Andre Cushing, Aldermen Maher, Peters, Ferguson, Kerr, Adams, Duffell, Brittain, Glasgow, and Wilson, E. Fisher, James I.

Fellows; C. H. Fairweather, treasurer; L. H. Harrison, secretary.

Executive Committee. — W. H. Tuck, Chairman; James A. Harding, George E. King, Andre Cushing, Gen. Warner, M. W. Maher, James Reynolds; L. R. Harrison, secretary.

SUB-COMMITTEES.

Shelter Committee. — M. W. Maher, F. A. King, John H. Parks.

Purchasing Supplies. — C. H. Fairweather, C. A. Everett, A. C. Smith.

Transportation. — Harris Allan.

Insurance. — John H. Parks, Harris Allan.

Sick, including Hospital and Interment. — William Bayard, M.D., C. N. Skinner, R. N. Knight.

Employment. — Harris Allan, E. McLeod, Henry Duffell.

Charitable Institutions. — T. W. Daniel, Andre Cushing, Boyle Travis, M.D.

Correspondence and Telegrams. — W. H. Tuck, L. R. Harrison.

Special Relief. — George E. King, James A. Harding, James Reynolds, William Peters, B. Lester Peters, George F. Harding, C. N. Skinner, Edwin Fisher, Robert Marshall, A. C. Smith, E. McLeod.

Reception and Storage. — William Magee, James Reynolds.

Audit. — Andre Cushing, George S. DeForest, A. Glasgow.

Printing. — Gen. Warner, John Kerr, E. McLeod.

A local paper published July 2 thus comments upon the new *régime:* —

" The new system of relief at the rink was entered upon yesterday, and, although at first working somewhat tardy, promises to be a great improvement on the former plan.

" The order on the commissariat is as follows : —

PROVISION ORDER.

Deliver to .... (name of applicant)
.... (present residence)

Signed

No. ....
Date...............................

" The following, copied from one of the tickets filled out yesterday, is a fair sample of what the committee consider good rations: One man, one woman, and four children, received as rations for fifteen days: 40 pounds flour, 20 pounds meat, 80 pounds potatoes, 5 pounds cheese, 1¼ pounds tea, 5 pounds sugar, 1 dozen fish, and 1 pound soap.

" On Tuesday the demand for out-door relief exhausted 18 barrels of flour, 14 barrels of crackers,

12 barrels of oatmeal, 13 boxes of cheese, 12 boxes of coffee, 12 boxes of soap, 4 chests of tea, 1 barrel of sugar, 24 barrels of potatoes, 6 barrels of beef, besides quantities of pork and other articles. A larger amount was given out yesterday, — enough to supply 1,500 for many days.

"The clothing department, under charge of Mr. A. C. Kerrison, is located on the floor of the rink, and, with the furniture department on the opposite side, separates the commissariat counters from the front half of the arena, in which are stationed the examining clerks and other officers.

"This department is enclosed by high board walls, on the inside of which are ranges of shelves, while down the centre of the enclosure is a double shelved counter. Every thing is in perfect order, and the goods are as carefully classified as in a first-class dry-goods store. Mr. Kerrison showed our reporter a lot of children's toys and picture-books, many of them the contributions of little folk in Canada and the United States, to the homeless and houseless children of Saint John.

"The furniture department is enclosed in the same manner as the one above described, and has similar interior fittings. The following is a copy of about the last order filled yesterday afternoon: one bedstead, four chairs, one mattress with pillows, a cookstove and fittings, blankets and quilts for three beds, crockery and cutlery for a family, and one table."

Although the number of applicants for food during the first twenty-four hours after the organization of the first Relief Committee is said to have exceeded ten thousand, yet the system of visitation which was soon adopted, and the exodus of the people, soon reduced the number to less than three thousand.

The most perplexing question which the committee had to deal with was in connection with the applications for shelter. It was no small problem to ascertain how so many houseless ones should be protected from sun and storm until they could in some way provide for themselves. This matter was partially settled by pitching a camp of government military tents on the parade-ground at the extreme end of the peninsula, and crowding them with people. Others were provided with passage into the country or out of the Provinces; and in several other ways a temporary covering or home was provided for all. At a later period, barracks were constructed on Queen's Square for the better accommodation of such as were more permanently destitute of homes.

A large number of people were too proud to ask for food or shelter, and suffered much before they were discovered; and some of the shelterless ones constructed on vacant lots temporary shanties of diminutive size, and occupied them until better quarters were to be had. Some of those buildings were most laughable combinations, and exhibited a conglomeration of material most wonderful to behold.

The following notice was published for the instruction of such persons as desired to obtain relief, and shows the methods adopted by the committee : —

" First, The receiving of applications. Parties can apply by mail or through friends, or by a personal interview at the office. This, of course, is only preliminary; and it is no matter how it is done, so that it is prompt and definite as to the name of the applicant and address.

" All letters from applicants or their friends should be taken as the basis of an application, and either sent out by visitors, or acted upon sooner, if the amount and quality of the information is deemed conclusive.

"Second, The preparation and recording and assorting of the applications, preparatory to sending them out by visitors.

" Third, Returning said applications as soon as possible to the office, with full report on each case, — comprehensive and reliable as to all particulars necessary to be known.

" Fourth, Checking them off, and delivering them

to the board of directors or general superintendent, to be passed upon as soon as possible, in order to be ready to issue on them (if approved) as soon as the applicant calls, which they will be cautioned not to do under a day or two; and the visitor will give each applicant, at the time of visitation, a card with the number of the application, to be presented at the office so that their papers can readily be found.

"Fifth, Prompt issue of orders for whatever is approved; the goods to be delivered on presentation of tickets to the respective departments.

"Sixth, Careful numbering and filing of all applications on appropriate indexes, and in packages of 100 in pigeon-holes; and the return of all tickets, on which goods have been issued, to the head book-keeper every night.

"Seventh, Complete indexes of all applications, in order that they may be instantly referred to on a second call by applicants, and so be able to check or prevent frauds and duplications in the books.

"Eighth, Three weekly or daily reports from all departments to the general superintendent."

CHAPTER XVIII.

REBUILDING THE CITY.

Character of the People. — Peaceableness of the Inhabitants. — Beginning to clear away the *Débris*. — Temporary Dwellings. — Temporary Storehouses. — General Clearing of the Burned District. — Measures for securing Money. — Speech of Mr. John Boyd.

THE people of Saint John did not long despair. They were a remarkably hopeful and courageous, peaceable people. As we look back upon the fearful devastation, and contemplate the vast number of persons turned out under such excitement, and in the absence of almost all lawful restraint, we do not cease to wonder at the law-abiding manner in which they universally conducted themselves. Their police force, though efficient, was very small, and would have been wholly inadequate for such a time as that when the fire was raging, had it existed in such small numbers in any other coast city. It is true, the artillery and a detachment of the Sixty-second Regiment of militia, and a small body from the Ninety-seventh regulars, stationed at Halifax, were ordered into the city, where for several days they encamped; yet, as far as the writer's observation went, they were of little actual service. They were handsome bodies of military men, and ably commanded beyond question; but the overwrought anxiety of a stricken people, and the unnatural fears which resulted from such a fright, were the only excuse for their presence. The city was wonderfully free from thieves, incendiaries, and mobs, in view of the opportunities and provocations.

It is a pleasure to record such a fact, and to let it go down to posterity to the credit of the people of Saint John. But another feature of their character, which secures respect, was seen in the courageous and enterprising measures for rebuilding the city, taken by them while the foundations were still hot. In order to provide a temporary home for their families, they began as early as the morning of the second day after the fire, to construct rude board structures, containing one or two rooms, in which they could sleep and eat until the cellars of their houses were cleared, and a new home constructed. Merchants ordered plans for new stores to be drawn before the smoke ceased to rise from the *débris*, and set workmen with teams upon the task of clearing the rubbish and laying the foundations. Meanwhile, to furnish accommodations for the stores of such as could find no rooms, the city granted them the use of King's Square, which was soon covered with temporary buildings, and made the centre of a most thriving trade in all classes of merchandise. Everywhere was the work of clearing prosecuted; and so soon were the streets cleared, the toppling walls torn down, and the reconstruction begun, that the visitor, four weeks after the fire, could obtain no idea of the ruins as they were when the fire left them.

Measures were promptly adopted to obtain assistance from the government, and loans from English capitalists; and the wheels of enterprise thus set in motion moved on with surprising speed. Public meetings were held to consult upon the best plan to raise money and rebuild; and the spirit of the populace was well represented in a speech made at one of these by Mr. John Boyd, a citizen of Saint John, whose portrait we present in our frontispiece. Suffice it to say here, that at the close of Mr. Boyd's speech, a committee, consisting of the following substantial citizens, was appointed and unanimously confirmed, to carry out the measures proposed by him: —

John Boyd, James Hegan, Robert Ferguson, W. M. Sears, A. L. Palmer, Andre Cushing, J. C. Ferguson, William Duffell, W. H. Tuck, Z. Ring, Alexander Lockhart, J. L. Dunn, Alexander Jardine, J. H. Moran, John McMillan, George F. Smith, William Magee, Henry Vaughn, J. S. Boies De Veber, J. P. C. Burpee, E. J. Brass, James Harris, S. Z. Earle (mayor), Joseph W. Lawrence, D. J. McLaughlin, W. H. Thorne, George McKean, Robert Cruikshank, Hugh Gregory, Alexander Gibson, Henry Hilyard, C. A. Everett, John Hegan, Stephen Hall, John H. Parks, W. C. Watson, D. V. Roberts, William Lindsay, T. R. Jones, J. V. Ellis, E. Willis, William Elder, James A. Harding (high sheriff), T. B. Barker, C. H. Fairweather, W. W. Turnbull, Richard Thompson, Jeremiah Harrison, Thomas Furlong, John Yeats, J. D. Lewin, Thomas Gilbert, George G. Gilbert, J. V. Troop, A. C. Smith, John W. Nicholson, Simeon Jones, Charles W. Weldon, J. K. Dunlop, R. T. Clinch, Oliver T. Stone, G. Sidney Smith, L. J. Almon, James Domville, and D. D. Robertson, with power to add to their number.

Mr. Boyd said he was there, as Chief Justice Ritchie had remarked, only as a listener and learner; but the presence of Judge Ritchie reminded him of an association in this city, of which the learned judge was a trustee, which had done its work well, of which there were twelve trustees personally responsible to the lenders. Of this association he had been a trustee. It borrowed at five per cent, and loaned at six per cent; had in its hands at one time $650,000; executed the trust liberally; and, when it gave up its operations into the hands of the Dominion Government, had profits of $42,000, which the trustees voted to the City Hospital; and thus ended the labors of an association which did great good in its day, and, in the grant to the City Hospital, has left a memorial of the economy, wisdom, and judgment of the trustees of the Saint John Savings Bank. The principle is the same in the association proposed by Mr. Domville, — to borrow on the lowest terms, and lend as cheaply as can be, retaining enough for ordinary expenses, risks of loans, and the payment of interest on the bonds. It would be impossible to get the government, as such, to make advances in this way. In extraordinary cases, governments might do extraordinary things; and it would not be going beyond their legitimate duty to guarantee the bonds of such an association as this, they seeing that proper trustees were appointed to work with the company, and to supervise the loans. The City Corporation acting with the local government in giving their indorsation of the bonds of this association, would settle the matter beyond all doubt; and he had the authority of a leading financier present, one of the keenest and ablest in the Dominion, that, in his opinion, the money could be had in this way at six per cent; and we cannot get it lower, and should be thankful to obtain it at this rate. These loan associations are no new thing: they have been in existence in Canada for many years, and a large part of Upper Canada has been built by the moneys procured through them. We cannot get money unless we have proper security to offer. These securities must be looked into and held by some one. These holders and managers must be paid, and no will work long or well unless he be paid; and the question is, Why cannot Saint John pay these investments, as well as Montreal, Toronto, Hamilton, and London? and why should Saint John, as some among us do, object to the receiving of these moneys, when no city on this continent has received more benefit than Saint John in proportion to the amounts so received? Objection is made by some to foreign capital being received here, as it was five and twenty years ago; but look at our lines of railways centring in this city, constructed by this money from abroad; and in the growth of our trade by means of these, have we not all benefited immensely beyond the six per cent which it has cost us yearly? The principle is the same which we apply to the most ordinary business operations. A shipyard is lying empty, — no money, and consequently no work. A Liverpool merchant says to Mr. Fraser, or Mr. Stewart, or Mr. Dunlop, "Here is £12,000 which I wish to invest in a ship. I'll advance you £4,000 to go on, and so on as you proceed, and charge you six per cent interest on the operation." At once the lumberman cuts down the trees, the millman saws them, the railways or the carters deposit them in his yard, the shipwright drives the bolts, the blacksmith the fastenings; the painter, the calker, the rigger — all are employed. That deserted shipyard becomes a scene of life and activity; and forth there goes the result of our united energies, to carry our name over every sea, and to bring back their wealth to us. And why all this? Because of this foreign capital idle before, busy now, stimulating every industry, and building up our city; while the lender receives good interest for his capital, and the borrower is able to pay it, and at the same time make a profit of $6,000 or $8,000 on his operation. Just as the shipyard without capital would have been silent, so will our city be; but take hold of this plan, and organize it properly with the right men, and these tall and blackened chimneys, and these falling walls, and sad-looking, poverty-stricken shanties, which now stare at us like ghastly spectres, where only three weeks ago stately warehouses, banks, churches, school-houses, and princely mansions were, will soon be taken away, and once more will the happy homes be seen, and the stately warehouses erected; and Saint John, of which we were all proud, — perhaps too proud, — will rear its head, and show to the world that its people are worthy of all that sympathy and aid which have been so lavishly poured into it; that they are worthy of help who help themselves, as we must do in this hour of stern necessity. These loan associations are easily worked. There is no mystery about them, and there should be none. Every practical banker understands their operations: they charge according to the nature of the security offered; and the security Saint John can offer is second to none. We have great reason to thank Mr. Domville for his action in this matter. He has gone abroad, and brought back intelligence most gratifying, — that the money can be had, and at a reasonable rate. It only rests with us to organize the machinery by which this useful information can be made practically available. Let earnest men meet, men of all shades of opinion, and do what is necessary, and we shall succeed. Let the same energy which built up this city in the past be displayed now; let the same holy brotherhood, which seems to have merged us all into one family since that terrible 20th of June last, continue us banded together to repair all our losses; and there will be no cause for repining; our disasters will all be repaired; and in a quarter of a century our beautiful city shall be all that its friends will desire; and no city on this continent will be better able to meet its obligations. Our noble river pouring its treasures into the city, our railways bringing in products from every point, cannot be turned aside from its course; and therefore why should there be one despondent heart among us? For the practical testing of this question, I beg to move that a committee be appointed to deal with this matter, and take such action as may be considered necessary under the circumstances.

CHAPTER XIX.

CHURCHES AND SERMONS.

The Sad Worshippers. — The Meetings for Consultation. — Sad as Funerals. — The Sermon of the Rev. D. M. Maclise, D.D.: "Shall there be evil in a city, and the Lord hath not done it?" — Sermon of the Rev. John Wills: "Shall a trumpet be blown in the city, and the people not be afraid?" — Sermon of the Rev. G. M. Armstrong: "I know, O Lord, that thy judgments are right."

WE made a sincere and earnest effort to obtain for publication, from the pastors of the churches, extracts from their sermons delivered on the sabbath succeeding the fire. We hoped thereby to find the free expressions of the people's feelings, and preserve them for future study. But the confusion incident to so great a disturbance, combined with the sad fact that there were but few rooms left in the city wherein they could congregate, caused such as there were of the church services to be very limited in number and duration. The assemblies of the members, whenever an opportunity offered itself for the purpose of discussing their future prospects, were sadder than many funerals. Every earthly thing connected with the sacred memories and the hallowed associations that had so long held them together was swept away forever. In such a time and in such a situation the words of the preacher have a peculiar interest to the public; and in order that future students of the history of this event may know something of the religious life of the inhabitants, and better understand the excellent qualities of that God-fearing populace, we add the extracts given below, and regret that the circumstances prevented the delivery and the publication of the sermons of other distinguished preachers.

The Rev. David M. Maclise, D.D., selected his text from Amos iii. 6, the first sabbath after the fire, and spoke as follows : —

"Shall there be evil in a city, and the Lord hath not done it?" (Amos iii. 6.) The word *evil* is one of very wide application. In a general sense it comprises all that is opposite to good, whether natural or moral. Pain, sickness, poverty, misfortune, loss of any kind, are natural evils; sin in general, crime of any kind, vices of every kind, are moral evils. Any thing that causes displeasure, pain, sorrow, suffering, or calamity, is a natural evil; while all that produces or is either the primary or immediate cause of natural evil is often, if not always, a moral evil or sin so far as man is concerned.

When we remember that God is holy, and that "in him is no darkness at all," that "he is of purer eyes than to behold evil, and cannot look on iniquity," we shall distinctly understand that the evil spoken of in the text is not *moral* evil, is not *sin*, but the suffering of evil, or calamity. "Shall there be calamity in a city, and the Lord hath not done it, hath not inflicted it?" This seems the proper meaning of the inquiry; and it does not in any way or the slightest degree attribute to God the commission or production of sin, which from *his* nature and *its* nature it is impossible he should do; but the infliction of that penal or corrective evil which God may lay on an individual, a city, or a nation, for the purpose, on the one hand, of punishing them for sin, or, on the other, of correcting them, and thereby bringing them back to God himself. But from this it does not necessarily follow that the most guilty are most severely afflicted: nay, the very opposite may be and often is the case.

With this understanding of our text, we may observe that the world is composed of good and evil: of good, as it came first, fresh, fair, and pure, from its Maker's hand, as he looked on its loveliness with delight, and pronounced it "very good;" and of evil, which entered it when it lapsed into sin.

As long as man maintained his allegiance to his

Creator and law-giver in its integrity, so long good alone remained unmingled in the world. But the moment the falsehood of Satan was believed, and preferred to the truth of God, evil entered into the world, commingled itself with the good, obtruded itself into the place of the good, and made the " very good " to be turned into evil; and consequently ever since, while we have in the world much that is *real* good, and much that is *imaginary* good, we have both commingled with much that is evil; and it becomes a problem of no easy solution, to tell which most generally predominates. And although we are generally ready to conclude that good prevails, and although in the end evil shall be exterminated, and good alone shall exist in the new or renewed earth, and unmingled righteousness shall alone rule, yet still there are times and seasons in the history of our suffering race, when we might find it one of the most difficult of tasks to persuade the sufferers that the evil of calamity is not greater than the good. There is a mistake into which we are all ready to fall, into which many have fallen; and that is, when we enjoy prosperity which we call good, we attribute it all to ourselves, to our own procuring. The possession of abundance is ever calculated to close the eye against the recognition of the Hand which ever open supplies abundance, and to lead us to place it all to the credit of our own prudence or business ability, or that of our ancestors who procured and bequeathed it to us; and in its enjoyment we are prone to ignore God, who gives it and all good gifts.

We see this characteristic of human nature admirably set forth in the case of the king of Babylon. When he stood on the top of his splendid palace, and looked around on the fair, far-reaching, and populous city, he said, in the pride of his heart, "Is not this great Babylon that I have built for the house of the kingdom, by the might of my power, and for the honor of my majesty?" Had he been about to engage in deadly conflict with his foes, he would doubtless have invoked the aid of his false gods, or perchance, in imminent peril, have been impelled to acknowledge the God of heaven, as the kings of Babylon sometimes did; but *now* when surrounded with affluence, peace, and prosperity, by the splendor of the city he had done so much to elevate to its present grand position, he looked upon it, and recognized not God from whom the power came, and at the tenure of whose will he held it, but saw himself as the originator and director of all: "Is not this great Babylon that *I* have built for the house of the kingdom, by the might of *my* power, and for the honor of *my* majesty?"

Trace human nature down through all the grades,

from the loftiest to the lowliest position, from the mighty monarch of Babylon down to the meanest digger in the mud, and you will find that whenever and wherever employment is plenty and remuneration ample, there is an inclination to forget God, and claim the credit of all to self. On the other hand, when evil comes upon us, when loss is experienced, or calamity of any kind crushes us, we at once look beyond self, and search for some cause to which we may assign the evil we endure. These causes are numerous and various. Some attribute all the ills they bear to *chance*. Many never go beyond a mere calculation of chances to account for all the afflictions of their lives: they look upon the world as a chapter of accidents; they consider the rise and power of nations, the wealth of a community or an individual, as merely their good fortune, while their poverty, their reverses, their ills of all kinds, are their ill fortune, and all alike the result of mere blind chance. Again, others more philosophical, more reasonable, because more considerate, who have discovered that chance is nothing, that there is no such thing as chance, that what so many call chance is merely "direction that we cannot see," search for some more satisfactory cause, and think they find it in what they denominate the *general* laws of nature. Or perhaps, if more piously than philosophically inclined, they will attribute all the causes that produce the changes to *nature's God*, but stop short at those general laws which, as they suppose, form and control the movements of Providence; but the particular actings, and the combination of circumstances which regulate the operations of these general laws, they take entirely out of the hands of God, and look only to this secondary and subordinate instrumentality by which, according to their ideas, the general laws impressed on the universe are found to operate, as they imagine, without any further care or control. The consequence is, that good is enjoyed, and self is honored; or, if perchance nature or the God of nature be acknowledged, the secondary cause will yet be their own skill, &c., that leaves God out of the account, and sets up humanity. On the other hand, if evil be endured, it will be assigned to any other cause than God; and it is not till man is renewed in the spirit of his mind, that he is renewed in the power of faith, and is led to accept the truth, that, "if there be evil in a city, the Lord hath done it."

If an evil, a calamity, is endured in the nation, in the city, in the family, in the individual; if it is found in the marts of commerce where the rich products of the earth are continually exposed for sale and profit, or in the dark and dreary lanes into which misery and want and woe retire to hide themselves from the light of day, in those wretched cellars or garrets, the last resort of friendless poverty, where the inmates are exposed to the fetid odors and deadly damps and malarious exhalations, or to the winds and the rains, and the snows and frosts of winter; whether it be in the palace of splendor, or the hovel of penury, — it is the Lord hath done it. If it be a calamity that comes to the treasury of a nation, and shuts up the fountains from which it was supplied; or that comes to the health of a nation, and lays its thousands or tens of thousands on beds of pain and death; or a calamity that has sent famine into the land, or one that has reduced to dust and ashes the hamlet, town, or city, — it is the Lord hath done it.

There are many phases of evil in the land at the present, which, did time permit their consideration, would all tend to illustrate the great truth indicated in our text; such as the commercial distress through which for nearly four years we have been passing, the general and protracted want of employment, its causes and consequences: but it does not. We would see in these and all other forms of calamity, that, while men usually limit them to second causes, the real and original cause of all is sin, — the sin of the people, and the righteous judgment of God on the people on account of it, to correct them for it, and reform them from it; but that men will attribute it to any other cause than this.

To come nearer home, and get away from general principles and considerations under the broad ægis of which we might feel inclined to shield ourselves from social or individual blame or responsibility, let us turn our attention more particularly to the terrible calamity which with one fell stroke has destroyed more than half of all the buildings in this city, and probably four-fifths of the value of the whole, and also much precious life; a calamity which has rendered homeless from fifteen to twenty thousand people; reducing multitudes of them from opulence or competence to poverty and starvation. Perhaps no such calamity, so extensive, so absolute, so complete, so utterly ruinous in proportion to the size of the place, and means of the people, has ever been experienced on this continent. Absolutely considered, indeed, far greater conflagrations have taken place; as for instance, Chicago. In that city a space one mile broad and two miles long was burnt, rendering homeless from one hundred and fifty thousand to two hundred thousand people; about ten times the extent of this conflagration, great as it is, with an equivalent of value in similar proportion. And in Boston twice as many women and sewing-girls were rendered homeless and out of employment by the great fire there, as there are here of all classes burnt out. There were about thirty thousand of that one class, probably not much more than fifteen thousand in all here. And yet, for the size and means of this city, fifteen thousand homeless ones is a startling and appalling fact to contemplate.

In returning from Halifax on Wednesday night last, I heard at Truro the startling tidings, " Half of Saint John is burnt; all the business part of the city is gone. It commenced at York Point, passed up Dock Street, burning all the way down to the docks, and many vessels in the harbor, King Street, Prince William Street, Water Street, Germain Street, past Saint Andrew's Church and the Victoria Hotel; and it is still raging, passing on to Lower Cove." That was sufficiently alarming; it was startling and stupefying; but it did not convey to my mind half of the terrible reality. There were many Saint John men on the train, and the excitement was intense; while at each station the telegrams not only confirmed the truth of the awful tidings flashed on the lightning's wings along the wires, but gave new and still more terrible accounts of the conflagration. It was passing eastward toward Courtenay Bay. Now it had reached Charlotte Street, Sydney Street, then Carmarthen Street, and was passing up Leinster Street, thence northward in the very teeth of the furious gale that was sweeping the fire before it with irresistible fury, to King Street, east. More than one hundred miles distant we saw the heavens lighted up with the lurid glare of the great burning going on in the homes of tens of thousands of our fellow-citizens; and oh, how helpless we felt, as we gazed with beating hearts and bated breath on the surging symbol! Oh, how we longed for power in a moment to transport ourselves to the place where our friends were in agony looking on ·their consuming houses, and all of earth they possessed, perhaps themselves perishing in the flames amid their burning homes, in the vain endeavor to save something from the general ruin!

But we had no such power; and, even if we had, it would have been of no avail, for, had we been here, we would have been as helpless as all the rest. The train rushed on with its usual speed; but it seemed to us that express-train never before moved so slowly, nor stopped so often or so long. At Moncton, where we stopped the apparently interminable time of an hour, waiting for the northern train, a railroad employee told me that both the Congregational and Calvin churches were consumed; that he had read the telegram which said so a few minutes ago. It seemed as if that information must be true. The man was intelligent, and said he could not be and was not mistaken; and yet I did not, could not, would not, believe it. It was *apparently* true, and caused a strange, startling sensation to thrill through my whole being as I heard it; but yet I held it as an idle tale. I reasoned rapidly thus: "The wind is north-west; starting from York Point, it has passed up Dock Street to King Street, and onward south towards the bay. According to all other telegrams, part of the north side of King Street below King Square still stood: that could not be, and those churches gone; for with such a wind in such a direction, were those churches gone, all south of them to King Street, and including it, must be gone too." And yet it was not till I saw the tower now over our heads, that I was fully persuaded that my reasoning, and not the telegram, was correct. When I saw it, and saw the black cloud rising from and resting over the ruined city, and thought of the unimaginable woes that lay beneath it, my heart was too full for utterance; and the friends who gathered round me at the depot, all telling me of the destruction that I knew only too well already, may have thought me heartless and unfeeling as I silently listened to the excited and exciting utterances. Appearances often deceive, and "things are not what they seem." It was because just then speech was impossible. I could not bear the strain, and maintain my manhood's fortitude; and therefore abruptly turned away to hide the tears that *would* well up, although "not much given to the melting mood." Hastening home with mingled feelings, — feelings of devout gratitude that this my church and home were spared amid the general overthrow of twelve or thirteen other churches and pastors' homes, feelings of profound grief for the fearful losses and sufferings of so many of my own people, and other people residing in the burnt district, — I could not wait a moment to rest after a night of sleepless excitement, till I went over the ruins of the city but yesterday morning so fair, and apparently so safe.

As I walked alone amid thousands among the ruins, and looked on the wide-spread total destruction of the greater part of all the homes and all the business houses of the city, so lately full of life and hope and happiness, I felt as I had never felt before, and hope never to feel again. It was soul-sickening beyond conception, and still more beyond description; and therefore I shall not attempt to describe it. Nor do I need to make the attempt to you, who have doubtless, most of you, felt the same; and even those views and feelings and sickening sensations utterly fail to realize the magnitude and the far-reaching consequences of the stupendous calamity.

A few months ago this community was startled when four or five business-houses with their contents were consumed, and five men perished in them, bringing sorrow and bereavement to as many homes; and no wonder, for it was a great disaster. How much greater the present calamity is, no living man can yet tell; greater in the loss of property a thousand-fold perhaps. How many lives are lost, is not yet known. It is not surprising that the boldest stand aghast at the overwhelming catastrophe. The whole scene, men say, is very blue. It is worse, much worse than blue: it is black; black beyond description or imagination, both metaphorically and literally. And yet it is not *wholly* black. There are some bright spots and some rifts in the black thunder-cloud; there is not only a silver lining to the cloud, but a golden glory lights up its heavenward side. The news, flashed across not only the continent, but around Christendom, of this calamity, has excited an amazing sympathy among the nations, which is bringing to our aid a vast amount of relief in provisions and other necessaries, including large sums of money, which will doubtless afford at least temporary means of support to the most necessitous; so that none need perish from hunger, or otherwise.

It is truly cheering to see how much there is of genuine goodness in the human heart, in spite of sin; to see how the tale of sorrow and suffering can stir up, and has stirred up, the beneficent sympathies of the souls of men and women, not only in the whole Dominion, but in the Fatherland: nor there alone; for our brethren of the great American Republic are coming to our aid with a heartiness and a liberality that is worthy of them; and that is saying all that I need say, except that, living among them as I have done for more than half my life, and knowing as I do the grandeur of their generosity, I am not surprised at their beneficence, but would have been surprised had it been otherwise.

For all this our hearts should be profoundly grateful, — grateful to our kind benefactors for their sympathies and their gifts; above all, grateful to our gracious and most merciful Father in heaven, who gives them kindly dispositions, and hearts overflowing with charity in the highest and best sense of the term; and I doubt not that our hearts *are* grateful for goodness granted us in the past, in the present emergency, and in the prospects of the future.

While we are grateful for all this aid, and properly appreciate it as demonstrated in the kindness and beneficence of others, let those of us who have not suffered so severely as others, but have been mercifully spared, endeavor practically to show our gratitude to God for sparing us, by doing our duty in this great crisis of our history, in affording such relief as may be in our power to those who, in the providence of God, are not so well provided for as ourselves. Let us not exclusively rely on the beneficence of others, but manfully put our own shoulders to the wheel, and help along our destitute brethren by sharing with them our spare rooms, our food and clothing.

As a congregation, we have great reason to be grateful to our God for his kindness and his care in sparing and preserving our church edifice, which has cost us so much, not only of material wealth, but also of the more precious coin of the heart, while so many other churches have been reduced to dust and ashes. And, what is still more precious than this fair building, precious as it is, the lives of all the congregation, so far as I know, have also been spared; not one life lost. It is true, many of you have lost your all — no, not your all; only your earthly all; nor even all that: you have each other; and, by the blessing of Him to whom belongs the silver and the gold, you may yet obtain more of earthly good than you ever owned before. And, above all, you have not lost your Saviour. You cannot lose him, nor will he leave you. He is the Friend that is nearer and dearer, and sticketh closer, than a brother.

Other congregations have suffered more severely than we, — suffered, not only in the loss of property more extensively, but also in precious life. But yesterday I heard one brother-pastor make lamentation over five members of his church cut off by the devouring fire. Let us sympathize with them in their losses, their bereavements, and sorrows; and bless our God who has dealt so tenderly with *us*, and preserved us so well. Afflictions, however severe, are really blessings when they lead to reformation of the errors which led to their infliction.

There are several lessons which we may learn from *this* affliction, and which, properly learned and practised, will make us safer, wiser, and better. Let us glance at a few of them. One lesson we may learn, and benefit by, is the necessity that exists for using materials in building that will not be inflammable as a tinder-box. This use of so much wood, and that of the most inflammable kind, as has prevailed in this city and elsewhere, has been undoubtedly the immediate cause of this and similar disasters on this continent. Even when the walls were properly constructed of brick or stone, so much pitch-pine and other combustibles were employed in and about the eaves and roofs, that the destruction of the whole structure was rendered inevitable.

No such conflagrations as are common in this country have occurred in the old countries of Europe for ages, nor in the nature of things are they possible. Why? Because there the people build with a view to safety from fire. They construct no wooden houses, and no wooden and pitched roofs; they build the walls, solid walls of brick or stone, and put solid slate or tiles upon their roofs: hence a fire scarcely ever extends beyond a single building, and in that the fire almost invariably begins with its inflammable contents. It is the wisest economy thus to build, and cheapest by far in the end, for a house thus constructed lasts for ages, descending from generation to generation; insurance costs the merest trifle, in many cases literally nothing, as it is wholly unnecessary; no danger from within, and none from without. It is earnestly to be hoped that our civic authorities will learn wisdom from the experiences of the past, and absolutely prohibit the erection of such structures as those which have provided the fuel for this most calamitous conflagration. It is also "devoutly to be wished" that others in other towns and cities may learn a lesson of wisdom in this respect, from the bitter experience of us and others who have similarly suffered from the infatuated course we have pursued in erecting buildings apparently designed, and certainly especially adapted, to make magnificent bonfires. Wooden buildings in cities, and particularly wooden roofs, whether mansard or not, are too costly, because so eminently dangerous and destructive, to be any longer indulged in. If men *will* violate, so determinately as they have done, the well-known and inexorable laws of nature, or rather laws of God, they must continue to bear the terrible consequences of such violation of law. " Oh that men would be wise, that they would understand this!" Had this city been constructed of proper material, it had not been consumed, and thousands, and tens of thousands had not been left homeless and wretched; those bodies of men, women, and children, had not been left broken, bleeding, and burnt, done to death by a terribly mistaken, expensive, and ruinous economy. What Carlyle said of England is true in a much more intense degree of us on this side the Atlantic.

I quote from memory, and do not attempt to give his *exact* words: " We are growing more and more selfish, and prone to slight and show and sham. A few ages ago England was wont to awake right early in the morning to the fervent prayer, 'Grant, O Lord, that we may this day do our duty to our best and utmost; that we may be useful to ourselves, each other, and to God, for Christ's sake, Amen.' But now it awakes to the prayer, or rather the abnegation of prayer, though the inward inspiration of the heart which is genuine prayer may be properly thus expressed: ' Oh that I may get through this day with the minimum of care, labor, and expense, and with the maximum of self-indulgence, sham, shoddy, and profit, for the Devil's sake, Amen.' Unless some gospel be preached and practised more elevating than the dismal science of to-day, this cannot long endure. It is only too likely to end in petroleum, and that ere long."

We have the proof of all this but too plainly demonstrated. What has caused this terrible disaster? Sin, no doubt you will say, and that is true enough; but what kind of sin? Many kinds; but mainly the sin of covetousness as seen in the miserably mistaken economy. For cheapness and saving, and hastening to be rich, using material for buildings that is almost as dangerous as dynamite; saving thereby a few hundred dollars at first, but at last to result in the loss of as many millions, and lives worth more than the millions,—is not this sin? Yes, "a sin to be punished by the judges." Would that it were everywhere made penal to commit it! and there are probably few of us that are not guilty of it in some of its aspects; and therefore has this calamity come upon us.

From the nature of things, this disaster will press more heavily on some people than on others; from which we are by no means to conclude that *they* were pre-eminently guilty, or sinners above others in these respects. Speaking of the Galilæans whose blood Pilate had mingled with their sacrifices, the Saviour of sinners asks, "Suppose ye that these Galilæans were sinners above all the Galilæans, because they suffered such things? I tell you nay; but, except ye repent, ye shall all likewise perish. Or those eighteen on whom the tower in Siloam fell, and slew them, — think ye that they were sinners above all men that dwelt in Jerusalem ? I tell you nay; but, except ye repent, ye shall all likewise perish." They were judgments brought on them on account of their sins, — general and individual sins. All were guilty, all deserved death; but on only a few was the death penalty inflicted, that proper proof of the divine displeasure might be manifested, and that those who were spared might be warned, repent and be saved, while yet there was time and space for repentance, reformation, and salvation. And they made a poor improvement of the admonitory dispensations in those days, who failed to benefit by them, through repentance and reformation, as most of them did fail, and as many, it is to be feared, will fail to benefit by the calamities of the present day. There are people, some of them in high places, who, as it would appear, cannot be taught, are apparently incapable of learning. Thus some of our civic rulers still advocate wooden buildings, claiming to be thereby the poor man's friend; and one of them actually affirmed that it was the flames from the stone and brick of his neighbor's buildings that consumed his dwelling, not knowing apparently that it was the irresistible fury of the fire of thousands of wooden buildings, by which those stone and brick buildings were surrounded, that set on fire and consumed the *wood* of these buildings whose walls were brick and stone, and that the wood in its consumption set fire to his home. When will our rulers learn wisdom? One lesson that we may learn is, that we cannot violate the laws of God, whether physical or moral, with impunity. Another lesson is, that God manifests his mercy when he causes calamity to awaken us from our sleep of forgetfulness and unconcern, when he snatches us from this world's folly and infatuation, when he drags us from our self-delusion, and shows us our need of a Saviour, by the suffering of evil.

The mercy of God in inflicting individual calamity is great, and is often seen and acknowledged by the afflicted ones to be very great: more probably are drawn to God from a sick-bed, than from a condition of the most perfect health; thousands have blessed the God who laid them on beds of suffering and sorrow, and consequently separated them from the sins in which they had been indulging, and gave time and inclination of heart to seek his favor which is life, and his loving kindness which is better than life. Nor is God less merciful in social, civic, and national calamities. The business tendency among men is generally running towards forgetfulness of God: it forgets him in the energy and intensity of its employment; it has not time for God, and often "he is not in all their thoughts;" it forgets him in the calculation of its losses, and still more in the calculation of its profits; and in every way it is disposed to forget him, until calamity becomes so great that its profits and its losses are equally put out of sight, and God, the inflicter of the calamity, comes into view. As long as men have their minds engrossed with losses and profits, as long as they are wholly actuated by the hope of avoiding the one, and obtaining the other — so long they are continually in danger of forgetting God. Therefore does the all-wise and merciful Father, from time to time, paralyze the power of their commerce, and strike terror into the civic or national heart, and dries up its numerous channels and sources by calamity, in order that the individual, the city, or the nation may turn from their infatuating idols to himself.

Sometimes men wonder at the magnitude of a calamity, and doubt whether there can be wisdom, goodness, and mercy in any thing so widely ruinous to worldly interests. We must ever remember that God's thoughts are not as our thoughts, nor his ways as our ways; "for, as the heavens are higher than the earth, so are my ways higher than your ways, and my thoughts than your thoughts, saith the Lord."

What seems very great to us seems very little to God. When, more than a hundred miles away, I saw the reflection of the great burning going on here, it was only because I knew the exact direction to look that I found it at all : had I not known it was there, I would not have noticed it at all, or seeing it would have attracted little or no attention. Great as it seemed and really was to the on-lookers, to those one hundred and fifty miles away it seemed a comparative speck on the distant horizon ; and I, knowing its extent, wondered at the littleness, and thought how small a thing must even this great calamity appear to God, who has all the countless worlds of creation under his control and care. Is there any thing in that lurid spot to show why it should not exist, if there are great moral or spiritual purposes to serve by its existence ? What is all that, great as it is, to the value of a soul ? What is that in comparison of the great day that is coming, when not only a part of a single city of no great extent, but the whole earth, shall be in flames ; when " the heavens being on fire shall be dissolved, and the elements shall melt with fervent heat," and you and I and all mankind shall stand before the great white throne to give account of the deeds done by us, whether they be good or bad, and be judged in accordance therewith, and to then enter on our endless condition of weal or woe ?

Permit me, then, in conclusion, to direct you all, in this time of trouble, to the true and *only* remedy for all evil. There is but one remedy for the evils of the land, for the evils of the city, for the evils of the individual, and the sins which bring them, — the Lord Jesus Christ. He is the remedy for all our evils. Nothing will or can cure those evils but uniting our souls to Jesus: .that alone can give us light and power rightly to use this world without abusing it. Nothing else will enable us to meet any and every disaster without dismay, even grim death itself in any form; but leaning on the arm of the Beloved we need fear no evil; clothed in the robe of his righteousness, we shall calmly contemplate " the war of elements, the wreck of matter, and the crush of worlds;" for

" 'Mid flaming worlds, in this arrayed,
With joy shall we lift up our head."

Beloved friends, let me, then, commend you to Christ, the physician by whom alone " the ills that flesh is heir to" can be alleviated and remedied. Oh that I could lead every one of you to Him who is the King of kings and the Lord of Lords, and induce you every one, and *all* men, never to trust in the prescriptions of men for remedying the evils of your hearts and your lives, the evils of the city, the nation, and the world.

There is but one Saviour, the help and the hope of

Israel in the time of trouble, — the Lord Jesus Christ, who calleth not the righteous but sinners to repentance, and is calling on us loudly by public, social, and individual affection in various forms, and entreating us by his word, his spirit, and his providence, saying, "Turn ye, turn ye: why will ye die?"

"Shall there be evil in a city, and the Lord hath not done it?" God is now giving us a call to take his word, to take his character, to stand up for him, to endeavor to remedy the evil sin has brought into the world and into this community. He is giving us a call to be his stewards, his agents for the dispensation of his bounties: let us seek to be faithful in our stewardship. The time will come, and come soon, much sooner than many of us suppose, when notwithstanding all our bodily health, strength, and property, "we shall be no longer stewards." Let us contemplate and prepare for that time, by being faithful in our stewardship to which God has called us, — faithful unto death, and we shall receive crowns of life.

Let us give God the glory; give him glory in the attributes of his nature imperishable as they are, and shining as they do in the eye of faith, in moral and spiritual beauty. Give him glory by recognizing and obeying his wondrously good and glorious laws, physical, moral, and spiritual, by which he sustains, controls, and governs the universe of matter and of intelligence, and the violation of which inevitably brings disaster and ruin. Give him glory, for he is holy, glorious in holiness; he is the King in his beauty, the chief among ten thousand, and the one altogether lovely. Give him glory, for he is just: his justice demanded a glorious victim, and his glorious love procured and paid it, and paid it for us. Give him glory; for, notwithstanding all our sufferings, he is long-suffering, and waits to be gracious. Give him glory, for he is loving. We read of Codrus the Athenian, who died for his country, for his friends; and of Curtius the Roman, who died for his native city. These brave men died; and a grateful and enthusiastic people wept over them, and enshrined their memory as a precious memorial in their hearts and on the page of history. But our dear Lord and Master died for his enemies: he loved those that hated him, did good to those who despitefully used and persecuted him and crucified him. He is fairer than the children of men, the rose of Sharon, the lily of the valley.

But if you will not give him glory *now*, by repentance of sin, and faith in Jesus the Saviour of sinners, and love for him, the time will come when you must bow to his sceptre; for he is as glorious in his power as in his holiness and truth. He has said, "The wicked shall be turned into hell, and all nations that forget

God;" and his own right arm shall get him the victory over all his incorrigible enemies. And as stiff-necked and rebellious sinners are cast forth from his presence, and as they fall from the heights of heaven, and the burning pit yawns to receive them, the chorus song of millions of millions of adoring saints and angels shall peal around the throne of God, saying, "Great and marvellous are thy works, Lord God Almighty; just and true are all thy ways, thou king of saints; who shall not fear thee, and glorify thy name?"

The following sermon was preached July 1, 1877, in the Unitarian Hall, Saint John, by the Rev. John Wills, from the text, "Shall a trumpet be blown in the city, and the people not be afraid? Shall there be evil in a city, and the Lord hath not done it?" (Amos iii. 6.)

Self is the universal idol before which every one bows down in abject adulation. It is in obedience to its oracles, so superlatively deceptive, that we lay the onus of all our misfortunes on the shoulders of others, instead of on our own. In casting about for their cause, we scarcely ever light upon the true one, namely, our own culpable inattention to the requirements of nature's changeless laws; and when, blinded by our idolatry of self, we can find no adequate cause for our greatest troubles outside of ourselves, our egotism, our self-sufficiency, our pride, all unite in making God responsible therefor. So we call them judgments, when, in fact, they are mercies, messengers of love, sent to us from our Father who is in heaven.

There are times, however, when the idol self is hurled from its pedestal in the human soul; when the brighter, the better side of our nature triumphs over our self-hood, and compels us to be generously disinterested, unselfishly benevolent. We have had full proof of this since the wholesale destruction of our city by the late tornado of fire, that swept away, in its desolating progress, so many of our beautiful homes, hallowed by the associations of the past, by the memories of childhood, and by the best affections of the heart. The universal sympathy that our great calamity has called forth leaves us no room to doubt that there is a God-like spirit in man, to which the Almighty imparts his inspiration. Indeed, if we of this stricken city do not perceive the unearthly beauty of the inner courts of humanity, and if we fail to fathom the great reservoir of unselfishness that fills its deepest springs, ready to burst forth at the anguished cry of our brother-man, we are either the most blinded, the most imbecile, or the most ungrateful, of created intelligences. But, whether we see it or not, the star of human nature shines out most brightly in the darkest night of human woe. Say not, *then*, that the world is governed solely by self-interest. There is within every child of man a seed of divinity, that, when developed by circumstances, dwarfs his littleness to an almost invisible point, and magnifies his greatness almost to the dimensions of a god.

We short-sighted mortals are, unfortunately, too prone to regard the things as wholly evil which are often instruments, in the hands of Omnipotence, by which he is working out for our race an exceeding and eternal weight of glory.

Calamities are not, as some imagine, necessarily judgments: rather, indeed, should we esteem them mercies.

Hawthorne once said, "Perhaps, if we could penetrate nature's secrets, we should find that what we call weeds are more essential to the well-being of the world than the most precious fruit or grain." Even so it might well be said, that, if we could unravel the mystery of life, we should find that what we call evil is perhaps more essential to the welfare of mankind than what we esteem to be our chiefest good. There can, indeed, be no evil in the sense in which we understand the word; for God is the Author of all things, and he is wholly good. To assert, therefore, the existence of evil, save only as the negation of good, if not in some mysterious way its germ, is to libel the Almighty, to call in question his omnipotence, and to proclaim that there is a mightier still than he, another deity besides the Eternal, usurping his thorne, dashing from his brow the crown of goodness, and wresting from his grasp the sceptre of righteousness. Such a thought is too intensely absurd, too manifestly impious, to be entertained for a moment by any rational creature who pauses to consider the full meaning of the word "omnipotent." Every thing that happens must be in strict conformity with the all-wise, all-perfect laws of the "great directing Mind of all." Whoever attempts to violate these is made to feel that they cannot be violated with impunity. In the very nature of things, the laws of the Eternal are — what the laws of the Medes and Persians were merely fabled to be — "unchangeable," fixed as the pillars of the skies, immovable as the foundations of the everlasting hills. Evil is often used by the sacred writers, as in our text, to represent a state of war and its attendant misery.

"Shall a trumpet" — the signal of alarm and invasion — "be blown in the city, and the people not be afraid? Shall there be evil in a city, and the Lord hath not done it?" If the people take *not* the alarm when it is sounded, and provide not for their defence and safeguard, there will, of course, be evil in the city; i.e., the enemy will come in like a flood, and prevail against it. Such is the natural order of things in both the moral and the physical world. So the Eternal has ordained that the indolent, who disregard the warnings of approaching peril, shall suffer for their criminal contempt of his righteous laws.

Thus, when we read in the book of the prophet Isaiah, who represents himself as the mouthpiece of the Lord, "I am Jehovah, and none else; forming light, and creating darkness; making peace, and creating evil: I, Jehovah, am the author of all these things," we are to understand the son of Amoz as teaching the children of Israel that the natural, inevitable consequence of their departure from the law of their God, in the observance of which their national safety lay, would be the triumph of their enemies, and the ruin of their nation. So we see that there *is* a sense in which it may be quite truly said that Jehovah is the author of good and evil, as of light and darkness.

All things happen according to the good pleasure of his will, in conformity with those eternally unchangeable laws written with the finger of omnipotence on every page of the wondrous book of nature.

"Shall," then, "a trumpet be blown in the city, and the people not be afraid? Shall there," *then*, "be evil in a city, and the Lord hath not done it?" No, a thousand times *no!* for the Lord doeth all things; causing the fire to burn, and the water to drown, by the unerring operation of those natural laws that he has imprinted on both. As men sow, they shall assuredly reap; and yet it is God that giveth the increase, whether they sow the world-wide field of humanity with the brazen tares of vice or the golden wheat of virtue.

If they sow the seeds of national weakness, how can they expect to reap the fruit of national strength? All the evils that were threatened by the ancient prophets of Israel, from Moses to Malachi, were the necessary consequences of inattention to or wilful neglect of the laws that were instituted for the benefit of the people, by observing which peace would undoubtedly have been preserved within their borders, and prosperity in their palaces. But, by the non-observance of the means ordained for their defence, they were sure to fall before their enemies, just as the ripe corn falls before the sickle of the reaper. The Almighty was said to create the evil which results *now, as then*, from disobedience to the law that is written by nature, and therefore by God, on every human heart. As for those who impiously or ignorantly assert that every great calamity is a special visitation of the Almighty, for the wickedness of men, their impiety is only exceeded by their folly, and their ignorance by their presumption. There is no evil of which man can be guilty, that can prevent the glorious sun from rising, and the blessed rain from falling, upon him. And we would do well to consider, that, whatever was said "*by them of old time,*" this great truth was most distinctly taught by Him who brought life and immortality to light. Did he not assure his disciples that the heavenly Father maketh his sun to rise on the evil and on the good, and sendeth rain on the just and on the unjust? In the nature of things, apart from any immediate interference of Deity, righteousness exalteth, and unrighteousness debaseth, a nation. But the notion so prevalent among the Jews, and not less prevalent among the loudest-voiced professors of Christianity, that those who are overtaken by great calamities must necessarily be great sinners, was combated strongly by Jesus, as quite as dishonoring to his heavenly Father as it was contrary to his righteous government of the world. What did he say when told of the Galilæans whose blood Pilate mingled with their sacrifices, slaying them at the altar? Did he say that their slaughter was a special judgment from the Almighty? No, indeed; but he queried of those who were discussing their terrible fate, "Suppose ye that these Galilæans were sinners above all the Galilæans, because they suffered such things?" "Or those eighteen upon whom the tower in Siloam fell, and slew them, think ye that they were sinners above all men that dwell in Jerusalem?" And to both questions he replied with an indignant negative, saying, "Nay; but except ye repent ye shall all likewise perish." It is only when men's calamities can be clearly traced to their sin, that the former can be justly attributed to the latter. If one of the fiendish incendiaries who were prowling about our city, as the late terrible conflagration was mowing down our habitations, had been caught in the act of applying the torch, and then and there summarily executed by the infuriated multitude, his fate might have been reasonably regarded as the God-awarded penalty of his crime; for in such a case the *vox populi* might have been fairly assumed to be, as it sometimes is, the true expression of the *vox Dei*. But the helpless condition of the houseless thousands that thronged our flaming streets on that never-to-be-forgotten night of the 20th of June forbade the conclusion that they were suffering specially for their sins. The pure Christian religion rejects such an idea, not only as un-Christlike, but as monstrous and unnatural, heartless and inhuman. If a man be assaulted and maimed by a villain, or if sickness invade his household, and his dear ones are cut off before his eyes, shall such calamities be attributed to the finger of God, specially lifted up to inflict them? Shall the innocent man or the suffering family be pointed at as an awful example of the retribution that overtakes the godless? Scribes and Pharisees only, who well deserve to be denounced as hypocrites, could reply to these questions in the affirmative.

Are other cities, where the fire-fiend has not held high carnival as with us, less sinful than we are? Was it our wickedness that called down fire from heaven to consume our city? Was it the greater purity of its northern portions that exempted them from experiencing the fury of the fiery tempest? Did some good angel guard the Roman Catholic cathedral, and drive away the fire-fiend from its sacred precincts?

How strange that in this enlightened age, as we are fond of calling it, men are just as much lovers of the marvellous as the superstitious disciples who asked the Master, "who sinned,"— the man blind from his birth, "or his parents, that he was born blind"!

In this age of scientific wonders, of steam and electricity, when we train the sunbeam to paint our pictures, and harness the lightnings to the chariot of science, that they may carry our messages from one hemisphere to another with the rapidity of thought, and enable us even to audibly converse with our absent friends, is it not passing strange, that in such an age as this, there are men just as superstitious as those of whom Shakespeare, in his day, tells us that there was

> "No natural exhalation in the sky,
> No scape of nature, no distempered day,
> No common wind, no customèd event,
> But they will pluck away its natural cause,
> And call them meteors, prodigies, and signs,
> Abortives, presages, and tongues of heaven."

And is it not still more strange, that there are to-day ministers of the gospel who gravely tell us that it was the breath of God, miraculously applied, that kindled the flames of the recent terrifically destructive fire; that it was a judgment sent to us direct from heaven, as though we, in this city, were sinners above all the dwellers on the American continent? It would not be at all surprising, if ignorant, half-civilized men were thus to dub every great misfortune a fiery tongue of heaven, a judgment on the stricken.

But to my view it is, to say the least, most extraordinary, that the enlightened inhabitants of such a city as Saint John could be guilty of the egregious folly of attributing the partial destruction of their city by a fire, to the judgment of Heaven for the sins of the wicked within its borders, as if a just God would punish the innocent with the guilty, the righteous along with the wicked. If so be that the Lord sent his angel to destroy our city, were there not even ten righteous men in all its churches, for whose sake he would have recalled the angel of destruction? Has God forgotten to be just, as well as gracious? or is Saint John worse than the city respecting which we read in the book of Genesis, that the Lord said unto Abraham, "*I will not destroy it for ten's sake*"? Oh! it is very sad to think that such a mean idea of "the Judge of the earth" should be not only sanctioned, but encouraged, by some who claim to be — *par excellence* — our spiritual leaders.

If, indeed, all that has occurred within the last fortnight could be reversed, if the fire had not burned the inflammable materials with which it came in contact, *then* surely there would have been ample grounds for supposing that not the Eternal who loveth righteousness, but some extraneous power, foreign to the universe of which we are natives, had lifted up his finger in our midst; that we had been visited by some supernatural, supermundane, super-celestial agent, who had no respect for the universal law in obedience to which the flames consumed our habitations. Oh! it is monstrous, it is impious, it is blasphemous, to attribute the burning of our city to the direct agency of the good God, whose tender mercies are over all his works. If, knowing the properties of fire, we build houses of materials, that, so far from offering any resistance to its action, actually invite its destructive embraces, providing fuel for its flame, how *can* we, how *dare* we, charge upon the Almighty the natural consequence of our own foolhardiness? In an open country where houses are isolated, and the burning of one does not, under certain unfavorable circumstances, necessarily involve that of many, man may please himself in the building of his house; but he has no right to do so in a populous city, where the lives and property of thousands may be jeopardized by his independent action. This is one of the great lessons of the terrible calamity that has befallen us; and I trust that we shall not altogether fail in reading it aright, while it is my earnest hope that we may embody its teaching in the reconstruction of our city.

My friends, I see no reason for despondency, much less for despair, in our present circumstances. As wrote the apostle, " We are cast down, but not destroyed." Might I venture to prophesy, I would say, Soon shall the winter of our loss be succeeded by the summer of our gain. Soon shall our night of misfortune melt into the morning of prosperity.

The brightest flash issues from the darkest cloud; and oh, how beautiful is the hope-tinted bow of promise that spans the horizon of what seems to me to be our not far distant future!

I was forcibly struck with a beautiful passage in yesterday's "Banner of Light." "The heavier the loss," said the writer, treating of our misfortune, "the greater the gain. Burnt districts may easily be rebuilt; but the energetic play of sympathy, generosity, energy, and courage, which they have evoked, these go to the perpetual strength of human character, and remain always to illustrate the capacity of human conduct."

Our great calamity has, like all our trials, its counter-balancing compensations. It has brought out in bold relief the divinest traits of our much-maligned human nature. And how refreshing it is, as I remarked last Sunday, to be reminded by the almost universal sympathy that our great misfortune has elicited, of the unselfish benevolence, the secret springs of affection, that underlie the superficial selfhood of humanity, so seldom brought to light because it is only on such exceptional occasions as that of the recent conflagration, that these emanations of the divinity that dwells within us are evoked from the inner depths of our nature. Such traits redeem it from its littleness. When its depths are thus stirred by the angel of mercy, the artificial gives place to the real, and the earnestness of those who hasten to the relief of their suffering fellows grades all our petty differences to the high level of that Christlike charity which always finds its best expression in alleviating the common distress, in sharing each other's griefs, and in bearing each other's burdens.

Thus to do, is to fulfil the royal law of love. Thus to do, is to elevate the human to the divine, — to crown our manhood with the glory, honor, and immortality, which constitute the inalienable inheritance of the sons of God. The first and most spiritual lesson of our recent calamity is, that we are all brethren, that one great life pulses through all our veins, that one common nature links us all together with the golden chain of a common affection, so that, if one member of the great human brotherhood suffer, the pang that rends his heart finds a responsive chord in many another human breast. We are unapt indeed to learn, if our great disaster has not taught us that, although we are many members, we are, after all, but one body. This is the Christ theology as it existed from the foundation of the world, and as it was taught both by Jesus and by Paul. Thus we read in the first Epistle to the Corinthians (xii. 12), "As the body is one, and hath many members, and all the members of that one body, being many, are still one body, so also is the Christ. For by one spirit — the spirit of love — we are all baptized, not with material water, but with the water of the river of life, into one body, and united into one sacred fellowship, — the fellowship of the spirit of humanity, which is truly and essentially divine."

The laws which govern the whole realm of nature, and especially human nature, are not partial but general, not local but universal, not of the earth earthly, but of the heavens heavenly. And the greatest of all these laws is the law of love. He alone is poor who has not a soul to give to him that needeth. He is rich beyond the dreams of avarice, though poor in the world's estimation, whose great soul can only be satisfied by sharing with the needy the little that he possesses.

This, doubtless, was what was meant by Jesus when he said, "He that hath two coats, let him impart to him that hath none." "Now," said the great apostle of the Gentiles, — "now abideth faith, hope, charity, these three; but the greatest of these is charity."

"One faith, one hope, one Lord,
One God alone, we know:
Brethren we are; let every heart
With kind affection glow."

The following is an outline of the sermon preached in the Saint John's Church, by the rector of the parish of Saint Mark, the Rev. G. M. Armstrong, on the Sunday after the fire, from the text, "I know, O Lord, that thy judgments are right, and that thou in faithfulness hast afflicted me" (Ps. cxix. 75).

In preparing to address you after the fearful desolation which has come upon our city, I feel quite unable to do so, as I believe you are scarcely able to give a continued attention to any poor words which I might speak to you of the dreadful ruin which has befallen so many of your homes, and for the present at least has blighted your fondest prospects. I shall not attempt, therefore, to dwell upon the lowness to which our once lofty city has been in one short day brought, nor upon how the more lofty flames triumphed over the riches, the pride, and the glory of it, showing us how useless and vain all our efforts must prove, unless under the Almighty's guardianship and care. How is pride confounded, and hope even overthrown, so that the hearts of many are sinking under the struggle! but, to those who look to God, He will in this terrible hour come forth and reawaken their courage, and strengthen them with might, enabling them to sustain their trial, and rise above it. It may help you to do so, if I can lead you to consider the Lord's dealings with his people, which are always profitable subjects for meditation, prayer, and thanksgiving. By his dealings, I mean the manner or the means by which we are brought to know his name, to taste of his salvation, to be directed to his service, and trained up for his glory. These dealings are various, they are often mysterious, they are sometimes most painful; but the object and result of them all is to bring those who are rightly exercised by them to know and love the Lord. Times of tribulation are often blessed to this end; but at such times we have need of earnest prayer, that our trials may be thus sanctified; and most suitable in this respect is that petition in our litany, "In all time of our tribulation, . . . and in the day of judgment, good Lord, deliver us."

The Christian, viewing all his trials as the dispensation of his heavenly Father, is perfectly satisfied with them; and instead of repining and fainting on the one hand, or hardening himself and affecting to despise them on the other, he looks at himself and his present circumstances in the light of the word of God, and, having arrived at his conclusion, expresses it in the language of the text, "I know, O Lord, that thy judgments are right, and that thou in faithfulness hast afflicted me." The Bible affords us abundant proof of this blessed assurance on the part of the Lord's people. The cases of Aaron, Job, Eli, David, the Shunammite, and Hezekiah were referred to as those who yielded to God's appointments in dutiful silence, being fully confident of his wisdom and goodness.

The souls of some of you, who are now especially subject to the divine chastisement which has so recently befallen us, may sometimes be cast down within you, and you may be ready to despair; you would give any thing, perhaps, to be able to take a bright and solacing view of your troubles. Most earnestly, then, do I pray — and will you not join me in doing so? — that it may please God, the Holy Spirit, who is the Comforter, to bless at this time the consideration of the text before us, that we may enter into its precious secrets, and be enabled to join in the pathetic but joyful affirmation of the Psalmist to which it introduces us.

There are three points to which I would especially draw your attention, — the nature, the author, and the source, of the sufferings to which David refers. As to their nature, he calls them *judgments* and *afflictions*. In the former sense he regards them as those divine arrangements and decrees whereby the Almighty vindicates his character and holiness. He cannot see his name dishonored, and his character forgotten, without vindicating them. Thus, where sins are public, there are sooner or later public judgments; while if committed in the secret of a man's heart, before God, the judgment will be such as will mark out most distinctly God's hatred of that sin, clearly enough, at any rate, to strike the mind of him who desires the glory of the divine character, and would see, in all God's dealings with him, the purpose he has in view. God's judgments are intended to convince us of his holiness, and to show us that he will not bear iniquity.

Again, David regards the sufferings referred to as afflictions, the bitterness and painfulness of which were very trying, and intended for correction. This, however, has nothing to do with punishment. The people of God, properly speaking, are never punished, because punishment implies the exacting of a penalty; but God's people have no penalty to pay, for the penalty has already been paid for them: but they may be, and are, corrected as a means of improvement, and every child of God needs correction at times. The holiest and most advanced Christian has many lessons to learn; nor is there one who would venture to say he needs no correction, not one who ever thinks that he is sanctified enough. There is a need before such trials. They are blessings in disguise. They are intended to smite our lusts, and develop our graces; to make us humbler, wiser, holier, more grateful, more sympathizing; so that we may well look up and say, "I know, O Lord, that thy judgments are right, and that thou in faithfulness hast afflicted me."

As to the author of these sufferings, they are attributed by the Psalmist to the Lord, — "*thy* judgments;" "*thou* in faithfulness hast afflicted." Similar exclamations of the Old Testament saints were here spoken of. "Is there an evil in the city, and I have not done it?" says God. "I will smite her corn, and wine, and oil; I will lead her into the wilderness," &c. God reserves to himself the authority to execute judgment or visit affliction upon his creatures. All trial is his doing. We need not be afraid of attributing it to him. It does not spring out of the ground; there is nothing of chance about it; it is not man's doing, though men may be the immediate instruments. It matters not what means may be used. It signifies little whether it be the fiery trial through which we have just passed, the fearful pestilence, or the terrific war-cry which is now sounding in distant lands: God uses persons and things alike as his instruments to fulfil his own purposes, and carry out his own designs. They are, however, only instruments and second causes; they can go so far and no farther; they are under the control of the Almighty, and in his hands his people are safe; they can look up to him as their heavenly Father, and in the language of our text refer all such things to him as their author.

Then, as to the source of their sufferings, they are traced up in the text to the faithfulness of God. Their true origin is to be found in God's justice, wisdom, and faithfulness; and there we may rest. Whatever he determines must be right. It may be very mysterious, very irksome, very excruciating, to us: nature may shrink from it; but the child of God has implicit confidence in his Father, so he curbs his will, and orders his tumultuous passions into silence, and says, "It is right, I am sure of it. I cannot see the why and the wherefore now; but God is his own interpreter, and in his own good time he will make it plain: what I know not now, I shall know hereafter." Thus David sets it down to God's faithfulness, that he is afflicted. God would have been unfaithful, had he not afflicted him. Affliction is a covenant blessing, and one which God gives without requiring us to ask for it. It is a special token of God's love, and therefore a matter of repeated promise, in the fulfilment of which the faithfulness of God is gloriously displayed; and it is by trials of one kind or another, suited to our various temperaments, that God graciously and faithfully perfects the Christian character in his people. Of this the Psalmist was assured: he knew it by his own experience, and so felt absolute confidence in God. Here, then, is joy and peace in believing, even in the midst of tribulation. We cannot escape the waves of this troublesome world; but here we have in the character of God our rock and our high tower, in which we may safely hide. Happy are they who can take this view of their afflictions. If only we can learn to trust God as our Father in it, then at once we shall receive beauty for ashes, the oil of joy for mourning, and the garment of praise for the spirit of heaviness. Then we shall see that these cheerless and desolate days, these hours of bitter tears, come not by chance, but are sent us in faithfulness and love.

"They come to lay us lowly and humbled in the dust,
  All self-deception swept away, all creature hope and trust;
  Our helplessness, our vileness, our guiltiness, to own,
  And flee for hope and refuge to Christ, and Christ alone.

They come to draw us nearer to our Father and our Lord,
  More earnestly to seek his face, to listen to his word,
  And to feel, if *now around us a desert-land we see,*
  Without the star of promise what would its darkness be?"

The afflicted Christian does not envy the portion of those who are living at ease in the indulgence of this world's good things; nor would he give up what he has, for all they possess. But they, on the other hand, will surely, one day, grieve over their folly in having neglected his. Their riches are becoming poorer every day, and their pleasures more insipid; and what will they do, and how will they appear, when eternity is at hand?

Should the attention of any such here this morning have been arrested by the words they have heard, I would entreat them to forsake their lying vanities, and to unite themselves with the true Israel, who are journeying to the better country, even the heavenly, and who drink by the way of the fountains of living waters. Come and join us; and, though you may suffer with us now, you shall reign with us hereafter. Jesus will be with you in whatever he ordains for you; and, once within those gates of the Jerusalem which is above, there shall be no more sighing forever, for God himself shall wipe away all tears from our eyes.

I beseech you therefore, by the mercies of God, by the mercies which he is able and willing to dispense to you in the midst of your trial, by all the necessity and the piteous helplessness of souls stricken by the hand of God, that you present yourselves unto him, your souls and bodies, a living sacrifice.

Give him your hearts, give him your love, give him your confidence; and so you will be enabled humbly and gratefully to acknowledge the righteousness of his "judgments," and the "faithfulness" of his corrections.

CHAPTER XX.

MISCELLANEOUS MATTERS OF INTEREST.

The Newspapers of Saint John. — Historical Notice. — Biographical Sketch of the Life of Lieut.-Gov. Tilley, C.B. — The Life of John Boyd, a Private Citizen. — Examples of Saint John's sterling Men. — The City Government. — The Fire Department. — The Insurance Companies. — Little Wanderers' Home. — Incidents of the Fire. — Conclusion.

THE great haste with which a work of this kind must be prepared, in order to reach the hands of the reading public while the matter is still a prominent topic of interest, precludes the possibility of writing a book that would be as complete as the author might earnestly desire, and makes it impracticable to publish a book in which there will not be many serious and manifest errors. But with a feeling that we have made a sincere attempt to do our duty, and believing the character of our intentions will cause our scrutinizing readers to overlook accidental omissions or mistakes, we shut our eyes, and send this volume out to take its place among those productions to the making of which there is no end.

The newspaper publishers of Saint John suffered exceedingly; not only by the loss of their buildings, types, and presses, but by the destruction of all their private files, libraries, and editorial paraphernalia. The fortitude with which they met those irreparable losses was only exceeded by their enterprise in getting again in publishing order. Their printers were at work in the few job printing-offices which were spared; and their editions were on the street for sale while the buildings in which they took refuge were still clouded with smoke from the ruins. A sketch of the journals published in Saint John, printed about a year before the fire, furnishes us with some interesting information concerning this peculiarly afflicted profession.

"'The Saint John Daily News' had the honor of being the oldest newspaper. It was started in 1838, as a tri-weekly morning paper with a weekly issue, by George E. Fenety, Esq. Its price was one penny, — being the first penny paper ever established in the British Empire. It was originally of about foolscap size, but from time to time was enlarged, and in 1863 was the largest morning paper in Saint John. Its founder was an advocate of liberalism, and was especially earnest in his advocacy of responsible government, which he had the satisfaction of seeing an accomplished fact. Mr. Fenety became Queen's printer for New Brunswick in 1863, and placed the 'News' in charge of Mr. Willis as editor and general manager, himself still retaining ownership.

"In December, 1865, Mr. Fenety sold the 'News' office and paper to Messrs. Edward Willis, James Davis, and Stephen Smith, the latter soon retiring; after which the establishment was conducted by Willis & Davis till 1872, Mr. Willis still retaining his former position on the paper. In December, 1868, it started out in a daily issue, in addition to its tri-weekly and weekly issues, which it has continued till the present. It was soon after enlarged to its present size. In 1872 Mr. Willis purchased Mr. Davis's interest, and managed the paper until July, 1873, when he gave Mr. Mott, who had been accountant in the concern for several years, an interest in the paper and printing establishment. Mr. Willis manages the editorial, and Mr. Mott the business department.

"Mr. Willis has represented the city and county of Saint John in the local legislature for five years, being elected for a second term of four years at the 1874 election. He has been for three years, and now is, a member of the New Brunswick government. The 'News' was among the first advocates of confederation, and is a strong supporter of free non-sectarian schools. It has three issues, — a daily, tri-weekly, and weekly.

"Mr. Willis was formerly editor of the 'Courier,' and manager of the office when he left to assume charge of the 'News;' and, still previous to that, was editor and proprietor of the 'Western Recorder,' which he published in Carleton for several years.

"Next in age was the 'Globe,' a daily evening paper, which was started in 1858 by Mr. Ross Woodrow. A few years previous he had been engaged in publishing the 'Morning Times.' Newspapers then were not published oftener than tri-weekly, and he conceived the idea of publishing the paper in a daily issue; but as public opinion was not ripe for such an enterprise, and his means were limited, he failed in the undertaking.

"In 1856 he commenced a weekly paper called the 'British Constitution,' which meeting with a fair success, he started the 'Daily Evening Globe,' which was in the interest of the regular Liberal party, which was headed by Hon. S. L. Tilley.

"After running it about two years, he sold out to John V. Ellis and Christopher Armstrong in December, 1861. Mr. Armstrong came from Ireland when very young, and learned the printing trade in the 'Morning News' office with Mr. Fenety. Mr. Ellis is a native of Halifax, where he learned the printer's trade. He came to Saint John about eighteen years ago, and served as reporter on the editorial staff of the 'Morning News' and other papers.

"The 'Globe' occupied premises at the corner of Princess and Canterbury Streets, in rooms formerly occupied by the 'Colonial Empire' (and the 'Telegraph' was in the same building), in November, 1864, when both were burnt out; but neither lost an issue. The office was then moved to the premises recently occupied by the 'Tribune;' but in May, 1871, the proprietors purchased and moved into the spacious building on Prince William Street, which they now occupy.

"Both being practical printers as well as writers, success attended their enterprise; and the paper in May, 1867, was enlarged to pages of seven columns, and in July, 1874, to eight columns, with proportionate increase in length. The 'Globe' maintained the political character with which it started, until the Liberal party divided on the question of confederation, when it sided with the opponents of the confederation policy. The 'Globe' has a weekly issue.

'The Daily Telegraph' was the product of the union of two papers. Mr. John Livingston in 1862 started the 'Telegraph' as a tri-weekly and weekly. In June, 1864, it was issued as a morning daily, and continued thus about a year; and, though a credit to the enterprise of the proprietor, proved ahead of its time. It then went back to its tri-weekly issue.

Mr. William Elder started the 'Morning Journal' in May, 1865, as a tri-weekly and weekly. The proprietors of the two papers, conceiving that the time had come for the permanent establishment of a daily morning paper, effected a union in 1869.

"The 'Telegraph,' being the elder, led off in this union; and the new paper was designated 'The Saint John Telegraph and Morning Journal,' with Mr. Livingston as proprietor, and Mr. Elder as leader-writer.

"By this union a large list was secured for the daily and weekly issues, and improved machinery was introduced. But its journalistic was greater than its financial success. In 1871 Mr. Livingston sold the establishment to Mr. Elder at a pretty high figure, and retired from the paper. The editorial staff was then re-organized in all its departments; and the establishment has been under Mr. Elder's sole proprietorship and management since. In 1873 the compound name was changed to the more simple title of 'The Daily Telegraph.'

"During the year past Mr. Elder was ably assisted by Mr. Livingston in the editorial department, till the latter started 'The Watchman.' Mr. James Hannay, a barrister by profession, and deeply versed in the history of the Maritime Provinces, as well as in their staple industries, now occupies the chief place in Mr. Elder's staff. Mr. Elder is well read, and a forcible writer, and is a member of the Provincial legislature.

"The 'Telegraph' devotes itself not only to politics, but gives a large share of its attention to trade and commerce and the great industries of the city and Provinces. The circulation of both the daily and weekly attests the fidelity with which all these interests have been cared for. The office is finely organized in its mechanical department, which is in charge of Mr. Hugh Finlay; and connected with it is a finely appointed job-office, under the supervision of Mr. A. F. Lugrin.

"Hon. Timothy W. Anglin, who was born and educated in Ireland, came to this city in 1848, and the next year, as proprietor and editor, started the 'Morning Freeman' as a weekly paper, and shortly after issued a tri-weekly, both of which he still continues. Mr. Anglin sat for Saint John County in the New Brunswick Assembly, from 1861 to 1866, when he was defeated on the question of confederation. He has sat for Gloucester in the Dominion House of Commons, since the confederation, being returned by acclamation at the last general election. He was elected speaker in March, 1874."

For the purpose of giving the readers of this volume, who will be nearly all strangers to Saint John, a better acquaintance with the character, enterprise, and ability of the people of Saint John, we select two citizens from the hundreds whose biographies ought to be written, and present one from the circle of public life and one from the business classes. The danger of such a sketch is found in the tendency among superficial thinkers to take the men mentioned to be exceptions, rather than examples, which would be a result very far from the writer's intention. Hon. S. L. Tilley, C.B., Lieutenant-Governor of New Brunswick, whose portrait appears on the first page of this book, was born at Queen's County in 1818, and is now in his fifty-ninth year. He went to Saint John in 1830, and was engaged in business there for nearly twenty years. In 1850 he was called to represent the city in the legislature; and in 1854 he was chosen a member of the government, where he continued for eleven years as a member of the executive council, and most of that time filled the office of provincial secretary, being the leader of the government. He was a Liberal in politics, and, when in the legislature, carried measures for the extension of the franchise, the construction of a system of railways, and other important measures bearing upon the progress of the country. He was also a member of the delegation which devised and carried out the confederation of the Provinces, and assisted in framing the Constitution of the Dominion. He was elected to represent Saint John in the Dominion Parliment, and for six years was a member of the government as minister of customs, and later as minister of finance; filling the duties of each with great ability and practical sagacity. He was appointed lieutenant-governor in November, 1873, for the term which expires in 1878. This appointment was received with satisfaction by all parties; and the numerous banquets given to him, in which all shades of politics united, and the hearty words of admiration for his personal character and moral worth there uttered, were indorsed by the entire population, with whom he is a great favorite. He has ever been an advocate of temperance principles, and is the first governor who carried his principles into Government House, where he had the courage to entertain his guests of every degree without violating the solemn pledge of his youth. He is well known to many throughout the United States, by his addresses at public meetings in various parts, and is especially endeared to the people of the Northern States, because that throughout the whole of the struggle with the Rebellion he was ever the defender of the Constitution, and a firm friend of the Union cause. He is a forcible and pleasant speaker, a keen debater, and, when roused by opposition, there are few who can carry their audience with them more effectually. He is genial, kindly, sympathizing, and a true friend. At the news of this great calamity, he at once put himself in communication with his Government, to devise means for alleviating the distress, and, by personal intercourse with his old friends and fellow-citizens, cheered them in their great trouble. He was also a loser in the great fire, but to what extent cannot yet be ascertained.

Mr. John Boyd, a private citizen of Saint John, and a member of the prominent mercantile firm of Daniel & Boyd, presents one of those examples of sterling business integrity, and social worth, of which it is always pleasant and profitable to write. His influence in the Province of New Brunswick, and especially in the city of Saint John, is hardly exceeded by that of any public official; and it has been obtained by steady and careful industry, combined with an eminent desire, everywhere apparent in his acts, to be useful to his neighbors and countrymen. He has a brilliant genius, which fits him for any position, and a happy, genial manner in his intercourse with strangers, which secures them at once as life friends. Mr. Boyd is a native of the North of Ireland, and a descendant of the race of sturdy Scottish Presbyterians, so many of whom have made their mark in every land. Mr. Boyd is now fifty years of age, and entered into business in the house with which he is now connected, known as the "London House," in 1838, and has been there nearly forty years. His partner, Mr. T. W. Daniel, has been associated with the firm forty-two years.

Mr. Daniel is foremost in nearly every good work, and universally respected and beloved. He, too, is a *gentleman* in the highest sense. He is a native of Bedfordshire, England. Mr. Daniel was in Saint John at the great fire of January, 1837, when the South Wharf, Water, and Prince William Streets were burned; also at the great fire of August, 1839, when the North Wharf, Nelson Street, Dock Street, and Market Square were burned, and the "London House" in it; and at the great fire of 1841, when Mr. Holdsworth, one of the founders of his firm, was killed. His residence is at Rockwood, outside the city, one of the most charming spots in the Maritime Provinces, laid out with consummate skill; one of the favorite visiting places of the tourist to Saint John, seeking its lovely scenery.

Mr. Boyd has also come through these fires, but this of which we write has been the most severe to him. His residence, a noble brown-stone front on the Queen's Square, and one of the most elegant and noticeable in all the city, was destroyed; and in it were many rare and valuable works of art, statuary, paintings, engravings, &c., collected by him during his many visits to the Old World. He also had one of the finest private libraries on the continent, not a volume of which was saved.

In that beautiful home, presided over by a wife who was almost as universally endeared to the people as himself, leading men from all parts of the world had been entertained; and in it were to be found also many valuable mementos of these visits, not one of which has been saved. The lectures which Mr. Boyd had written, and had delivered in many parts of the Provinces, in the United States, and Great Britain, during thirty years, were all destroyed. Not a fragment remains, as his dwelling was burned before he knew it, and while he was engaged in attempting to save his stock and warehouse. Mr. Boyd used his spare hours with marked advantage to all around him: his letters of travel published in the "Boston Journal" from 1852 to 1869 have been read by many in New England; and leading articles on general questions in the press, for a year past, were from his prolific pen. He wrote a valuable report on the railway necessities of the Province of New Brunswick, years ago. That report was adopted by the Board of Trade, and its suggestions carried out. From his lectures, readings, and speeches, he is said to have raised for public and private charities $28,-

000, besides giving largely to them from his own means.

He is a favorite on the lecture-platform, and his name always attracts large audiences. At the time of the fire he was so arranging his business that he should have more leisure to give to literary work, which he loved so well and performed so admirably. He has been a member of the school-board since the new law came into operation, and was chairman of the Saint John school-board, one of the most important trusts in the city; and to his conciliatory method, judicious counsels, and liberal views, is the country largely indebted for the recent settlement of those vexed questions of difference between Protestants and Catholics, which are now happily nearly forgotten.

Messrs. Daniel & Boyd lost heavily in this great fire, but they were largely covered by insurance. It is said they will receive directly and indirectly, in insurance, some $350,000 in gold; their losses over their insurance will probably reach $20,000, a small proportion compared with many. Mr. Boyd's private losses will be heavy: he had only $14,000 insurance on his house, which with what it contained was worth not less than $30,000. The sympathy for them is universal and genuine; and it was a happy announcement that they intended at *once* to rebuild,

on the old spot, the widely-known "London House."
We are told that one of the inspectors of the insurance companies who was settling insurance claims stated publicly, after inspecting the books and statements of this house, that he had "been through the fires of Chicago and Boston, adjusting claims, but the best kept and most correct set of books he had ever seen were those of Daniel & Boyd." Such men as these are a necessity to the growth of a country; and such as these are many of the merchants of Saint John, who will yet make their city even more prosperous than in the past. Mr. Daniel is a quiet, cautious, unassuming English gentleman, — while Mr. Boyd is a genial, genuine Irishman, always ready for a joke, but ever with his eye on business, far-seeing and keen, not easily daunted, ready for work at all times; knows what to do and how to do it; is not afraid of taking hold of the whole himself; and in the midst of this overwhelming calamity, while surrounded by all kinds of people asking his advice or assistance, he was courteous and kind to all, the poorest receiving his chief attention, while on the street his pleasant smile and cheery word to all he meets makes his presence sought by all. The Rev. George M. Grant of Halifax is said to have remarked, on a public occasion there, that there were three things in Saint John of which they were proud: "the

Skating Rink, the Victoria Hotel, and John Boyd;" and that brilliant preacher, and author of "From Ocean to Ocean," might safely have said the same with regard to the feeling and pride of the inhabitants of the other Provinces also. Many deserving young men of business capacity, who had some capital of their own, have been assisted by them; and throughout the Provinces these are to be found in large numbers, now grown independent, but who ever in the strongest terms express their gratitude to the friends who first gave to them the helping hand.

The roster of the Saint John City Government at the time of the great fire included the following officials : —
Mayor, Sylvester Z. Earle, Esq.; *Recorder*, W. H. Tuck, Q. C.; *Common Clerk*, B. Lester Peters, Q. C.; *Aldermen*, Michael W. Maher, James Adams, John Kerr, Henry Duffell, Samuel L. Brittain, H. Adam Glasgow, William Peters, John C. Ferguson, Jarvis Wilson. *Councillors*, Elias S. Flaglor, Edward T. C. Knowle, Richard Cassidy, Bartholomew Coxetter, William A. Quinton, J. Alfred Ring, Thomas B. Harrington, George H. Martin, Charles Emerson. *City Chamberlain*, William Sandall; *Clerk to Mayor's Office*, Hiram G. Betts; *Deputy Common Clerk*, J. Austin Belyea; *City Engineer*, Hurd Peters; *City Auditor*, Thomas V. Raymond; *Superintendent of Streets*, James J. Lawlor; *Assessors of Taxes*, John Wilson, Uriah Drake, James Sullivan; *Harbor Master*, Charles S. Taylor; *Harbor Inspector*, Joseph O'Brien; *Chief Engineer of Fire Department*, Thomas Marter; *High Constable*, George Stockford.

The list of members of the Fire Department at the time of the fire included the following : —

Thomas Marter, Chief Engineer ; Samuel Dunlap, No. 1 District, engineer; George Drake, No. 2 District, engineer ; John Wilson, No. 3 District, engineer. No. 1 Engine : G. M. Matthews, engineman ; Henry Brazillian, assistant engineman ; Elias Belyea, driver. No. 2 Engine : Samuel Piercey, engineman ; Thomas McChristal, assistant engineman ; John Lane, driver. No. 3 Engine : James Melick, engineman ; Hiram Webb, assistant engineman ; George Corbett, driver. Hose Company, No. 1: J. T. Magee, foreman ; Robert Magee, assistant foreman ; Alfred Carr, William Kee, John Kee, John Magee, Stephen Munford, William Griffiths, sen., William Griffiths, jun., Charles Magee. Hose Company, No. 2 : William Neal, driver ; Andrew Lawson, foreman ; William Quigley, assistant foreman ; Joseph Duffell, secretary ; Robert Lowe, William Reed, W. H. Drake, G. T. Whitenect, William Melvin, William Reed, 2d, Herbert Spiller, John Robertson, David Stockford, Thomas Rankine, Frank Barnes. Hose Company, No. 3 : William Cummings, foreman ; George Blake, assistant foreman ; Joseph Mason, Robert Torrens, Joseph Noble, Samuel Laskey, John Knollin, John Shields, Charles Fletcher, George Jackson, Edward Lantalum, Dennis Costigan. Hook and ladder : W. A. Smith, driver ; John Jackson, captain ; John Rankine, secretary ; James Carr, John LeLaseur, William Bowman, George Baldwin, W. A. Magee ; driver of coal-wagon, Walter Welsford.

The insurance companies, who had losses in the fire to the amount of nearly seven millions of dollars, were very prompt in adjusting losses; and several of the more prominent companies contributed liberally toward the relief fund. Their promptness and liberality received the commendation of all English-speaking people. They nearly all united in an agreement not to insure frail wooden buildings, and thus contributed very materially toward the permanent character of the buildings which succeeded those destroyed. The companies having the largest losses and the estimate risks are stated to be the following: Queen, $700,000; North British and Mercantile, $600,000; Lancashire, $400,000; Provincial, $57,000; Liverpool, London, and Globe, $480,000; Guardian, $400,000; Canada Fire & Marine, $47,500; Citizens', $140,000; National, $123,000; Royal, $500,000; Commercial Union, $400,000; Royal Canadian, $350,-000; Western, $96,400; Imperial, $300,000; Ætna, $220,000; Hartford, $190,000; Phœnix of Brooklyn, $60,000; British America, $22,000; Stadacona, $320,000; Central of Fredericton, $60,000; Saint John Mutual, $75,000; Northern, $200,000; Canada Agricultural, $4,000.

An editorial notice of the insurance companies and their losses, published in Saint John soon after the fire, contained the following item of interest in this connection: "The Maritime Mutual Fire Insurance Company (capital $1,000,000) went up in the smoke of the big fire, and no vestige of it remaineth. The premium notes and assessment and stock-books were burned up in the safe, and there is nothing left of the company except the policies in the hands of the insurers. Notice is given that 'it has now ceased altogether.' The fire has staggered several of the companies. The Mutual, which is a Saint John institution, has made an assessment on its shareholders. The Central of Fredericton is taking measures to meet the indebtedness incurred. The Provincial of Toronto has suspended business, but declares it will pay up. The Stadacona is asking time from its creditors. English and American companies, and some of the Canadians too, are meeting their liabilities, and proceeding with business."

Those unfortunate people who insured their dwellings in local mutual companies, and who were left with worthless policies, were the especial subjects of sympathy; and they presented a numerous class. Many a humble home on leased land was insured in such companies, and utter destitution followed as a consequence. The true principle of fire-insurance is seen in the distribution of losses as widely as possible, and each city ought to insure in companies established in other cities. Insuring in "home companies" comes too near the act of "insuring our own property," which means having no insurance at all.

The charitable measures adopted by the Little Wanderers' Home of Boston, U. S., were thus mentioned in a daily paper published in that city: "Mr. R. B. Graham, agent of the Baldwin Place Home for Little Wanderers, arrived home on Friday from Saint John, with a large company of poor children, who will be cared for at the Home until arrangements can be made for their support here. Ten of the number are from the Protestant Orphan Asylum. Among the others are four sisters of a family reduced from a position of comfort to extreme want. Three of them, who are young women, have already found employment in Boston families, and another will remain at the Home. There are four children of another family, and three of another in the party, which numbers twenty-six in all. They went by rail, free tickets having been given by the European and North American, the Maine Central, and the Eastern Railroads. At Bangor the children were furnished with refreshments by Mr. Nye, keeper of a restaurant in the Maine Central Depot, and Mr. J. L. Crosby, city treasurer, was at hand looking after the wants of the little ones. The depot-master at Vanceboro', Mr. Robinson of Saint Andrews, and the conductor on the European and North American Railway, also aided in providing food for the party. Saint John and other places in the Provinces have contributed liberally for the support of the Baldwin Place Home in former years; and its managers cheerfully volunteered to open the doors of the house at this time."

A prominent gentleman of Saint John, in a letter to the author, mentioned the following incidents of the great disaster: —

A resident on Queen's Square sent her little son, aged nine years, for help. When he had gone a short distance, he was surrounded on all sides by the burning houses; the firemen poured water on him, and he continued on his way, and accomplished his mission.

When asked why he went on under such circumstances, his reply was worthy of a true soldier: " My mother sent me; and *I had to do what she* told me."

Everywhere one hears incidents illustrative of the courage and devotion of the noble women. We cannot recall them all; but after depicting scene after scene, every husband praising his wife as the best, they would end with the exclamation, " No use talking: one woman is worth six men at a time like this." And it was so; for when strong men were quivering before the blast of this terrible whirlwind of disaster, and almost sinking under the weight of their losses, these brave women would cheer them with their hopeful words, "Never mind: we are saved to each other, and what more need we care for?" Had these been the words of enthusiastic young lovers, one could have understood them; but they were the utterances of many a one going down the hill of age, and who had not the energy which nerved their hands in the years gone by.

Among the applicants for relief, one receiving an order for a barrel of flour stopped to ask the question, "Shure, and wud yez be plaised to till me what brand it is to be?"

Another says, "They till me that there's to be a thousand dollars for ivery man that was burned out; and, feth, whin I wint down for my share, all that I got was only a dhurty matthress."

Such are some of the applicants; but among others would be seen the tenderly reared lady, who had every comfort in her beautiful home, now reduced to the hard necessity of begging for the supply of her daily wants and for a little clothing, having lost all but the garments in which she stood before them.

Thus ends our story of the great fire in Saint

John. And if other similar disasters shall be averted by the lessons which the foregoing pages teach, and if the sympathy and aid for the unfortunate but brave inhabitants of the devastated city shall be extended or strengthened hereby, the highest purpose of the author will have been gained, and he will feel that his efforts herein contained were not without their measure of success.

www.ingramcontent.com/pod-product-compliance
Lightning Source LLC
Chambersburg PA
CBHW020302240426
43673CB00039B/675